Richard James Burgess

the art of music production

OMNIBUS PRESS
London/New York/Paris/Sydney/Copenhagen/Madrid/Tokyo

Cover designed by Chlöe Alexander

ISBN: 978.1.84449.431.6

Order No: OP50314

Exclusive Distributors
Music Sales Limited,
8/9 Frith Street,
London W1D 3JB, UK.

Music Sales Corporation,
257 Park Avenue South,
New York, NY 10010, USA.

Macmillan Distribution Services,
53 Park West Drive,
Derrimut, Vic 3030,
Australia.

To the Music Trade only:
Music Sales Limited,
8/9 Frith Street,
London W1D 3JB, UK.

Every effort has been made to trace the copyright holders of the photographs
in this book but one or two were unreachable. We would be grateful if the
photographers concerned would contact us.

Typeset by Phoenix Photosetting, Chatham, Kent
Printed in the United States of America by Vicks Lithograph & Printing.

A catalogue record for this book is available from the British Library.

Visit Omnibus Press on the web at www.omnibuspress.com

Contents

Acknowledgments

To my sons Ace and Blaze for making every day an adventure, Chris Charlesworth for making the project possible in the first place and his continued enthusiasm and sharp, editorial, eye, Chloe Alexander for the cover design, the artists who have allowed me to produce them and unknowingly cook this book along the way. The many producers, engineers, managers, label people, colleagues, friends and crazy people I have been so fortunate to work with over the years and who so generously contributed their experience, time, and tales.

Special thanks for this edition to: Ace and Blaze Burgess, Peter Collins, Lauren Christy, Cathy Fink, Pete Ganbarg, Don Kaplan, Bill Laswell, Anna Loynes, Arif Mardin, Marcy Marxer, Wendy Page, Linda Perry, Perry Resnick, Sandy Roberton, Daniel Sheehy, Lydia Sherwood, Katrina Sirdofsky.

Comments, corrections or casual conversation to Richard James Burgess, PO Box 646, Mayo, MD 21106-0646, USA. Email: rjb@burgessworldco.com for further information: www.burgess worldco.com

Introduction

Welcome to the third edition of this book, which started life as *The Art Of Record Production* and was transposed for the second edition to *The Art Of Music Production.* The substitution acknowledged the passing of vinyl records into history and niche status. During the evolution of the record producer many things have changed – Stereo, eight-tracks, cassettes, multi-track, Quad, digital, random access, CDs – all came and in many cases went. Most of the major labels have changed their names from Blah-de-blah Records to Blah-de-blah Music Group but people in the industry still call them the record company or record label. Music producers still get referred to as record producers even if what they are making ends up as an MP3. Whatever form or formlessness recorded music takes it is still a record – a document. Dictionary.com says that the noun, record, means something, such as magnetic tape, on which sound or visual images have been recorded. The word 'something' pretty much covers it for me. Then there's that beautiful moment at the height of creation when someone will lean back in their chair and say "sounds like a record", signifying that the whole finally transcends the parts. This is what record, audio or music producers, whatever we call them, strive for. It's why they work crazy hours, deal with difficult people, get ripped off and keep coming back for more. Suffice it to say that I will use the terms, record, audio, and music producer inter-changeably throughout the book.

Most people have no idea what a record producer does. Half the time the producers don't even know because the way they mix varying measures of art, science and magic becomes second nature to them and the particular blend is unique to each producer. Vinyl records intrigued me as a kid – the music that you can almost see locked in the shiny grooves, trying to decipher the hieroglyphics on the label, poring over the liner notes. I wanted to know who wrote the song, which musicians played on it, what a record producer was and how the whole thing came together. Gradually it dawned on me how special it is to be able not only to capture sound – moments in time, ideas, concepts, personalities and attitudes – but to be able to fashion these elements into something that excites and inspires people all over the world. This book offers a series of glimpses into that process of turning nothing into something that will make people keep on 'hitting play' again and again. I'll talk about the people, the situations and how one gets to be a record producer in the first place.

The patriarch of music producers, Sir George Martin, says that a record producer is like a film producer and director rolled into one. It's a good description.

Film production involves more people and much bigger budgets than music production. There may be multiple executive producers, co-executive producers, producers, co-producers, associate producers and line producers. Film producers very often put the whole project together, either raising the money or investing their own. Like record producers, they handle the administrative side of the process either directly or by delegation. Film directors on the other hand supervise the actors, direct the action, define the artistic vision and have creative control over the day to day shooting and editing of a movie. Record producers exercise overall and day-to-day creative control in varying degrees depending on the producer, the project and the artist. The independent music producer evolved out of the record company A&R position, which in the early days involved supervising artists and choosing material, being mostly administrative like a film producer. During the Fifties and early Sixties record producers became more involved in the actual recording process including engineering, arranging and even writing the material, gradually exercising much greater influence over the direction of recorded music and individual artist's careers. Some record producers do get involved in deal making and these days multiple layers of producer credits and production teams are more common but mostly the independent record producer is a lone gun for hire.

Music producers have to be versatile like the blank piece in Scrabble that can substitute for any letter. Producers have to supply whatever elements are needed to make a great recording. Referring to his changing role over four highly successful Simply Red albums, Stewart Levine said, "As a producer you have to be prepared to adapt to the circumstances. It's horses for courses and every day is different.

Mick [Hucknall] wanted to take a larger role on the fifth album. When you have a situation where the artist is growing, if you are wise, you help him to do just that."

"A record producer is responsible for the sound 'shape' of what comes out," says George Martin. "In many ways, he's the designer – not in the sense of creating the actual work itself, but he stages the show and presents it to the world. It's his taste that makes it what it is – good or bad."

GRAMMY award winner André Fischer puts it like this: "I know I'm here to be in the service of others. I can stand on my own, of course, but I'm a good accompanist. The nature of what I do as a producer is accompaniment."

Sometimes the production process can be more about discovery than creation. Just as an archaeologist uses sensitive techniques in trying to uncover precious artefacts, a great producer can gently coax moving performances out of the artist and musicians in searching for the perfect parts and fitting them all together. At other times, in other situations, the producer may completely control and define every aspect of the record. One thing's for sure – each production is unique.

Chapter One

What Kind Of Producer Do You Want To Be?

"The ability to deal with people is as purchasable a commodity as sugar and coffee. And I pay more for that ability than for any other under the sun." (John D. Rockefeller)

a) All-Singing-All-Dancing-King-Of-The-Hill

These producers could easily be artists in their own right. In the movies and theatre someone who sings, dances and acts is known as a triple threat. This type of producer is a triple, quadruple or quintuple threat. They will most likely write the songs, play the instruments, sing the demos and may even engineer and programme the computers into the bargain.

They are blessed with a natural, diverse musical talent, a rock solid sense of direction and their songs, arrangements, orchestrations, sounds and vocal stylings are instantly recognisable, even though the vocalists themselves may be unfamiliar.

That's not to say their records are 'samey', more that they have an identity that shines through no matter what.

They're not a good choice for a band that writes its own material and intends to play everything on the record, but they're perfect for the solo artist who either does not write, needs a co-writer or is short of hit singles. Much in demand by record companies, these producers are the answer to many an A&R man's prayers. In one fell swoop they solve the problem of having to find a song and a producer. Their names carry a huge amount of clout at radio since, in their care, an unknown artist can get exposure that would normally be available only to an established artist.

Traditionally the All-Singing-All-Dancing producer has been favoured by certain formats and, for that matter, only certain kinds of artists within those formats. In the late Nineties and early part of the new century those distinctions have been eroded. Hip-hop producers such as The Neptunes, Timbaland, and Kanye West have generated hit singles for many artists. R'n'B has always had producers such as LA & Babyface and Jam & Lewis who certainly fit into this category as has pop music. The Matrix penetrated the rock-pop crossover market with their production of 'Complicated' for Avril Lavigne. At this point, with the necessity for hit singles to promote an album and the difficulty of getting untested bands on the radio, all formats seem susceptible to the All-Singing-All-Dancing producer or production team. The 'All-Singing' producers almost invariably end up running their own production company or label. With the all around ability they have, it makes total sense for them to apply their time and energy to building a collection of valuable copyrights. And of course they can jump in and produce for another label any time a truly great artist comes along. Once the 'All-Singing' producer hits their stride they tend to have an unbroken run of hits for a number of years. Their style is usually very distinctive and can become a genre or, at least, sub-genre in itself.

The only possible downside is that when they finally drop out of favour or fashion it may be impossible for them to recover. Flexibility is not a hallmark of the All-Singing-All-Dancing-King-Of-The-Hill. The consolation, when it's all over, is the money. Unless they have been on a willful mission to financial oblivion they should be able to buy a small country to retire to. Having said that, the skills are very transferable and there is no better testimony to that fact than L.A. Reid who went on to run Arista Records and subsequently Island Def Jam after the L.A. and Babyface production team split.

'All-Singing' is a category you are either born into or start training for at an early age. The diverse skills need to be developed from a fairly young age, and the genre is often populated by production teams rather than individuals. Sometimes one of the partners is the creative genius, with the other being the sounding board, the big picture guy, or the business brains, but they come in all shapes and sizes. I asked Lauren Christy from the three-person production team The Matrix how their roles are defined. She said, "If people come around they'll see Scott sitting in front of a whole lot of gear, they see Graham with a guitar and they see me sitting with a book. They immediately go, 'oh that's what they do'. The truth is, the lines are so blurred and Graham will be singing a song to me (sings) 'la da da de da da, I'll never kiss your lips again, I'll never kiss your lips again' and I'll go, 'oh I like that'. So I'll just write it

2

down. And then Scott's doing the same thing and he starts singing some kind of lyric and I'll love that so I'll write that down. So everything goes in my book that everyone is saying. When Scott is starting to do drums, I'll say 'uh uh, I'm not feeling that groove against the vocal, the kick pattern is wrong'. And Graham is sitting there with his melody and Scott is saying, 'more like this at the top line of the chorus – swoop it up so that it starts higher than the last note of the verse'. We'll all just blur each other's lines and I guess that's what makes the partnership great. We're kind of like a monster with three heads."

Les Paul pioneered the concept of overdubbing (more like 'sound on sound' the way he did it) in the late Forties and early Fifties on the revolutionary 'How High The Moon'. On that record he played all the guitar parts and Mary Ford sang all the vocals. This apparently simple recording technique would change forever the way records were to be made. Previously, artists performed live in the studio. The aim of the first audio engineers and producers was to capture the sonic event as accurately as possible so that the original sound field could be reproduced in the consumers' home, just like a Cartier Bresson or Ansel Adams photograph – an idealised or optimised representation of reality. As artistic as these photographers may have been, their photographs were dependent on what was happening when the shutter opened. Likewise, early recordings were a representation of a single continuous event that took place in a single environment.

Suddenly, with the technique of overdubbing, it was possible to create an entirely artificial sound picture. It was possible to have multiple takes of the same musicians. Musicians and instruments that didn't play together could be recorded at different times in different sonic environments. This was more like the way Man Ray had used the photographic medium. Using his instincts as an artist he had manipulated the photographic medium directly by placing objects onto light sensitive paper and exposing it to light. There were a lot of inventions and innovations that had to happen to bring us to where we are now, but once Les Paul crossed that bridge from reality to artificiality the stage was set.

With the advent of multi-track tape machines the process became easier and more widespread. Through the early Sixties' records were still made largely by recording a band live in the studio. Overdubbing was mostly confined to vocals and additional orchestration. George

Martin's arrangements on The Beatles' records and Brian Wilson's elaborate vocal overdubs on classic Beach Boys' albums such as *Pet Sounds* represent the pinnacle of this era of recording. It wasn't really until the early Seventies that artists such as Stevie Wonder and Mike Oldfield made the first successful commercial records by multi-tracking all or most of the instruments themselves. At that time Tamla Motown and Virgin, respectively, had to take a huge leap of faith to allow an artist access to as much studio time as they needed to painstakingly piece those records together, and in those cases, without even the safety net of an outside producer. This was all the more remarkable since record companies are not renowned for embracing expensive, creative or technological innovations. (Digital recording took a long time to catch on, partly because of its negative effect on the bottom line; the same with stereo in the Fifties and Sixties.)

"I like to do everything," says Walter Afanasieff, producer of Mariah Carey and Michael Bolton, writer of hits such as Kenny G's 'Don't Make Me Wait For Love' and Gladys Knight's 'Licensed To Kill' and keyboard player on too many records to mention. "Some producers prefer to work with full bands and leave it up to the musicians to supply the music and the arrangements," he says. "I'll create the rhythm, the drum parts, the bass lines, the keyboard parts, the string arrangements, the horn arrangements, and the vocal arrangements. Even when the guitar players are in doing their parts, I'll be in their face every minute, every second, making sure they're giving me exactly what I want them to play. I like being responsible for every note on the record, which I suppose classifies me more as a producer/ arranger."

Very often the only thing All-Singing-All-Dancing requires of his artist is that they sing or rap. Teddy Riley says of his work with Michael Jackson and Bobby Brown, "Most of the vocal tracks were completed on the first or second try. If you can't come into the studio and sing a song the way it's supposed to be sung, then you don't need to be working with me. If the singer feels the music, and you've got the melody recorded beforehand, you're going to get the vocals down cold."

Timbaland is one of the most innovative and successful hip-hop producers. Among others he has worked with Missy Elliot, Jay Z, Memphis Bleek, Ludacris, Justin Timberlake and Ginuwine. Timbaland didn't beat around the bush in a January 2004 interview with *Billboard* when he said, "My producing style is this, 'I am the music.' The artist is the frontman for the producer."

In the case of the massive UK success of Stock, Aitken & Waterman, the artist's singing ability has often been secondary to prior fame. They laid the foundations for an empire by writing and producing a phenomenal run of hits for previously non-singing, but well-known soap actors, Kylie Minogue and Jason Donovan.

Nowadays the new, inexpensive digital technology makes it much easier, and more practical, to develop impressive studio skills at an early age. The influence of artists and producers like Prince, L.A. & Babyface and Jam & Lewis will hopefully inspire more kids to become proficient writers, arrangers and multi-instrumentalists. Those who choose not to become recording artists in their own right may well develop into the next generation of this very powerful and influential breed of producer.

Working as a team helps Jam & Lewis to handle several projects simultaneously. They have a saying, "We have no slack," that helps them to come up with a solution to any musical or technical problem. If one of them is experiencing a creative block, the other one will pick up the slack. Jimmy Jam calls Terry Lewis 'Vocalmaster' and Terry Lewis calls Jimmy Jam 'Trackmaster' which loosely defines the roles they play in the productions.

Although L.A. & Babyface no longer produce as a team, when they were collaborating L.A. Reid said of their highly successful and long-running relationship, "One of the biggest advantages of having a producing/songwriting partner is that you always have someone to bounce ideas off. Working by yourself can sometimes get a little stale, so it's better to have a collaborator around to help keep up the inspiration level. There are always ideas out there that you may not have thought of, and that your partner has humming around inside his head. Plus you don't have to second guess yourself when working with someone whom you trust. As my partner, Babyface, says: 'By working as part of a team, one always has the benefit of a second opinion'."

The vast majority of producers traditionally congregated in either London, New York, Los Angeles or Nashville. In fact, the job can involve a lot of traveling. You very often have to go to where the artist is, where the record company is or where the studio is that has been chosen for the project. One beneficial side effect of being in the All-Singing category is that the artists will come to you, wherever you are based. Max Martin (Britney Spears) is in Sweden, Jam & Lewis (Janet Jackson) are based in Minneapolis, Teddy Riley (Bobby Brown) is in Virginia Beach, as are The Neptunes. Walter Afanasieff (Mariah Carey) operates out of the San Francisco Bay area, and L.A. & Babyface (Toni Braxton, TLC) when they were working together, operated (in part) out of Atlanta, Georgia.

b) Sidekick

No one ever wants to own up to this stereotype. Almost invariably credited as a co-producer, this category of producer usually gets started as an engineer, programmer, musician or co-writer. They often connect with one particular artist early in their career. If that artist goes 'mega' the 'sidekick', having become an indispensable asset, is in line for a promotion. A co-production credit is the next logical step. Continued successful co-productions with one artist lead to full production credit with other artists.

This type of producer is the perfect choice for the confident, independent minded, self-directed artist who needs a right-hand person and someone to bounce ideas off. He will take care of the jobs that the artist doesn't want to deal with or doesn't have the expertise to handle; in particular the administrative, engineering and technical aspects of the production process. He is not a good choice for the artist who doesn't have a strong sense of vision and direction.

In the case of the musician co-producer, the attraction for the artist may be his more formal understanding of music and help with the arrangements, songwriting or organising and rehearsing the band. Mostly these relationships become long-standing, very tight and extremely lucrative, even though the producer may be on quite low royalty rates. Very often one early relationship with an artist who turns into a superstar can turn into parallel relationships with two or maybe even three superstars if the recording/touring schedules can be synchronised.

This is usually a very hands-on producing role, which for the right personality type is ultimately satisfying. If you are a hands-on detail person teaming up with an explosively creative artist could be one of the most fulfilling ways to do what you do best and succeed in a big way.

I don't normally give examples of producers who fit this mould because I detect that most prefer to think of themselves as collaborators. There are distinct differences between the 'sidekick' and the collaborator. The collaborator is usually more independent and has his own working methods that the artist will have to accommodate. He has undoubtedly worked with many different artists and didn't build his initial reputation primarily as the right-hand person of one artist. The sidekick is much more likely to fit in with the artist's style of working – freeing up the artist to concentrate more on the purely creative aspects of the production.

Steve Albini had something to say about humility in an essay he posted on the *rec.audio.pro* news group on the worldwide web. "Remember that nobody ever goes into a record store shouting, 'Give me the new album on label X, produced by producer Y, whose deal memo was hammered out by A&R guy Z and lawyers A,B and C!' People like records because they like music. Music is made by artists. You're just sitting in the chair with wheels and pressing the button. Do not forget your place! You are not the star, and you must be content with that. Do your job to the absolute limits of your ability – don't be a pussy about anything – but remember whose picture is going to be on the sleeve, and remember how much of their souls they're laying out for all to see. Don't get uppity, not even at three a.m. Don't demand more money or credit or attention than you deserve. As of right now, that's probably less than you're asking for, so start by taking a step backwards."

In many respects the 'sidekick' is the noblest of all the categories. Engineer/producers are the guys who garner the loyalty. These are the only producers other than the Merlin types who consistently make four or five albums with the same artist. Maybe the artists say about the Collaborator (the next category), "Oh we've collaborated with him now let's collaborate with someone else." But an artist can get addicted to a 'sidekick': "I love his drum sound, he knows how I work, we're comfortable, he doesn't get in my way." As Andy Jackson says, "You can roll into the next album and it's like riding a bike. You pick it up where you left off and you haven't got to reinvent the wheel."

For the right kind of personality and with the right co-producer the sidekick role is perfect. It takes a great amount of humility, which I believe every producer should have and good measures of independence and initiative. A great sidekick can, from time to time grab the bull by the horns and do what's needed independently, without looking like they're trying to take over the project, and then be able to seamlessly fall back into the support role.

c) Collaborator

I would say that the vast majority of producers not only fall into this category but would happily characterise themselves as falling into this category. Collaborative producers often come from bands themselves; rarely an ex-lead singer, most likely a drummer or bass player. This may be because they have a history of collaboration within their own groups. They don't see themselves as, or even desire to be, one man bands. They have most likely always enjoyed collaborative situations and they bring that band-member-mentality to their productions. Often they will fit right in, almost as an extra member of the band. They usually prefer to steer the band towards a unanimous decision and use their casting vote sparingly. The collaborator's hallmark is flexibility and a willingness to see the value in other people's ideas. Their own ideas are thrown into the pot with everyone else's and are not necessarily given more weight than another band member's. If the collaborator had a catch phrase it would most likely be "the whole is greater than the sum of the parts".

This relationship is ideal for the musically secure artist who nonetheless would like to have a seasoned ear on site, someone to bounce ideas off and a different, sometimes even opposing, point of view.

The producer's experience can save the artist time, money and frustration. Although there are very few 'can't be done's' in record production, there are a lot of *cul de sacs* that don't need to be explored and can be spotted easily by a studio veteran. The collaborative producer will steer the band away from time wasting situations and recommend methods and approaches that are proven to work for the particular genre in which the band is working.

Jerry Harrison is a good example of a collaborative producer and his approach to producing was characterised in the comment, "I might experiment in the future with playing with more of the bands I produce. But these bands I work with have all been so self-contained that I didn't want to step on anyone's toes. Most of these bands have keyboard and guitar players, and I'm really trying to get their performance down. My attitude is that it's their album, and I'm the one who's facilitating making that album."

8

d) Merlin The Magician

"The best leader is the one who has sense enough to pick good men to do what he wants done, and the self-restraint to keep from meddling with them while they do it." (Theodore Roosevelt)

Merlin is often an intangible force in the proceedings. Perhaps mysteriously, Merlin can garner great loyalty from the artist and record company even though he may spend most of his time on the tennis court, the phone, in meetings, in the car or wherever else producers go when liberated from the studio. In a way he acts like a hands-on A&R consultant, coming in with an objective/subjective view frequently referred to as 'fresh ears'. Peter Collins refers to Merlin as the svengali type of producer and it is true that they often perform a conceptual, almost guru-like role.

Successful Los Angeles based engineer John X (Black Grape) had the experience of working on a four-month album project with a very famous producer who managed to appear for half an hour in the entire four months. Despite this, when the band would go out at night after the session, if anyone asked what they were doing they would proudly announce that they were recording an album with XYZ (the famous absentee producer). I guess the only explanation here is that this particular producer had built such a level of kudos and the band were so impressed by his reputation and track record that, just by being associated with him, they felt that some of his success would rub off on them.

There are many other fantastic stories around about Merlin. One in particular relates to a band that had just delivered their album. In classic form their A&R person said "I don't hear a single". They were told to write more songs and come up with a hit single before the company would release the album. This is by no means an unfamiliar scenario. What followed was the common outcome of this kind of situation. The band holed up in a New York City hotel for about a month attempting to create the required commercial masterpiece. They were thoroughly confused. At the tail end of the month Merlin, who had nothing to do with this particular project, happened to come by the writing room with a mutual acquaintance, where the band were putting the finishing touches to the N'th hit-single contender. They were playing it through as he walked into the room. When they finished playing Merlin pronounced the song a smash. They relayed their depressing tale of what was going on with the album and their state of confusion over the last minute pressure to deliver a hit song. His response was: "I believe in this song so much that I'll produce it myself." He promptly picked up the phone, called the previously worried, but suddenly surprised and delighted, A&R person in England. He told him he'd just heard a number one song and that he would produce it himself. The A&R guy could barely contain himself. Normally, neither he nor the band in question would have had access to a producer of this calibre and reputation. Terms were agreed, the contract was quickly drawn up and security trucks were dispatched with Merlin's advance money. Production would commence a.s.a.p. Merlin would not be seen again for the duration of the project. The band recorded and mixed the single on their own without so much as a phone call from Merlin. It subsequently grazed the Top Ten and launched the group into a short cycle of reasonably healthy single and album sales. Not Number One admittedly, but everyone concerned was happy. Merlin took the money and the credit and moved on to even bigger and better things.

So what actually happened here? Was Merlin's power so great that his pronouncement that the song would be a hit was sufficient to drive it straight through the system into the charts? Was it his depth of experience that enabled him to walk into a room and immediately recognise a hit that might have been passed over by a lesser mortal? Was it his enthusiasm for the song that inspired the record company to market and promote the single effectively? Was it the mere presence of his hallowed name on the label copy that carried the record through to radio? Could he have walked in on any day in that month of writing, made the same pronouncement about any other song and achieved the same result? Who knows, most likely it was a combination of some or all of these factors, but it sure is a nice way to make a living.

If Merlin does decide to spend some time in the studio the direction he gives can range from the very specific, subjective and detailed to the vague, general and philosophical. Sometimes it can be quite obscure. Brian Eno rejects the idea that there are "correct" ways to do things and thinks that we should "learn and enjoy from all the different ways we *can* do things". In keeping with his philosophy, in 1975 he developed his "Oblique Strategy" cards. They featured over one hundred possibilities to help alleviate uncertainty and stasis in the studio. Tony Visconti first showed them to me after he had worked with Eno on a David Bowie album. The cards work on a similar principle to the I Ching. If you arrive at a point where you are unsure or there is some disagreement about what to do next, choose a card. The advice ranges from "consider a different fading system" to "look closely at the most embarrassing details and amplify them". If all else fails you might get lucky and pick the one that says "go outside and shut the door".

Eno himself says "Normally I don't stay with the project for the whole time. I deliberately keep out so I can come back in and hear things with fresh ears. Some things will seem completely obvious to me straight away. Like 'that doesn't work, that works brilliantly, this is confused'. I can very quickly, within an hour's listening, set up an agenda which says, 'This we must talk about philosophically, we have to look at that structurally, we have to look at this in terms of whether it's going anywhere like the direction of the rest of the record'. I set agendas like that, to the extent that I will say that I want to take control of this song for, say, half a day. For half a day I'll say what to do and we'll see if it works. Sometimes it doesn't. And of course any other participant can take the same role. It's very good to be in a working relationship with people and you can say, 'OK, I tried it and it doesn't work', and they say 'Yep, fine'. Fortunately most of the relationships I am in are like that. You have to have the respect for people who say 'look you're grown up, you can take an option and not pretend that it's interesting when it isn't'."

David Bowie once said about working with Eno, "It was a bit like being four-years-old again and having a rather fun uncle who could produce coins out of his ear." Flood (producer of P.J. Harvey, U2, Depeche Mode and Nine Inch Nails) who worked with Eno on the U2 project said of him, "His psychological approach is something that very much influenced me – the way that people can be encouraged, and how to judge a situation and discover what's happening, why it's happening and what its possible outcomes could be. U2's Bono said, "With him we discovered the spirit of our music and a new confidence in ourselves."

Talented and successful artists are not renowned for casually praising producers. As mysterious and obscure as Merlin can be, to be able to inspire these kinds of responses from major artists is a significant achievement.

Talking about his overall attitude to producing, Rick Rubin (Beastie Boys, Run DMC, Red Hot Chili Peppers and co-founder of Def Jam and Def American Records) said, "I look at producing in a very different way from most other producers. I think of it as being more like the director of a film or a play. By that, I mean that for the technical side of it, I hire engineers who I think are competent, much like a director hiring a cinematographer, and I let them do their gig. That doesn't mean I don't have very strong ideas about what I want to hear, but I don't technically know all the bells and whistles to make it sound that way."

Chili Peppers bassist Flea says, "Rick Rubin is an incredibly great producer. He keeps a balance between work and relaxing, maintains complete clarity and focus. He keeps his objectivity while we are completely caught up and so emotional. It might not be great for all bands, but we don't need that emotional push. We're just exploding and coming up with all kinds of stuff, and he helps us harness our energy. And he helps musically, making sure that every song is well crafted. He's had a great track record with hit songs, but you can't really compare any other situation with this one." Singer Anthony Kiedis puts it most succinctly, "Rick has encompassed all the things we need in a producer."

"And he knows when to lie back on the couch and not say a word," adds guitarist John Frusciante. "As a result of his coolness, we've found the accurate, well-rounded colours of music that represent what this band is all about." Flea continues, "Some producers look at little things as they're going on, as opposed to getting the big picture of a song, or an album. Rick's suggestions don't interfere with the emotional feel. The most important thing is the energy and the soul of the music."

There's a certain point at which a producer can simply put his name on a record, get paid and just not show up. This is more common in America than in Europe. Ros Earls says, "I'm not sure whether the Americans are more honest about it. It happens some-times that Flood is asked to mix something and before he's even done it they're saying 'you're great, you're great'. Flood is really adamant that he won't lend his name to something. He gets really angry about the way a name becomes public property, the way a name can help get a record on the radio. They're not really listening to [the work]. The kind of people I represent are very hands-on and involved. That's not to say I disapprove [of the more managerial approach]."

Merlin is undoubtedly the hardest producer-type to aspire to. Mostly we are the kind of producers we are because of our basic personality types. Age and experience are obviously modifying factors. It would be unusual for Merlin to be directly responsible for a great deal of the specific musical and technical content of the record. This is a high concept role, more to do with the overall direction and energy of the album, and the other intangibles that drive an artist's career forward. Merlin has to be able to identify talent and harness it. He is usually charismatic, powerful and extremely successful. A natural leader with an ability to see the "big picture", and not get bogged down in the details.

Merlin's occasional forays into the studio and casually dropped pearls of wisdom can earn him the same place in rock'n'roll immortality, and on the "500 richest" lists as weeks, months or maybe even years of arduous labour by a more conventional hands-on producer. For the producer who spends his waking hours head down over a hot console, the mere suggestion of the existence of these mystical free spirits can be alternately frustrating, infuriating and awe inspiring.

e) Other Ways Of Categorising Producers

There may be as many ways to describe the various roles that producers take as there are working producers in that everyone has their own unique combination of skills and talents. The four categories above focus on the interpersonal relationship between the producer and the artist more than the individual skills of the producer. The nature of this relationship can change project by project, as a relationship matures and over the course of the producer's career. Great producers can move back and forth adjusting their relationship with the artist as needed and as appropriate. You could focus more on base skills in describing production styles – engineer, musician, songwriter, arranger, programmer, DJ, but these days everyone does a bit of everything and the base skill is just a starting point.

Arif Mardin illustrated three categories that existed when he started, "the songwriter producer who is in control of his or her composition and records the song with an artist. We are talking about Gamble & Huff, Lamont Dozier, Leiber & Stoller – songwriter producers. Or you have music lover producers, like Ahmet Ertegun, Jerry Wexler, the Chess brothers, Berry Gordy. They don't have music training but they love music and they have a song sense, they know lyrics and things like that, they can analyse a song. Then the other would be engineer producer, Hugh Padgham, Tom Dowd, they sit behind the controls and help shape the sessions."

I pointed out to Arif that he had missed out his own category, arguably the most successful one of all that he would share with Quincy Jones and George Martin – the arranger producer. Each of these producers has a deep musical background and the very highest levels of formal arranging skills that have enabled them to maximise the potential in the material they are working with. In the terms I have used above these producers would be at the topmost level of the collaborator category. They don't dominate the artist as much as the All-Singing producer, they adapt to the artist's needs which enables them to work with the most powerful and opinionated artists on an equal footing based on their formidable musical prowess and the mutual respect that is thus engendered. Of course as you gain experience in the studio and work with other great producers, engineers, musicians and artists so you learn and grow into a more complex and cross-disciplinary role. Many skills are overlapping, the engineer's ability to identify pleasing or troublesome frequencies is related to the musician's ability to identify pleasing or troublesome notes they just use different language to describe what they are hearing. Arranging and orchestrating is as much about finding or creating space for a sound as is equalisation, compression and the use of effects in engineering and mixing. What it all comes down to is that you have to develop a set of skills that are attractive and complementary to the artist in order to keep working. These can range from the cut to the chase, hitmaking machines such as the 'All-Singing' ..., the complementary, fill in the gaps collaborator, the supportive sidekick or the high-concept guru role of Merlin.

Chapter Two

How Do You Get Started?

"Nothing in the world can take the place of persistence. Talent will not; nothing is more common than unsuccessful men with talent. Genius will not; unrewarded genius is almost a proverb. Education will not; the world is full of educated derelicts. Persistence and determination alone are omnipotent." Calvin Coolidge.

a) What Are The Ways In?

There are seven routes, or launching pads, from which most successful record producers choose to get started:

i)   The musician or artist
ii)   The audio engineer
iii) The songwriter
iv)   The DJ
v)   The self taught home studio hobbyist
vi)   The finding a new act route
vii) The who-the-hell-knows-how-they-got-started.

Eventually, like most British motorways, this seven-lane freeway narrows down to one classic, catch-22, bottleneck. You have to prove that you can actually produce a record before anyone will pay you money to do it or at least be a fast enough talker to convince someone to let you have a go. The fastest talkers usually come from the seventh category, but we'll take them all in turn . . .

i) The Musician Or Artist?
You could get your break if you have an impeccable musical reputation, possibly as an arranger or musical director, but it's more likely that you will have to produce your own very high quality demos or maybe co-produce your band's first few recordings. The latter is an excellent way to get started, largely because you have the benefit of

15

learning at the feet of a master (one hopes) before you are thrown in the deep end.

Producing your own demos is a tried and tested route. But there are several distinct disadvantages: you will be working in a vacuum without anyone to mentor you. You usually need some capital to get started and you will need to either hire a commercial studio or set up your own place – often in your bedroom, which is guaranteed to make you popular with your soul mate! Even in these times of incredibly inexpensive digital recording equipment, a decent home set-up capable of moving you into the big league will be somewhat damaging to your financial health (unless you have a trust fund you can raid).

Certain techniques that are common currency among the pros may take on the mysteries of the most arcane forms of alchemy when you are locked in your bedroom with your so-far disappointing demo and very big ambitions.

I'm biased, for sure, but I do think there are two major advantages in coming to producing from a music background: you speak the same language as the musicians and artists, and you know how it feels on the other side of the glass.

I will never forget the frustration of standing in the studio after having given my all on the last take and watching the producer, through the glass, either chatting on the phone, or having a discussion with someone in the control room. It's a very simple thing to push the talkback button and let the artist or musicians know what is going on, but it may not occur to someone who has never been a studio performer. A musician instinctively understands how much more enjoyable the session is when the engineer is aware of the musicians needs and has done his preparation.

Albhy Galuten who produced hits with The Bee Gees, Andy Gibb, Samantha Sang, Barbra Streisand, Kenny Rogers, Diana Ross and Dionne Warwick developed his career from his beginnings as a guitarist and keyboard player through string arranging, songwriting and eventually producing. His studio experience began at the legendary Ardent Studios in Memphis. He landed a job assisting Tom Dowd at Criteria in Miami by hanging out with friends who had been hired as part of the Atlantic rhythm section in Miami. During this time he learned his craft on records such as Eric Clapton's *Layla* and The Allman Brothers' *Eat A Peach*. The assisting job eventually led to a staff producer position with Atlantic. His musical training began with piano lessons through high school, a couple of years at Berklee in Boston and playing in several bands. He says, "There are two levels of learning: theory, notes, understanding what's going on, the technique. But there is also the development of the ears. I discovered that in the studio with Tommy Dowd and Jerry Wexler."

Another successful producer who got his start through arranging is Tony Visconti. He eventually worked with Procol Harum, The Move, T. Rex, Joe Cocker, David Bowie, Marc Bolan, Badfinger, Gentle Giant, Thin Lizzy, Boomtown Rats, The Stranglers, The Alarm, and U2. In 1967 he left America to settle in Britain. "In American studios at that time, it was still the old régime where you had to make an album in three days. You'd take six to twelve hours for recording, three hours to mix it. I was being trained as a record producer in New York by my publishing company, they'd tell me what budgets were available. And I was doing a little talent scouting. I was a rejected songwriter, so in one fell swoop I was fired as a songwriter and hired as a record producer because my demos were good. Anyway, it seemed like all the records I was buying were British records, and then I would read articles about how The Beatles took one week per song to make *Revolver* – like thirteen weeks on an album – and I thought, 'just give me two weeks and I'll make a great album!'

"Then, through very lucky circumstances, I met Denny Cordell who was the producer of Procol Harum and Joe Cocker and The Move and Georgie Fame. He had come to New York to make a record with Georgie Fame called 'Because I Love You' and he was hiring all these good players like Clark Terry to play on it, but he didn't have a chart. He thought he was just going to play them the demo, and then they'd write their own charts. So I said, 'That's going to cost you a fortune in New York City'. So I wrote a quick arrangement and copied out the trumpet line from the demo, and then the session went very well, and he hired me to be his assistant in London. I worked for Denny Cordell for two years and through him, I made a lot of contacts. I met both David Bowie and Marc Bolan during those two years. I met Bowie through his publisher, and Marc Bolan I found on my own – I went talent scouting and found him playing in a club one night. Then, through having hits with those two guys, people came to me."

Jerry Harrison of Talking Heads says that his co-production role on *Remain In Light* with the rest of the band and Brian Eno helped get him started as a producer. "By the time we did that album, the barriers between musicians and producer were being broken down because we were writing the songs in the studio. So there were times when Brian was playing parts and we would be saying, 'Well, Brian, that's not right. Try something else'. So there was a lot of back and forth at that point. I think it was those experiences making the albums with Brian that kind of gave me the knowledge, you might say, to go on to start working with other people as a producer."

Walter Afanasieff started as a musician and worked for Bay Area producer Narada Michael Walden. Eventually he stepped into the production role himself. Speaking about their working relationship in 1991, he said: "I've learned a great deal from Narada, but now it's time to leave the nest and set up my own shop. I will always draw upon what I've learned from him. However, I've been anxious to be doing things on my own for a while, and now's a great time for me to move on. We'll always be great friends and now we'll be working neighbours. He's a great guy and incredibly talented."

Danny Saber has risen to prominence with his mid-Nineties productions for Black Grape. When I first met him in 1989 he worked in a tuxedo store in Hollywood. He was playing in a band with unsigned artist Issa Joone and making eight-track demos in her garage. He started out wanting to be a musician – Jimi Hendrix was a big influence. As a teenager he would play rhythm guitar on one tape recorder, play that tape back and record a solo over it onto another machine. He says: "When I was 15, I would go in the studio and tell the stoned-out engineer from the Sixties that I wanted to double my guitar. He would look at me and think' 'who's this punk?' Then I would nail it. With recording, it was the one thing in life that I always seemed to get right, even before I knew what I was doing. So that all led to the producing thing. At first I would do tracks with little rap bands."

Around this time he signed a publishing deal with EMI. That led to writing opportunities with a number of artists in the US and UK. His first real break was when he produced Proper Ground, Madonna's first signing for her own Maverick Records. The record was not a hit but opened the door for more work. "Even when I first met you I always wanted to produce but I had a long way to go," he told me. "I've known that for a long time even since I was working with bands. I was always the one who said 'do this, do that'."

Unfortunately, simply having the desire to be a record producer is not usually enough. The known universe is loaded with would-be record producers. Clearly there is a groove in the time/space continuum because an inordinate number of these aspirants seem to have slipped into the greater Los Angeles area. Most of these characters will regale you with stories about how they just didn't get the breaks or the opportunities did not open up for them. They're frequently only one (very expensive) piece of equipment away from completing their home studio to the level that they can finally deliver the killer tracks.

To be sure, everyone needs a break. No matter how talented an individual may be, multiple unknown factors have to align themselves before raw talent translates into industry success. When it comes to opportunity I believe you have to create, finagle, prepare for and at the very least develop an eagle eye for identifying what will most likely be a fleeting opportunity; a brief, fast-moving window in time that opens up before you. If you are ready, you dive through. If you are not, maybe it'll come around again and maybe it won't.

I once played with a lounge band as a substitute drummer whenever the regular drummer wanted a night off. This was a pretty good band. They played all the old jazz standards and one of the guys had actually played with Charlie Parker. Some of the musicians were full-time and some of them had day jobs. I was very young at the time but I must have had an invisible sign hanging round my neck saying that I was going somewhere in the business. At every break one of the regular players would buttonhole me and tell me how much he hated his day job and that if he just got the right breaks he would "go pro". I probably played this gig once every two or three weeks over a period of about six months. This guy's favourite band (this was the Seventies) was The Carpenters. It gradually became apparent what he thought would constitute a lucky break. In this scenario The Carpenters would happen upon this establishment one evening having just lost their guitarist. In the middle of their fine dining experience they would gradually realise that the answer to their personnel problem was performing before their very eyes. Of course the happy end to this fairy tale is that they would whisk him away on a whirlwind agenda of tours, recording and personal appearances.

Now I may have stretched this story slightly but the basic elements are not only true but applicable in a wider sense to the actions of a lot of individuals supposedly wishing to break into the big time of the music business.

I've worked with musicians, engineers and even some record company executives who also seem to operate on the basis that a giant hand is going to reach down, pluck them from obscurity and thrust them into the forefront of the international record production arena.

I would never underplay the importance of luck, divine providence, good fortune or whatever you want to call it. However, without exception the success stories that I have encountered have been attached to individuals who not only exhibited raw talent but also persistence, determination and a willingness to take risks.

ii) The Audio Engineer

. . . you will generally start at the bottom of the pile, making tea and coffee for the stars, the assistant stars and probably the demi-friend of the assistant to the assistant stars. Short of an engineer dying on the job this can go on for several years. In my experience most tea-boy/tape ops/assistants don't take the best advantage of these weeks/months/years. Many assistants sit at the back of the room reading magazines, talking on the phone or just looking bored. This is the only time in your life that world-class engineers and producers are going to let you look over their shoulders, study their techniques and even write down their eq's and favourite reverb settings. The assistant also participates in the most intimate studio moments and has the opportunity to learn the unteachable secret of the record producer – how to handle the artist. The best assistants, the ones who go on to bigger and better things, don't regard the job as beneath them. They instinctively recognise that they are the lubricant that keeps the session from squeaking.

Flood got his nickname when he was assisting at Morgan Studios because he was so on the ball with tea making, a vital function anywhere within the British (ex) Empire. Flood said, "The first four years or so of my career were very important. In some respects, I think that what a lot of people are suffering from, certainly over in this country, is lack of grounding in learning a craft. From when I first started to when I first went freelance was almost six years, and I think that a lot of the time people don't have that luxury anymore, to get that experience in different situations."

"When Flood was head engineer, the tape op to assistant to engineer process was very strict," says his manager, Ros Earls. "You'd be looking for the sort of people that would turn into engineers and then producers. People like Steve Osborne (engineering partner with dance supremo Paul Oakenfold), I employed him as a tea boy, it's a difficult thing to do. You're wondering whether they're going to be easy people to have around. They're going to have intelligence, musical taste, personal creative ambition. And they're not necessarily the same sort of people you want to have making your tea and filling your papers in."

Ros thinks that there's an unhealthy pressure to move up through the ranks now. She says, "It used to be that people went through a strict training and it would be like getting your 'O' levels and 'A' levels via a studio. Up to the mid-Eighties people would do their apprenticeship in a studio and then, at some point, they would realise that they were capable of doing more than engineering. Engineers have always been regarded [in England] as 'just' an engineer which they aren't in America. People there may be engineers for forty years and they are formidable talents. What's happened recently is that people are looking for a manager earlier. Studios are taking on less permanent staff. There's a lot more competition at an earlier stage now, so some people will only have a year's experience in a studio and they'll be looking for a freelance manager."

Andy Jackson came up through the ranks at Utopia Studios in London. He subsequently engineered several Pink Floyd and Roger Waters albums. He says, "I was quite lucky when I came in. It was Utopia and it was quite new when I started. The place expanded very quickly. I got opportunities to engineer demos and jingles within a year. That was good discipline because you had to work very quickly. A lot of studios I would've had to wait two or three years before I got to engineer something." Although it is generally a slower way to get started, Andy feels that a period of assisting in a major studio is incredibly valuable. He says, "I was seeing good practice. Good sound stuff, classic techniques. I didn't get to work with that many bad engineers. It's very easy to spot them and it just reinforces the good techniques you have learnt."

It's not just the engineering tricks that you can pick up on, but the way the producer handles the session in general. Andy says, "Everybody has a different approach. You just pick up bits and pieces. Not just in terms of techniques but attitudes to the actual fulfillment of getting a record made and ways of handling people. Bob Ezrin (who worked with Pink Floyd) has been a good example. I may not agree with everything he does but he's a 'get things done' person, some of that's been really useful practice to have picked up. He has a little saying, which is 'do anything even if it's wrong'. What he's getting at is 'let's do *something* rather than sit around scratching our heads not knowing *what* to do. Let's do something and react to it.' You can say 'this isn't right and I can see why this isn't right so it gives me an insight into what would work.'

"Some projects I've worked on have been horrendously slow. People usually assume that's because the artist is being meticulous, but a lot of it is because the artist is being lazy and doesn't show up, or they'll show up and get two hour's work done in a day. One producer I work with takes the attitude that if the artist is not there then he'll get on and make the record and the artist will have to do something about it. The producer will sit down and compile the guitar solos and if the guitarist doesn't like it, then he'll have to come in and re-do it himself. It forces his hand. It's a fine line. It's the artist's record but that's why they hire a producer. In this particular situation the producer will get it done and he will stand up to the artist. He is not overawed by the fact that this is a multi-million selling artist. He won't be a 'yes' man to them and that is one of the big reasons why he is involved. At the same time he can be quite mercenary about it. He's not there because of the art of it. If by taking a stand it forces the artist to make a decision that moves things forward, then he's happy with that outcome. He'll argue his case but the artist will have the last word."

Smashing Pumpkins' producer Alan Moulder started as an assistant engineer at the world famous Trident Studios in London. He describes how he moved from engineering to producing. "I worked with bands and you end up getting a bit of a relationship with them. Then they decide to bypass their producer to do some B-sides so you get to do some tracks on your own with them." He adds, "It's mainly from co-production – where bands want to do the record and have a big input themselves. Most of them have a pretty good idea of what they want or how they want to sound and they have a lot of ideas in their head. I'll collaborate with them to try to get that and if we come across problems I'll act like a referee or be the one to point out that something's not working. I try to make things run as smoothly as possible, as quickly as possible, and I'll come up with ideas if they're needed. Maybe with the structure of a song or if the parts aren't working. So I'll act as an extra opinion."

I believe that, to some extent, you can predict an assistant's future in the business from the first time you work with them. Among other things it's characterised in the way they deal with the lunch order. The assistants that I worked with who consistently got it wrong didn't translate into successful producers. The assistants I've worked with, including Tim Palmer (mixed Pearl Jam's first album *Ten*) when he first started at Utopia, Alan Moulder at Trident (produced Smashing Pumpkins), Pete Walsh at Utopia (produced Simple Minds) and Flood at Morgan Studios, were always right there when you needed them. They seemed to have an ability to read the "vibe" in the room. Teas and coffees would arrive at precisely the right moment. They are extremely intelligent but they don't mind doing mundane tasks. They fit in very well without being too chummy.

Chris Lord-Alge spoke about getting started as an engineer. "Find the best studio in town and fight your way in. Get a job, whether you're pushing a broom or cleaning the toilets, and work your way up from there. Don't be scared to take a chance on anything. The only way you are going to learn is by watching the best at what they do."

Don Gehman (producer of Hootie & The Blowfish's 14+ million-selling début album) said, "When I was coming up as an engineer we were always told that we were supposed to guess what the next move was, and be set up for it, before we went there. Sometimes that means doing two or three things at once, but that's the mark of a good assistant."

Engineer to producer is a very natural route. As Mitchell Froom (who started as a musician) says, "Good engineers contribute a lot to the production. People need titles, but every record has production suggestions from other people."

One problem that engineers can face when trying to make the move to production is that record companies would sooner keep paying them as an engineer, knowing that in reality they are doing a lot if not all of the production work.

Jack Douglas' track record includes six Aerosmith albums, three with Cheap Trick, John Lennon's *Double Fantasy* and Alice Cooper's anthem 'School's Out'. Douglas started out in bands but while recording at A&R Recording found that the other side of the glass held more fascination for him. An engineer at New York's A&R Studio told him about a new studio opening up where everyone was going – Shelley Yakus, Roy Cicala, Jay Messina – The Record Plant. Douglas started out cleaning toilets and moving Hendrix tapes around during the period they were working on the *Woodstock* sound-track there. Gradually he worked his way up to tape librarian and eventually assistant engineer. His leap to engineering was sudden and dramatic. "There was an engineer there, Jack Adams. He was doing The Who sessions for what would be *Who's Next.* He did the R&B that came into the place and didn't like rock, no matter who the artist was. So we get the room set up and he says to me, 'I hate this rock shit, I don't care about any of it'.

"Now Jack lived on a houseboat on the 79th Street boat basin. So he tells me to go into the other room and tells me to call him on the phone and say his houseboat is on fire. He was like a method actor – he needed motivation to lie. So I'm twelve feet away and telling him his houseboat's on fire, and I can hear him screaming, telling Kit Lambert (the producer) and Pete Townshend that his boat's on fire. It's sinking in the boat basin. He tells them that I'm not the assistant but the other engineer on the session and that I'll be doing the sessions. Up till then, I had only done some jingle dates and one record session with Patti LaBelle during which I had set the old Datamix console on fire by knocking someone's beer onto the trans-formers. So I was a little nervous. Everything was all set up. The first song was 'Won't Get Fooled Again'."[*]

This is a particularly dramatic story but it seems a lot of engineers and producers who go on to be highly successful get thrown in the deep end early on in their careers.

Douglas made the move into production. "There were a few famous producers I was working with who had a habit of not showing up and calling to see how things were going. Bob Ezrin (Pink Floyd) made me aware that I was already producing because of that. He got me to do some Canadian records, like Crowbar, to get me to, in a sense, open out of town, so I wouldn't fall on my butt in New York. He was priming me for the next Alice Cooper album, *Muscle Of Love.*"

Greg Ladanyi also made the move from engineer to producer. He was a GRAMMY Award winning engineer (*Toto IV*) and was nominated as producer of the year with Don Henley on *Building The Perfect Beast.* Talking about making the move from engineering to producing he said, "I was working during a time in the record industry where artists became more involved. Engineers became

---

[*] In the event The Who scrapped the material from these sessions and re-recorded the tracks for *Who's Next* at Olympic Studios in London, with Glyn Johns producing.

more and more valuable, and I was lucky to be around. We became valuable because we could sit with the artist and help them as co-producers. That led me into co-producing, and later to producing because I got better at it, better at listening and capturing performances. And I learned about arranging songs from people like Jackson Browne and Don Henley."

The transition from engineer to producer is less painful if your engineering history encompasses mega-acts like The Beatles and Pink Floyd. Alan Parsons turned a glittering engineering career into an equally glittering production track record. "I think that producing was a fairly natural progression. I was in touch with a lot of people from EMI records, a lot of the A&R people. The first things I did were for Pilot and Cockney Rebel, both EMI projects. I think it evolved as a result of getting a reputation from the Pink Floyd album and just doing bits and pieces in a production capacity with other producers. The word just got out that I was capable of doing it. But I never actually went up to record companies and said, 'Will you let me produce this act?' They actually gave them to me, which is rather nice."

There is a story told about an engineer who was the only one from the production team in the studio throughout a particular project. He was the only one who had any day-to-day relationship with the artist and he took the brunt and the whole responsibility of the production. There were several other producers with huge names who would just dip in and out for a week and then disappear. One producer would come in and listen to a couple of tracks, give the band pointers on the mixes and take a substantial royalty. The engineer felt that he was holding the project together for not a lot of recognition. This production methodology had been set up by the artist who was already extremely successful. They obviously considered the royalties they were giving away to the consultant producers to be worthwhile. The engineer's contribution was eventually rewarded. On later albums he was given a co-production credit and his career made the leap to hyper-space. Talent, patience and paying your dues can pay off.

In fact, a great number of engineers make the leap to producing from having engineered a particularly successful record. Mike Clink produced Guns'n'Roses' *Appetite For Destruction* after engineering bands like Whitesnake for the same label. Brendon O'Brien went on to produce Stone Temple Pilots and Pearl Jam after engineering for Rick Rubin. Hugh Padgham's engineering career included Peter

Gabriel's seminal, third solo album. That was the project which gave the world the Phil Collins drum sound. Hugh went on to co-produce Phil Collins, The Police, Sting and Genesis. Now he commands production credits of his own.

"Flood developed from engineer to co-mixer to 'recorded by' credit which is always an interesting one," says his manager Ros. "It doesn't really mean anything but implies a better position than just engineer. 'Recorded and mixed by' doesn't actually mean that the person engineered the project. It implies an overseeing, chief engineer kind of position. There could be a dozen engineers on the project. 'Recorded and mixed by' says that you were in charge of the whole recording process but you don't get royalties for that. Some producers do millions and millions of different things and other producers grow with projects. Flood did all of the Depeche Mode albums but started off engineering. On the second one he was co-producing with the band and on the third one he was producing."

The producer of any hugely successful record immediately becomes massively desirable and, based on the good old principle of supply and demand, wildly expensive, but here's the scenario wherein an engineer might get his first big break. A new artist comes to discuss with his A&R person who he would like to have produce his first record. Inevitably the artist will suggest at least one producer who has a current big hit or a string of hits. Usually, while trying not to flinch visibly, the A&R person will say, "Well, I just spoke to him yesterday and he is not available for the next twelve months at least." If the A&R person is in a semi-honest mood he may say, "No, he's going to cost you at least $150,000 and you don't want to take on that much debt at this point in your career, but how about so and so who engineered the record and has been his right-hand person for the last two years." Well, if you happen to be so and so, that recommendation could be a very painless entrée into a major league production career.

iii) The Songwriter
Some of the greatest producers and production teams have used their songs as a foot in the door. It may be that the songwriter is not necessarily that interested in production – but enduring a couple of badly produced versions of your beloved songs is generally sufficient to convince you that you could do a better job yourself. Wendy Page who has produced songs she wrote for Hilary Duff and Lulu said she

got into production, "because I wanted to make the songs I wrote sound how I wanted to hear them."

The line between writing and producing has become blurred in recent years for a number of reasons. Writers almost invariably have well-equipped home studios and make very sophisticated demos. But at the same time publishers, artists, producers and A&R people have in recent years been spoiled by the high quality of song demos, and in too many cases can no longer "hear" the voice and piano or voice and guitar demos.

Unless you have a huge reputation, the opportunity to bang out your latest ditty on a piano in the publisher or A&R person's office just does not exist. They not only want to hear a high quality demo but one that is in the style of the artist for whom it is intended. In fact, if you happen to be looking for songs for a less famous artist during the six months after, say, Christina Aguilera, Britney Spears or Whitney Houston finish their album, the publishers will send you a gaggle of highly produced demos that sound just like Christina, Britney or Whitney. These are the songs that have just been released from being 'on hold' for the past six, twelve or eighteen months, waiting for one of the coveted ten or twelve places on these all but guaranteed multi-platinum albums.

The consistently successful songwriter producer is very powerful and usually becomes the All-Singing-All-Dancing type of producer. The Neptunes, The Matrix, Scott Storch, Timbaland, Max Martin, L.A. & Babyface, Jam & Lewis, Narada Michael Walden, Walter Afanasieff, Gamble & Huff, and Holland, Dozier, Holland are a few good examples.

Collaborating with an artist on their songs is a less hit and miss way of nailing the production job for a number of reasons. You get a chance to build a close relationship with them, you get a low pressure opportunity to establish your production abilities in their minds and if they enjoy working with you they will go to bat for you with the record company. The artist will also have a vested interest in songs you write and produce together going on the album.

Shep Pettibone was able to make the move from being Madonna's remixer to her co-producer on the *Erotica* album by collaborating with her at the writing stage. Obviously, he already had a good working relationship with Madonna because of the remixes he had done for her. Had he simply tried to write songs for her he would have been competing with the entire songwriting population of the free world. Instead he did what he does best: built tracks in the style of his remixes for which she could write the lyrics and melodies. The nature of dance music is such that the production ideas, the parts, the sounds and the song itself are almost inextricably intertwined. Once Pettibone and Madonna had written and demoed the songs together, not only was there little point in bringing in an outside producer, but they wound up transferring most of the stuff they had recorded on the eight-track demos over to 24-track tape and onto the final record.

Pettibone gives an example of how the process ran: "It took about two or three days to write a song from beginning to end. Still, sometimes even after they were done we'd want to change the flow of the song and ask the song a few questions: Where should the chorus hit? Should it be a double chorus? Sometimes Madonna would call me in the middle of the night and say, 'Shep, I think the chorus should go like this.' Or, 'I hate this verse, fix the bass line.' 'Deeper and Deeper' was one of those songs she always had a problem with. The middle of the song wasn't working. We tried different bridges and changes, but nothing worked. In the end, Madonna wanted the middle of the song to have a flamenco guitar strumming big-time. I didn't like the idea of taking a Philly house song and putting 'Isla Bonita' in the middle of it. But that's what she wanted so that's what she got."

iv) The DJ Producers . . .

DJ Producers have been around since the early Eighties and are now pretty much a fixture of the club and hip-hop scene, spilling over into R&B and pop. Usually they specialise in dance or rap records. Being a successful music producer has a great deal to do with understanding how music affects people and you can learn a lot about exactly that from being a DJ. There are the DJs that just spin and their appeal is based on programming the right music for the occasion and keeping the flow going throughout their set. They learn a lot about pacing and audience reaction to certain beats, tempos, artists and song types. DJs very often become experts in certain genres and subgenres of music. The DJs that scratch are really producers in training even if they don't know it. Beatmatching, beatmixing and beatjuggling as well as blending a cappella vocal versions with other instrumental tracks in a live situation teach all the basic techniques for the way many records, particularly the loop based ones such as hip-hop and dance, are put together. Not only that but many DJs use samplers and drum machines live to augment the vinyl or CDs they are spinning as well as all the various scratching techniques which are really just ways of using turntables and vinyl to add percussion to an existing track. So they are developing technical skills, a great understanding of repertoire, a good understanding of the history of, at least, their genre of interest, as well as how the audience interacts with what they play. Very often DJ producers will continue to DJ long after it ceases to be a fiscal necessity. They know that it is this umbilical connection that keeps them at the cutting edge of club trends.

Arthur Baker started off working in a Boston record store, went on to spin records at a local club, where he met Tom Silverman of Tommy Boy Records. Baker moved to New York City in 1980, working with some of the early hip-hop artists, Afrika Bambaataa and New Edition. His work as a producer and writer led to remix work with artists such as David Bowie, Mick Jagger, and Cyndi Lauper. He now prefers to concentrate on production rather than remixes.

Rick Rubin started producing without any training or background in bands or studios while he was still in college. He had been DJ-ing at clubs and was fascinated by rap because he saw it was a whole different sound. He says, "Being a fan and understanding what rap was really about, I just tried to capture that on record, and ironically part of the answer was not knowing anything about the technology and what was considered right or wrong in the studio. It was about capturing some really awkward sounds at times. Looking back they're pretty funny-sounding records, but that was what was going on."

Cypress Hill's DJ Muggs has written, produced and mixed tracks for The Beastie Boys, Ice Cube, House Of Pain, Funkdoobiest, Daddy Freddy, YoYo and Mellow Man Ace. He has done remixes for Janet Jackson and U2. His own band's 'Black Sunday' went straight to Number One in the *Billboard* charts. DJ Muggs (real name Larry Muggerud) grew up in Queens, New York, and moved to Los Angeles during high school. It was his love of rap music and break-dancing which eventually led to DJ'ing. He started producing his own tracks using a pair of Technics SP1200's while in tenth grade. In the mid-Eighties he formed the 'Spanglish' rap group DVX with B-Real and Sen Dog, the three of whom would eventually become Cypress Hill. When DVX broke up less than a year later he joined forces with the rappers 7A3, released an album on Geffen and got a song on the *Colors* soundtrack. When Muggs decided to get back with B-Real and Sen Dog to form Cypress Hill, he sent the early demos to Joe 'The

Butcher' Nicolo, a young engineer from Philly. He had liked his style when they worked together on the 7A3 album. Nicolo signed the band to his newly formed Ruffhouse Records and got distribution through Columbia.

Talking about his working relationship with Nicolo, Muggs said, "Joe taught me a lot. He's a hell of an engineer. Now, I go to mix with Joe. When we're mixing songs, he'll add an idea here and there, and he'll ask me if I like it or not. And some things I like and some things I don't. He doesn't mix my records, he engineers my records, and he'll add a few ideas in the mix. Me and Joe have a good vibe together, that's why I stick with him."

DJ producers often work with samples in a montage or collage kind of style that is based on the way they might put a mix together live with two turntables. In a completely different musical discipline this way of working was pioneered in a purer, more intellectual form by Stockhausen in his *musique concrète* work in the Fifties. The obvious advantage of working with samples is that you are not starting with a 'blank sheet of paper'. You don't have to build a groove up from nothing and hope that it will work. You simply take a groove from a record that is already proven, add another sample from a different record on top of that and build up a new track from there. Eno says of this, "I admire people like Howie B who turn up with their record collections and they don't bring a single instrument with them. They just patch together other bits of music. This is so intelligent. You get all the cultural resonances of one sound, and then you stick it with all the complexity and cultural resonances of another. I really admire economy more than anything else: elegant ways of making big things happen – which is the opposite of what normally happens in a studio, where you have clumsy ways of making small things happen."

Although Jack Douglas came up through the traditional tape op/assistant way he says, "There's guys out there that just walk into a studio from a club where they're DJ-ing and they sound phenomenal." He attributes this to the fact that a DJ spends so much time listening to records.

Part-time DJ and record storeowner Shep Pettibone capitalised on the Eighties remix craze by rebuilding tracks for dance artists such as Gloria Gaynor, Alisha and Loleatta Holloway. The new wave of British acts such as Pet Shop Boys, Thompson Twins, New Order and Erasure were generating music primed for Pettibone's explosive mixes. Suddenly radio discovered dance music and the remix sound became 'the sound'. Janet Jackson, Paula Abdul, MC Hammer, Lionel Richie, Prince, Cyndi Lauper and Madonna had all been re-created for clubs by Shep Pettibone. "By the time I worked on 'Like A Prayer' and 'Express Yourself'," says Pettibone, "it looked as if Madonna liked the remixed versions better than the ones that were on the album. That was great, but producing was still at the top of my wish list." Finally she asked him to write and produce a B-side for the single off the *Breathless* album. That B-side turned into 'Vogue' and became the biggest selling single of 1990. Pettibone had arrived as a producer. Madonna encouraged him to continue writing and a single evolved into the album *Erotica.*

The advantage and disadvantage of working with superstars is that the album is not done when you run out of money, it's done when they are happy with it. "Madonna's attitude was 'Either make the song work, or it's not going on the album. That's that'. Patience was not one of her virtues either and if some sequencing was taking a little time she would say, 'What are you guys doing that's taking so long?' And that was just after the first few minutes," says Pettibone. "We'd tell her to go downstairs and make some popcorn or phone calls so that we could put the song together and she'd do that for about five minutes before screaming, 'Come on guys, I'm getting bored!' I had to keep things moving as fast as possible because it's one of my jobs to keep Madonna from losing interest in what she's doing."

Undoubtedly part of the key to being a good producer is having an instinctive understanding of what a good record really sounds like, and how it works on an emotional level with the audience. DJ's are invariably huge fans of their particular genre of interest. They have huge collections of vinyl, CDs, and MP3s, they know the history and they have a real feel for what works and what doesn't. Knowing how to produce a track that will excite an audience enough to pay money for it is a matter of either acquiring the skills to do it yourself or assembling a great team that has complementary skills to yours.

v) The Self Taught Home Studio Hobbyist

I'm not even sure that hobby is a word anymore. It conjures up images of ancient sheds filled with shortwave, ham radio equipment. This category used to be the domain of the solitary tech-head, the mid-twentieth century predecessor of the geek, the one with glasses on the right hand end of the evolutionary chart. Nowadays, because of the proliferation of inexpensive technology everyone has a home studio. And geekdom is cool. These days the home studio hobbyist is usually a musician also, so this has now become a sort of DIY engineer/musician route. It is possible to be a non-musical, home studio hobbyist. If you don't have musical training or experience, in order to get started from home you will need either an aptitude for figuring out software and all things technical or an innate ability to manipulate your musician friends. In the latter case forget the years of apprenticeship – jump straight into the Merlin style of production.

If you are a natural, technical, programmer/home studio geek, then you are really treading a self-trained engineer route without the benefit of the mentoring you would get in a studio apprenticeship. You're on your own and you'll have to figure it out for yourself. Books, magazines and trial and error will be your main source of information. As will the musician-with-the-home-studio, you will spend ages working out things that are basic to the pros. Fortunately, in the past 25 years, there have been many books and magazines published that give blow-by-blow accounts of how to record vocals/drums/saxophone and so on. The upside of the self-teaching method is that you will have the opportunity to develop a unique style.

Jack Endino, the Godfather of Grunge, used a home studio to develop a unique style and to create a place in rock and roll history. He was certainly instrumental in shaping the early Seattle sound, having recorded over 80 albums, 110 seven inch singles and 300 EPs, from more than 200 bands, including Soundgarden, Mudhoney, Screaming Trees, Afghan Whigs, L7, Babes In Toyland and, perhaps most famously, Nirvana. He started out in his basement using a TEAC quarter inch four-track machine to record his own band, then around 1983, he started recording other bands such as Soundgarden and Green River for five dollars an hour. He got a track on a popular compilation called *Deep Six,* which led to a job, engineering in a new local recording studio.

Many of the clients he had in his basement days followed him to the new Reciprocal Studios. "During '85 and '86 there was nobody in Seattle who was good at recording grungy rock bands, and especially for cheap," he says. "It's a small town and when people found out I was making decent sounding recordings for next to nothing, they beat a path to my door. I was recording frantically – about a single a week. It seemed like everybody was coming to me with or without Sub Pop, with or without a record deal."

Although Jerry Harrison came into producing through the musician route and credits Eno with demystifying the production process for him, he did say, "I think that's a process that's gone on a lot now that people have home studios and home equipment. When I work with bands now, everybody is much, much more familiar with the options one has in the studio. People know about delays, they know about reverbs, because they all have home versions of the more expensive items in the studio. Whereas when I first started making records, the studio was more of a mystery. You went in there and they did what they did. You went out in a room and played and then came in and listened to it. If you went back to the time of The Beatles, the engineers used to wear lab coats because they considered themselves technicians."

If self taught seems like your only option I would encourage you to do anything you can to get some outside input, take a course at a local college or a summer school, go to seminars and panels, hang out in the back of the nearest pro studio. Confucius obviously knew a thing or two about producing when he said, "By three methods we may learn wisdom: first, by reflection, which is noblest; second, by imitation, which is easiest; and third, by experience, which is the bitterest." Save yourself the agony and learn as much as you can from the most experienced people who are available to you.

vi) The Finding A New Act Routine

One way or another, a successful production career is dependent on being able to find good acts. Later on you will have to pick from the plethora the labels or your manager bring you. At the beginning of your career knowing who the best local artists are can be a rocket to the stars. When your career is adopting a belly-up posture pulling a hit act out of the hat can be a lifesaver.

George Martin signed The Beatles. Tony Visconti discovered Marc Bolan. John Kurzweg produced Creed's multiplatinum album *My Own Prison* for $6000 in his home studio before they had a record deal. I got my first real shot at producing by becoming friends with Spandau Ballet well before they were signed. Being there early and seeing them live, understanding what they were about and being able to build a relationship with them before the feeding frenzy happened, all helped when it came time for them to choose a producer. Labels like to think that they choose the producer, but ultimately it's the band that chooses.

Russ Titleman's highly successful career was based on finding an artist. He produced his first album in 1969 by taking a musician friend's band over to another friend, Lenny Waronker, who happened to be at Warner Bros at the time. The musician friend was Lowell George and the band was Little Feat. Lowell and Bill Payne (Little Feat keyboardist) played a couple of songs and Lenny said, "Great. Go talk to Mo (Ostin) and let's make a record."

These days deals are not usually done that fast. Clearly, it is not 1969 and most of us don't start out having friends like Lowell George and Lenny Waronker. The principle, however, remains the same. Find a band or artist that you really believe in. Convince a record company that the artist is hot. Establish your own credibility as a producer – make great sounding demos, be hip, inexpensive and come across as if you understand the new scene and you have your foot in the door.

The producer who uses this route, especially early in his career, can do well in the music business. Finding raw talent and developing it into a successful act is at the core of the industry. One bona fide superstar can carry you to the higher echelons of the music business.

Peter Asher is a producer who has inhabited the stellar regions of the music business for many years, partly because of his production abilities and partly because he was able to discover, sign and develop an artist who became a megastar. He has produced 28 Gold albums, 18 Platinum and won two GRAMMY Awards, 21 years apart. His introduction to the music business was as a member of the pop duo Peter & Gordon. After nine Top 20 records he moved into A&R for The Beatles' Apple label. He actually credits Paul Jones, the ex-Manfred Mann lead singer, with giving him his break into production. "I owe him a lot because he was the first person who said he liked my ideas and asked if I would produce his record.[*] It was a bold step on his part, for which I am grateful."

Right after Asher started working for Apple he made the connection that would secure his place in the Producers' Hall of Fame. Danny Kortchmar, who would also go on to become a successful producer in his own right, had played in Asher's backing band. Kortchmar's childhood friend and partner in a band called The

---

[*] A single, "And The Sun Will Shine"/ "The Dog Presides", featuring Jeff Beck on guitar, released by Columbia in 1968.

Flying Machine was James Taylor. When The Flying Machine broke up, Taylor decided to move to London. Danny Kortchmar had given Taylor Peter Asher's number. The rest of the story is rock'n'roll history: they hooked up, Taylor played a tape for Asher who was knocked out and said, "Listen, it so happens I've just started working for this new label – I'd like to sign you to the label and produce your new record. It all fell into place very easily."

The finding a new act route is a great way to turbo charge any one of the other routes including the next one. The right new artist will take you from zero to sixty in no time flat.

vii) Who-The-Hell-Knows-How-They-Got-Started
Believe it or not there are producers who don't engineer, don't play an instrument or sing particularly well, weren't DJ's and didn't work at a record label. For better or for worse they are hustlers par excellence. They can talk up a storm and they know enough about what they don't know to surround themselves with talented engineers, programmers and musicians. The trade off for the programmers, musicians and engineers who will actually make the record is that the hustler (sorry – producer) pulls in the work. These guys (I have never met a woman of this persuasion) will usually claim to have a music background meaning they were in a band at school (wasn't everyone in a band at school?) or worked in a record store one summer vacation. Required skills are to be a born leader and have the gift of the gab.

b) OK – So You Want To Be A Record Producer – What Next?

Brian Wilson has called Andy Paley a genius. Having been a staff producer with both Warner Bros. and Elektra Records, Paley advises young producers to, "Knock on doors. And go where the action is. Don't stay in the middle of nowhere and expect to be discovered, because it's not going to happen. Anybody can sit around and be a tortured artist in a garret someplace but that's not going to get you anywhere. You should go out and knock on doors, show people what you can do where the business is – New York, Nashville, London, L.A. I've met quite a few people who said, 'I'm great, and the world doesn't know it'. Well so what? Where's that gonna get you." He adds, "I used to do that – but I got over the hump and got to work."

This advice is consistent with my experience. I grew up in New Zealand, which is a truly wonderful place to live but about as far as you can go from anywhere. It's the ultimate small town. And back then it was further away than it is now. I wished that I could have learned the things I've learned and done the things I've done from my hometown in New Zealand but at the time it was all but impossible. With a population of around three million (in the Seventies), the music business there was very small. The knowledge base was not available to develop the various skills I needed, so I hit the road. I took private music lessons in Sydney, Australia, went to music schools in Boston, USA, and London, England, lived and worked all over Europe and, eventually, New York City and Los Angeles. Everywhere I touched down, I learned something new. A slightly different attitude here, an alternative technique there, new ways of looking at the same old problems.

It's a movie and not music but *The Lord Of The Rings* is a shining example of how, today, people living in remote places can acquire the knowledge, experience and equipment necessary to compete on a world-class level in the entertainment industry. In music as with movies many factors are making this possible. Firstly, digital technology means that a well-mastered CD sounds very close to the original master. Anyone listening to that CD anywhere in the world on decent equipment will be getting a very good impression of what the artist, producer and engineer were striving for. I know there is still a lobby out there for vinyl, and at its best it certainly did sound nice (Deutsche Gramophon discs always sounded excellent) but assuming you could afford a great turntable, you needed a Ph.D. to set the thing up properly. Then there was the surface noise, the lousy pressings and the substandard, recycled vinyl that companies would use for rock and pop records, not to mention the degradation after repeated plays and the potential for damage by mishandling. Not only that. If you lived somewhere other than the country of origin, the record would have been remastered by a local mastering engineer who might or might not have known what he was doing. Your local version would almost certainly not sound like the original. CDs get remastered too, but with digital domain copies, discs manufactured worldwide can sound remarkably consistent.

So someone living in the outback of Australia can toss a CD they ordered online into their stereo or surround sound system and hear very nearly the same thing that the producer heard when he mastered it in London, New York or Los Angeles.

Back in the bush, while our hypothetical person is listening to the CD, the chances are they can read an article by the engineer and/or producer about the techniques they used to make the record in a magazine or online. Unfortunately MP3s and all the various compressed download formats are a step backwards in terms of quality. Whilst they are great for portability they are not adequate for critical listening. MP3s are the cassettes of the digital age, convenient but not quality audio. Hopefully we'll be moving to the lossless formats such as FLAC in the near future.

There are many pro and semi-pro audio magazines that are now available worldwide, both in paper and electronically on the internet. There are many, many more books available about music, the music business, producing, engineering etc. than there were even twenty years ago. In the Eighties there was an explosion of video tutorials and master classes. Add to that the advent of multi-media, the best applications of which have to date been educational. Engineers of the calibre of Allen Sides are preserving and sharing their knowledge and expertise on CD Rom. On his 'Allen Sides' Mic Locker' he shares his incredible knowledge of microphones and demonstrates specific uses using his private collection of the best new and old microphones in the world. So you can not only read about the mikes and their applications but you can see, hear and compare them in action in a world class studio. Many remixers have put out sample CDs of the drum sounds they use, enabling someone in, say, Turkey to have access to the same samples as their favourite artists.

No matter how good you get at what you do, you will still run into the problem that Andy Paley was talking about: how do you let people know what you are capable of. In effect, how do you market yourself? Well, that is still a problem. Highly influential and successful scenes have emerged within the last 15 years in non-standard music business locations, There are very active hip-hop scenes in Atlanta and St Louis. Grunge put Seattle on the rock'n'roll map in the Nineties. Seattle is not Los Angeles or New York but neither is it the Outer Hebrides or New Guinea. A&R people can easily fly in to Seattle. We are now at the point, as I predicted in the first two editions of this book where some enterprising kid from a truly obscure place can launch himself into the world music arena without setting foot on a plane. But more of that later.

c) Are Qualifications A Help Or A Hindrance?

"An investment in knowledge pays the best interest." (Benjamin Franklin)

You won't get hired as a producer in rock, pop, hip-hop, R&B or country because of any degrees you might have. A&R person, Pete Ganbarg said, "You could be an unemployed high school drop out and produce a great record, everyone's going to want that guy. You could be musically illiterate as long as the record sounds great and you come up with amazing stuff, that's what people are looking for. They're looking for the magic that they hear on certain records."

What would a relevant qualification be? A music degree preferably with a concentration in arranging and composition will definitely help you to excel in the studio. An audio engineering certificate or degree from a new reputable school will reduce the trial and error factor. Some people think that a psychology degree wouldn't be a bad idea. When producers have educational qualifications, they don't make a lot of noise about them. The knowledge that they acquired from their studies may be working well for them in the studio but labels and artists don't hire someone based on the letters after their name. Some very successful producers receive honorary doctorates because of the quality of their production work during their career.

In 1960, Columbia Records in New York City ran an actual A&R producers course. Goddard Lieberson, who was the president of the company at the time and was an A&R man himself, took a great personal interest in it. Mike Berniker, who went on to produce Barbra Streisand, Eydie Gorme, Brenda Lee, Perry Como, many jazz artists and GRAMMY award-winning Broadway shows, was tested for various aptitudes and then given a crash course in how records were made. He says, "It was wonderful, because we not only learned the nuts and bolts of what records are – how they're manufactured and all – but we went into the studio and watched other producers at work, and in effect learned what to avoid , as well as what to do. It was a great training ground." Peter Collins talked about starting as a producer trainee at the world famous Decca studios in North London. "In those days labels owned their own studios and they groomed people to become staff producers. Gus Dudgeon, John Burgess and George Martin, all those guys came through the studio systems. And I was destined to become a staff producer when it all started going pear shaped for Decca financially."

Speaking of relevant qualifications, Jerry Harrison's education was typically oblique for someone who would subsequently become a producer of note. He took a course at Harvard that could have led into either painting or filmmaking. From there he joined Jonathan Richman's Modern Lovers, taught a little at Harvard, worked for a computer company and was eventually asked to try out for Talking Heads.

Having an opinion is probably one of the most important qualifications for success as a producer. (Although one of the many answers to "How many record producers does it take to change a light bulb?" is "I don't know, what do you think?") Neil Finn of Crowded House said about producer Mitchell Froom, "In some cases he does hardly anything, but he's got a solid opinion all the time. In the studio, when everyone else is wavering, he's good for a consistent opinion." Neil's brother Tim adds, "Even if you don't agree, it's good to have someone who is clear, someone you can bounce ideas off."

Unfortunately, unlike brain surgery and the design of missile guidance systems, when it comes to the music production process, everyone this side of the black stump has an opinion. And they can't wait to give it to you. You spend months cocooned in Rock'n'Roll Heaven Studios out in the wilds of nowhere surrounded by much of the technology man has hitherto created, and the best musicians in the galaxy. When you emerge blinking into real life, clutching your masterpiece, anyone and everyone will have an opinion.

The reason why one producer gets paid the big bucks for his opinion and another one doesn't is because the big money producer has 'taste' that is proven. You may not think it is 'good taste' but it is one that is consistent with millions of other people's: the same millions of people the label hopes will go out and buy the record. The skill is in understanding your taste and knowing where the project should sit relative to what you like and dislike. You have to be able to trust your instincts and opinions and know what action to take to achieve the results you want.

Whether you have a hit or not will depend in the first instance on getting an enthusiastic response from the people in A&R, promotions and marketing. If they don't get excited about your work of art, then the only other person who will get to hear it will be your mother. Assuming your musical baby manages to squeeze its way down the record company birth canal and arrive in the world alive and reasonably undamaged, in any week of the year, it will find itself competing with at least a half dozen other, very hungry, siblings for the record companies' affections.

The record company expresses its affection, as so many of us do, in monetary terms. This money manifests itself in the amount of promotion and marketing dollars they spend on your record. Only with the label's blessing will reviewers and radio programmers get to hear your brainchild. If you're one of the fortunate few and you pass the media frisking, the general public will cast the final vote with their hard-won moolah. The public has its own collective opinion which can diverge greatly from industry and media consensus.

How efficiently and frequently you can translate your opinions into hits will determine how long before you qualify for 'Lifestyles Of The Rich And Famous' or need to find a proper job. The means you use, and exactly how you translate those ideas is not necessarily important but it will certainly affect the type of projects you produce.

So educational qualifications won't directly get you projects. Your hairstyle may be more of a factor. A good education will enable you to do a better job. But since most people, including those who've actually worked with you, have no idea what you do or how you do it, you will be judged by your results. For results read – how many copies your last three records sold. Many successful producers have come up via the practical experience route. I believe this will change over the next few years with the reduction in the number of major commercial studios and the subsequent loss of opportunities for aspiring producers and engineers to work their way up from the bottom. More and more engineers, musicians and producers will recognise the need to get some training at the universities and engineering schools. School can give you the basics but you still need the talent and you still have to put in the hours in a studio. Tom Lord-Alge says, "Recording schools can't teach you how to hear, how to mix. They can only teach you how the equipment runs. I learned in the studio, under pressure; deal with the people, sit in the chair, you sink or swim. You don't learn until you're put under that pressure and you learn from someone who is great." He then adds, "Music is hell."

Studio 'street qualifications' come from working with great people and seeing how they handle things. But, there are situations where at least some formal knowledge comes in very handy. Alan Moulder wishes he could read music at times. "When I'm recording an orchestra, for instance, and trying to follow the score blindly," but, he adds, "I was lucky in that I got into an area of music that I've always been interested in so I wouldn't say it was too much of a hindrance." He doesn't think having a basic musical training would be an obstacle, but, "Having worked in America, I can see that sometimes having a formal engineering training can cause people to get hung up on what is 'good' and 'bad'." Alan tried to get as much technical training as possible when he was assisting. He thinks it can be good to have a more formal training as engineers tend to in America, providing that you use it as a tool not a rule. "Sometimes it's just better to get it on tape than to worry about the technicalities too much."

Andy Jackson feels that music qualifications can be useful, "you can always farm things out. You can get people in to write dots but it's more direct if the producer can do something that's outside of the ability of the artist like writing a horn arrangement."

You don't learn people skills in school. The assistants who can come into the studio and be helpful but invisible at the same time seem to do well in the business. Andy says, "Something that was always put across to me as being very important was to at least not be destructive to the session. In those days as a tape op essentially you were sitting there operating the tape machine, being invisible and helpful at the same time."

It's an interesting combination of qualities. You have guys who seem to have all the potential in the world, they are confident, enterprising, quick and smart but they are a pain in the butt to have in the room. They are not the ones who usually go on to be successful. I've had assistants who are so aggressively confident that I think they're either going to be hugely successful within three months or they'll be out of the business. Almost invariably they quit. One assistant, who worked in a studio where I was encamped for a couple of years had natural ability, was comfortable around people and very confident in everything he did. The chief engineer and myself would give him advice and help but generally he seemed to know it all anyway. The one thing we kept reminding him about was to be extremely careful when lining up the record side of the tape machines, especially when the record pad was at the head of someone's master tape. I told him stories about famous projects that had been erased by assistants. I came in one morning, and his face was as white as a sheet. He'd erased a master. I breathed a slight sigh of relief when I found out it wasn't my tape. It was a track for a famous artist who had been working on his album for about three years. It turned out that the

41

master could pretty much be rebuilt from samples the artist had on disk. In this instance not too much permanent damage had been done. We pointed out that if he'd taken our advice this wouldn't have happened. He stayed on at the studio for another two months but he was never the same again and he dropped out of the music business altogether.

Qualifications are useful if they are tempered with a certain amount of wisdom and humility when it comes to dealing with people. Andy Jackson says he has had situations where he's worked with assistants who've had substantial amounts of knowledge but who are confrontational to the main engineer. "That's an appalling situation," he says. "The schools can allow people to come into the studio with more confidence but that may not be such a good thing. It may be more useful to come in somewhat overawed by it all. It makes you mind your P's and Q's more."

Wendy Page learned most of what she knows "sitting with other people watching them do their jobs and looking, listening and learning." Wendy was in the British band Skin Games and has subsequently written and produced for Hilary Duff and Lulu among others. From producing their own demo recordings, Wendy and her producing partner, Jim Marr, learned to "comp" vocals and guitars, record drums and position microphones by trial and error. Along with the experimentation and what she calls "studio patience" they were lucky enough to also work with other professionals. "Necessity is the mother of invention. You need to make your demos compete with records so you have to learn. Obviously, when you have your own set up and are not working to a record company deadline, you can take your time learning new software. I think this is the reason home studios are so popular as you can be very free and creative."

This combination of experimentation on your own schedule and the apprenticeship or mentor-apprentice relationship with talented and experienced professionals is an excellent way to develop the necessary skills.

Quincy Jones studied at Berklee for a time and later with Nadia Boulanger in Paris. Most of his education was from the people around him and fortunately he was surrounded by the best musicians of the time. He said in an interview on wordiq.com, "I had a good ear, so I realised that printed music was just about reminding you what to play . . . but the creation of music has nothing to do with that at all. That's a divine sense in a way." I think the same applies to producing.

You can learn a great deal from school but you still have to have that spark inside of yourself.

Maybe formal qualifications won't actually get you any production work. But training is essential. A good college course, reading books and magazines, watching videos, or working alongside experienced and proven talent will save you from wasting huge amounts of time reinventing ways of doing things that others have been doing for decades.

d) So Exactly How Much Technical Knowledge Do You Need?

It depends what kind of producer you want to be (see Chapter 1). The full spectrum of possibilities is available, ranging from super-tech-head to 'can't-stop-the-clock-on-your-video-recorder-from-flashing-on-12:00.' Your technical ability or lack of it won't affect your ability to make a hit record but it will affect the way you go about making a record. Lack of technical ability will in some ways make your life in the studio easier. If the computer crashes it's not going to be your problem. If the artist doesn't like the eq on his voice – you can fire the engineer.

George Martin has managed to produce a few hits yet he does not consider himself to be a very technical producer. Talking about the all-important communication with the engineer he says, "You might say that the drum sounds a bit dull or [you'd] like it to be 'snappier'. When it comes to other sounds, like horns and orchestral sessions, then I will be very particular about the kind of sound I want. The engineer has to realise the kind of sound you're looking for, in [terms] of clarity and good 'liquid' sound from the strings."

Surprisingly for someone as technically adept as Steve Albini, even being referred to as an engineer makes him uncomfortable. "I don't have a degree in electrical engineering like some engineers I admire have, and I never had any formal apprenticeship as an engineer. Recording engineering used to be a black art – you had to know everything involved in building a tape recorder, a loudspeaker, a mixing desk and so on before you could effectively operate them. Only since the Seventies have electronics been user-friendly enough for people who don't know what they're doing to make records. These days, you have people being paid huge sums of money as 'producers' who don't know how to align a tape machine, they couldn't find a burnt resistor on a circuit board or even tell if their monitors are out of phase. Get this – I walked into one of the biggest, most expensive, classy studios in Chicago to mix a tape recorded somewhere else, and their main monitors were 180 degrees out of phase – they'd been living with them that way for weeks and nobody noticed! That really blew my mind."

[Author's note: when speakers are 180 degrees out of phase, if you listen to music while sitting between them at the optimum position for the stereo image, you will feel like your head is turning inside out. In addition to that, most of the low frequencies get cancelled out so the whole thing will sound very thin and trebly. Inconceivable as it is that a major studio could do this I have had a similar experience at a record company. I found an A&R person's system wired out of phase and he had been critiquing mixes and productions with his stereo equipment in this condition for some time.]

Albini seems to have a healthy sense of the absurd, on a more recent news group posting he said, "On every session I've been involved with, I've considered the band to be the actual producer. I've been credited as a producer, but so what. I've been called a 'Gypsy dago creep' too and neither one bothered me." Maybe the humility is a little overstretched when he said that being referred to as an engineer makes him uncomfortable because he doesn't feel qualified. He goes on to knock himself out of the credits game completely in his final sentence on a rec.audio.pro news group posting when he says, "If somebody calls himself a 'producer' who isn't qualified to call himself an 'engineer' then he is a fraud."

If you were searching for an engineer or producer using Steve Albini's criteria, these days you would search long and hard. I would guess that well in excess of 90 per cent of successful recording and mixing engineers have only a very basic knowledge of the inner workings of studio equipment. We live in an increasingly complex world. Knowing how to build, repair and tune a car will not necessarily make you a world champion racing car driver. However, if you have the potential to be a world champion driver and you take the time to understand the inner workings of the vehicle, I'm sure you would be a lot more help to the support team that does build, maintain and optimise the vehicle. Likewise, in the recording studio the engineer or the producer who has an in-depth knowledge of music and technology is likely to be able to identify and eliminate both creative and technical problems more quickly.

Al Jourgensen and Paul Barker, the production team behind the cutting edge band Ministry, spin-off group The Revolting Cocks and outside projects such as Anthrax, Nine Inch Nails, Mind Bomb, The Jesus & Mary Chain and The Red Hot Chili Peppers (sometimes credited to their pseudonyms Hypo Luxa and Hermes Pan), have an interesting approach to all things technical. According to Jourgensen: "We are knob turners, we are button pushers. We don't know what it's gonna do half the time, but damn it, we're gonna do it. We'll take a day off to slave five compressors together, all overloaded, just to see what will happen. And half the time, the board blows up ... but so what?" Barker adds "Yeah, we don't know any better, but it takes us places that no one else would go."

Chris Lord-Alge, GRAMMY-nominated engineer/producer, has a healthy attitude to technology. "Give us the toys, and we will play them. We take the manual and throw it in the garbage and turn the knobs until it blows up."

Classical producers may be somewhat more conservative in their attitude towards equipment but even they don't need much technical knowledge. GRAMMY award winning Andrew Cornall, Senior Executive Producer at Decca, says he rarely gets involved in decisions about mic preamps or microphones. He adds, "What I want is to hear the timbre of the instrument replicated back in the box [control room]. If it doesn't sound the same then I have a problem because essentially it's these timbral sounds that I am trying to capture. The skill of the crew-especially the engineer on the desk – is by far the most important element."

T-Bone Burnett has produced albums by Los Lobos, Elvis Costello, The Bodeans, Marshall Crenshaw, Bruce Cockburn, Counting Crows, the *O Brother Where Art Thou* soundtrack along with albums as an artist in his own right. Obviously this is someone who has rubbed shoulders with his fair share of studio equipment. In spite of that he says, "I know what I want to hear in my music and when I produce other artists. I use everything and I know when it's working, but I don't know what any of it is called or how any of it does what it does. I'm interested in poetry, and all of that equipment is logical. Chesterton said, 'Logic is the natural enemy of poetry. The poet wants to get his head into the heavens, and the logician wants to get the heavens into his head'."

André Fischer says, "I'm technical to the point where there's no engineer who can lie to me, because on one level I know what they know. I can do engineering myself. When I was in Rufus, I'd occasionally find that the engineers were lying to me, and they'd try to give me this technical explanation of why something I wanted to do couldn't be done. So I'd stay after they left and experiment and find out that it *could* be done."

So it is definitely possible to survive and prosper with virtually no technical knowledge at all. The less technically inclined you are, the more dependent you will be on your engineer for all the engineering and sonic aspects of the production. So you will need to make sure that he or she is not only good at their job but is someone who you can communicate and get along with, since you will spend many hours together.

Bob Ezrin's credits include albums for Pink Floyd, Peter Gabriel, Rod Stewart and Kiss. "I come from a very musical background," he says. "I'm only a tech head in the sense that I've always loved toys. When I was growing up in Toronto, my best friend was my transistor radio. I owned one of the first ones, and I used to listen to all these faraway stations. That's what got me hooked on music and sounds. Over the years I've learned enough to be dangerous, but I couldn't build a circuit if my life depended on it! I just know how things work from having studied it, and if you showed me a schematic, I could only barely read it. But I have an instinctive feeling for technical things, and I have an innate understanding of how things work, if not why."

Different types of records require different skills. Life, radio and MTV would be extremely boring if there was only one type of record being made. I was very happy to see the fresher, more spontaneous kinds of recordings the Nineties brought. The Noughties seem to be bringing back the Eighties Lego style production techniques (some of which I was responsible for), which homogenised and manicured the artist. Computers have permeated every area of production. Once you have the ability to endlessly tweak things most people can't resist.

What a producer really does need to know about technology is how it can best serve the music. Knowing precisely how it all works can cut at least one link out of the creative chain. If a producer doesn't have a clue, then his ability to communicate will be vital. He will have to be able to explain what he is hearing in his head to someone who knows exactly how to achieve that result.

What makes people go out and buy a record is the emotional impact it has on them. Music can make you happy, sad, angry, peaceful or reflective. It can become a soundtrack for a particular period in your life. It can stimulate or relax you. Whatever it does, it must do something. What matters from a production point of view is not how the record was made but what it 'says' to people or how it touches them and their lives.

Flood is no techno-slug. Engineering is his background so technical matters are not a problem for him but he definitely has his priorities. He gives a practical example, "Let's say you have a great part, and you want it to be on your record. You can put it through an amp and go through all the business of doing so and find the sound you want, but by the time you do that you can have easily lost the spark of the moment. I tend to weigh things up like this when recording – what gains priority: sound tinkering, the original idea, or the song itself? First impressions mean a lot for the artist. Essentially, I believe that modern technology is an instrument in the music. I am an advocate for technology as long as it's something that's used rather than something that somebody is used by. It's very easy to become a slave to technology and do something over and over again. Even though you have the ability to try a lot of options with a computer that doesn't mean that it will be done any better or quicker. It is important that you make sure you use technology to your advantage and don't ever let yourself become used by *it.*"

e) How Much Musical Knowledge Do You Need?

The type of producer you will be is going to be defined in large part by your musical knowledge. If you have perfect pitch, a Ph.D. in music and you write songs you will most likely become the All-Singing-All-Dancing-King-Of-The-Hill. At the very least you will be contributing to the arrangements and probably playing and singing backgrounds on the album as well. You don't necessarily need perfect pitch and a Ph.D. to be this producer type, but if you do have those attributes it's highly likely you're going to get frustrated working with bands that don't know where middle C is and can't hold a note. You're probably going to gravitate towards a very self-contained world where you can write, arrange and play all the instruments unless you are able to work with artists at your level.

Conversely, if you have minimal musical knowledge you will be dependent on others for musical input to the project. You can cope with this by working with bands who are self-contained musically and who either need technical, logistical or philosophical help. You will be able to control the musical input by building a team of musicians, arrangers and composers that you work with on a regular basis. This can be a yes/no, I like it/I don't like it process.

Marcus Miller, co-producer of many platinum records by Luther Vandross and a phenomenal multi-instrumentalist himself, doesn't think it is absolutely necessary for a producer to have a musical background. "The most important thing is to be able to really hear music and love music. People who love music make the best producers. A lot of times musicians don't make good producers because they're too focused on the mechanics of playing their instruments, and sounds. Those things are important, but the most important thing is the overall music, and I think the best producers don't play any instrument. I think I've gotten very good at listening like a regular person as opposed to listening like a musician. You need to take an overview. The first thing you should hear is the saxophone or the singer, whatever is out front, and how the music supports that. People who don't play instruments really have that naturally. Musicians have to come around full circle to come back to that. I just try to spend a lot of time listening to music, in non-musician situations – in the house, in the car – listening to see what grabs people. When somebody listens to a Luther Vandross record, they're not listening to the bass, at least not at first. They're listening to Luther."

Talking about the amount of musical input he has on a session Steve Lillywhite (Peter Gabriel, Rolling Stones, Big Country and U2) says, "I'm not the kind of person to tell a bunch of Latin players what notes to play, though I get in the right people, the people I know will play what I want to hear."

"When I first became involved in music I couldn't play instruments," says Brian Eno, "but I could manipulate sound with technology – tape recorders in the first place – and then synthesisers and recording studios in general. New technologies have made it easier to cheat. Cheating is the name of the game in a lot of ways now, and is often the name given to new ways of doing things. So it's not really cheating, it's just that we have had a traditional picture of audience/ artist, observer/creator, and the new technologies challenge this. They ask us in particular to acknowledge the possibility that someone who rearranges other people's materials is also an artist. I became a musician through cheating for 20 years. I can't play any musical instrument, but what I can do is work with many of the interesting new devices that enable people to put music together. It was called cheating when I started doing it. Now it's what everyone does. It's called using a recording studio."

Eno defines a producer's role as well as anyone I have come across. "What has become interesting is the idea that artists are people who specialise in judgment rather than skill."

f) What If You Have Neither Musical Nor Technical Skills?

Not having any specific musical or technical skills will put all the emphasis on your ability to manage people. You will have to communicate your ideas through the musicians, the engineers and programmers. This can work by choosing people who have the right instincts and abilities and who can come close to the results you are looking for – without you having to define precisely every detail that gets recorded. If the project is not going well you will either have to convey to the musicians and/or technical crew what it is that is not right – or change the crew. This can be advantageous. Since you have not been hired for your musical or technical abilities you can be extremely flexible. Providing the budgets will stretch to it, you can change musicians and engineers to suit the situation and needs of the project.

In fact, as a successful production career develops, most producers will pull back from direct hands-on involvement to a more managerial style. It helps with the objectivity, improves your status somewhat and claws back five of the 10 years that you took off your life when you were putting in 72 hour days during your early years in the studio.

When I asked Danny Saber about the musical or technical qualities a producer needs, he said, "That's a tough one. For everything I name, there's someone producing who doesn't have that. There are no rules." He recounts the story of a very famous producer who was in a panic doing a track for TV. "He kept saying I want it to be sharp, I want it to be sharp. It turned out what he wanted was distortion. He doesn't have a clue [about the specifics and the details] but he turns out excellent records."

Once you start spending time in studios, especially if you are lucky enough to be around a great producer, then you will naturally acquire a certain amount of technical and musical skills by osmosis. In my first year or so I would hear the producers talking about timing and tuning problems that I simply could not hear. Gradually, these subtle nuances became more and more obvious. Eventually, working with producers who were apparently unaware of horrible tuning and timing discrepancies started to drive me crazy.

"In terms of my early education at home, I guess my parents didn't know how often you were supposed to tune a piano," says Albhy Galuten. "In the studio, while tracking, we tune the piano every day, but in suburban middle America, you maybe tuned the piano every couple of years. I didn't really know what 'in tune' was, and here I was in the studio, never having played guitar, and just took tuning for granted. Jerry Wexler was saying something to Aretha during the session for 'Spanish Harlem' about her pitch being a little flat, and I was thinking, 'I didn't even hear it.' Today's technology has made it much easier to hear, so contemporary records are much more in tune and much more in time. The pitch microscope was not so finely tuned back then, and we've learned over the years to look carefully at pitch, make adjustments with harmonisers, look at the meter, use razor blades and delay lines. But around 1970, it was a new world to me – suddenly hearing careful tuning. If you listen to records from that era, many of them are way out of tune. The opening chord comes in, they're singing, the choir comes in and hits that chord, and you go 'Ow!' But back then it sounded normal. To be in this environment with Jerry Wexler, Arif Mardin – their ears were fabulous, well educated and well tuned."

g) The Door's Open, The Foot's In, Now What?

You need to be extremely pro-active. You need to control the shape and direction of your career to the best of your ability. This is difficult but becoming more and more necessary. Many producers take a passive approach to their careers. This works fine when you are in a hot period, not so good when things are cooling off and not at all when you are trying to get started or when your career is being examined for vital signs.

The first project you did you probably had to move hell and high water to get. You might have got involved with the group at an early stage before they were signed and built that all-important relationship with them. Ideally you should pursue your entire career with the vigour and enthusiasm with which you pursued the first project. That way you never get typecast or stuck in a rut. A good manager can really help out here by planning each move, actively pursuing projects that are suitable for you and not letting you get suckered into vampire projects that are living on your reputation. A lesser manager will tend to take the path of least resistance, which exposes you to the risk of enforced early retirement. Peter Collins credits his longtime manager Andy Kipnes with enabling him to have a long, varied and successful career. When Andy started managing Peter in the Eighties he sat him down and said 'where do you want to be in five years with your career.' He also made one of the most insightful observations that I have heard, "It doesn't matter how many records you've sold. Nobody in the industry cares about that. It's how cool was the last artist you worked with. We can do the Bon Jovi's occasionally but if you want to stay working and stay cutting edge it's got to be young and it's got to be cool." Peter says Andy helped him in the selection of those sort of acts.

Huge sales will obviously keep a career healthy but nobody can guarantee multi-platinum albums every time out, there are too many factors that the producer does not control. The music business is a cut-throat business and other producers, or their managers, will pursue artists with whom you have an established relationship. It is a reality that you will have to deal with. The key thing is that there is some strategic intent behind your career. Things rarely go according to plan for better or worse. Either way having a plan is a good idea; you can always change it to suit the circumstances.

Chapter Three

What's The Job Description?

"When two men in business always agree, one of them is unnecessary."
(William Wrigley Jr.)

In any human interaction there are at least two points of view. Very often pursuing one or both of those points of view brings you to an irresolvable impasse (in the studio that's an argument). Bands have a tendency to argue. The producer can represent the unspoken third or higher point of view, which is 'what would be the best solution for all concerned.'

A great producer sometimes does very little. The producer who knows when to butt in and when to put his butt on the couch is, in my opinion, the very best kind. The great Jerry Wexler said in *Rolling Stone* magazine about the late Ray Charles, "We talked once every few years. But I was very happy this time when he said, 'Pardner' – he always called me that – 'those were my best years, with you and Ahmet.' But when people say, 'You and Ahmet produced Ray Charles,' put big quotation marks around produced. We were attendants at a happening. We learned from Ray Charles. My dear friend (*writer*) Stanley Booth once remarked, 'When Ahmet and Jerry got ready to record Ray Charles, they went to the studio and turned the lights on, Ray didn't need them.'[*]

Of course one of the hallmarks of greatness is modesty. When discussing how to keep the creativity going, Flood says, "Some days [that] can mean just sitting there and saying, 'Sounds great, just carry on'. Then other days, it's constructing a situation that you hope will spur people on. It might be a really bad idea, but if it gets the ball rolling, then it's a good idea." He's absolutely right: sometimes you

---

[*] Rolling Stone, July 8–22 2004

need to take a step sideways to get out of a rut or a stagnant way of thinking. It may be that the place you initially step to is all wrong, but all wrong is usually more obvious than not quite right and that can give you the stimulus to find a way, a thing or a technique that you positively do like.

W. Somerset Maugham probably wasn't talking about a record producer when he said, "Like all weak men he laid an exaggerated stress on not changing one's mind," but he could have been describing certain dictatorial and de-motivating producers that I have encountered. Just because all eyes are on you as the producer to come up with the next brilliant idea, it doesn't mean that your ego has to be permanently attached to the first thought that comes out, especially if it should stimulate a better one from someone else. A famous scientist, Linus Pauling, emphasised the merits of not being precious when he said, "The best way to have a good idea is to have lots of ideas." Industrialist John D. Rockefeller in turn stressed the benefits of reaching for the stars by saying "don't be afraid to give up the good to go for the great."

Some producers do almost everything. In the case of the All-Singing-All-Dancing type, the producer will be the songwriter, orchestrator, engineer, producer and vocal arranger. All the artist has to do is sing the song and occasionally they won't even do that (remember Milli Vanilli). With less experienced singers it's very common for them to copy the producer's guide vocal note for note, inflection by inflection.

Sometimes the producer acts as a stimulant or a catalyst. Bands and artists have a habit of trotting out their clichés (or even worse, someone else's clichés). Quite often they get lazy and settle for the first possibility that comes along. In some cases the first idea is the best, sometimes it's total crap but most frequently it represents a good starting place. Just having someone in the room who asks "What if we tried this?" can be enough to kick things off. A good producer can be the little bit of grit that irritates and stimulates the artist to create the pearl.

Production can sometimes be about arranging or optimising arrangements. This is about coming up with, and organising, all the bits that will comprise the finished record. Quite often the way different sections of the song are put together on the demo may be a little convoluted. It's not uncommon for an artist to underplay the best parts of a song and overplay the least interesting bits. In this case the producer needs to edit and reorganise while treading gingerly through the exploding ego field.

Finding and choosing material can also be a part of the production process. With an artist who doesn't write, this can entail sifting through piles of publishers' demos. Even when the artist is the writer, it may be that the material being put forward for the record is not even the best available. In this case it's necessary for the producer to go through several old demos and bits of songs to find the best material. There have been many occasions when the only hit single off an album was a song that had been buried at the back end of the tenth demo, unrecognised and unloved until the producer or A&R person spotted it.

Jerry Harrison of Talking Heads assumes nothing. The first thing he will do at the pre-production stage is to say, "Let's hear everything you have, not just what's been decided on." Then he will listen through to everything no matter how rough it is. "Sometimes you'll see that the raw way that they play something sounds better than the way they did it on a demo. A lot of times you'll hear the raw beauty."

You have to be aware of the conditions under which the demos were made. Did the band or a friend of the band produce them? Did their lack of experience create more problems than they solved, such as stilted arrangements, bad sounds, lumpy feels or inappropriate production techniques. A lack of money or expertise can push a demo in a weird direction. A band whose main appeal is their rhythm section might have chosen to use a drum machine because they couldn't record live drums in their house. Demos are often the first thing a band does when they get together. A year later when they have done 200 live shows they will be much tighter. Nothing sharpens up a band's material as much as a full gig sheet.

Sometimes production is about mediating, moderating and protecting the democratic process, other times you need to allow yourself or someone else to be a dictator. "Usually what people are practising is not democracy, but cowardice and good manners," says Eno. "Nobody wants to step on so-and-so's toes, so nobody wants to say anything. The valuable idea of democracy is that if there are five people in the room and one of them feels very strongly about something, you can trust that the strength of their feelings indicates that there is something behind it. My feeling about a good democratic relationship is the notion that it's a shifting leadership. It's not, 'We all lead together all the time', it's 'We all have sufficient trust in one another to believe that if someone feels strongly then we let them lead for that period of time.' And this is what typically happens. Somebody will say, 'No, I really think we should do it this way,' and I'll say, 'OK, let's try it, let's see what happens'."

Sometimes you have to protect one person's creativity from another's stupidity. There is a story about a world-famous percussionist and a not-so-world famous producer. Supposedly the producer was not happy with what the percussionist was playing on a particular track, so he hit the talkback button and said 'Could you make it more Cuban'. The percussionist reputedly rose to his full 5′ 6″, said 'I am Cuban' and walked out of the studio. So, we know he's a little touchy. Shortly after this happened, I was working with an artist who claimed to be a huge fan of this percussionist. The drummer in particular wanted him to play on their album. I knew the percussionist so I called him. This musician is an incredibly instinctive player. On a previous session for me he had nailed a complex part on the first run-through of a song he'd never heard before. He didn't even look at the chart. Fortunately we were in record.

For this new session the guy arrived at the studio with four truckloads of stretched, dead-animal skins and things filled with dried beans. I ran the tape and our captive Cuban played the most beautiful part. It was perfect, and very exciting. Just over my left shoulder I sensed someone moving toward the console. I looked up in time to catch the drummer making a beeline for the talkback button. I rugby tackled him (figuratively speaking) and asked him what he was up to. He said that he had a different part in mind, which he sang to me. It was probably the most clichéd bongo part I had ever heard. A book one, page 1 idea, "Bongos 101." Sometimes the obvious thing is the right thing, but we could have done this part on a drum machine for much less than triple scale. Fortunately the rest of the band agreed with me and we kept the first take and avoided another Bay of Pigs incident.

The point is you book musicians for what they can do. That's not to say they don't need some guidance or can't be pushed. The producer can't afford to be intimidated by a musician's reputation. On the other hand, although the best players can take a lot of direction, it's possible to disempower even the greatest musicians by not allowing them the space to do what they do best. If a session becomes too much of a struggle then you've either got the wrong guy or you may be getting in the way of the creative flow.

Probably the worst thing that can happen in the studio is for things to descend to the lowest common denominator; to compromise in order to keep everyone happy. Excitement and passion are more likely to produce a great record than conciliation and compromise. Sometimes the producer needs to protect a more vulnerable member of the band while he or she tries out an idea. Creative notions are incredibly fragile. It's very rare that anyone has a fully formed creative thought. More often there's a vague sensation of something to be reached for, and only by actively reaching can the idea be pulled through. It only takes a single disparaging comment ("It's shit," {UK} or "It sucks" {US} seem to be perennial standards) from another band member in the early stages of the creative process to completely slam the door on an idea before it fully manifests. Bands are often riddled with internal politics, jealousies, factions and cliques. Part of the producer's job is to instinctively understand these forces within the band so he can analyse exactly why certain comments are being made. You need to understand whether they represent an honest and valid opinion about the subject in hand or a deeper underlying agenda related to historic events, feuds, long-standing resentments or the fundamental power structure of the band.

Sometimes producing is about defining the parameters, sketching out the boundaries or as Eno puts it "establishing the cultural territory". There are times in a band's career when they are at the centre of what is happening, they instinctively understand who they are, what they represent and how they relate to what is going on around them culturally. Usually this is early on in their career. They have grown up at one with the influences of their generation, they are still carrying the confidence of youth and they are unburdened by an overly wide base of knowledge, so they are able to generate consistent, relevant music of their time. It may be trend-setting, trend-related or trend-following, all three can work. Personally, I would sooner be involved with trend-setters but they are not always the projects that make the money for the record company and they are not hiding around every corner.

Artists are not always focused. The producer in this case needs to direct the artist's attention, and a good way to do that is by limiting their options. Eno tries to do that by asking, "Where are we culturally? What are we trying to be? What books? What films? OK, if this is where we are, then we are not going to do that or that. What are the things that we're not going to do? Let's just get them out of the way and narrow the field a little bit." He adds, "Obviously you don't want to create a situation where you stop all creativity. But you want to create a situation where there is a meaningful amount of attention on something, rather than a small amount of attention on everything."

Andy Jackson thinks that a good producer can liberate the artist, allow them to do what they believe in and break through their inhibitions, fears or preconceptions to fulfill what they potentially could have done anyway. "He's acting as a therapist in some way. He's helping the artist to zero in on what they *really* want to do, rather than what they *imagine* they want to do – to free up their creativity. In that context the producer can say 'OK, you know what you are doing now so go and make the album.' [At that point] he doesn't even have to be there. It's something I have a tremendous amount of respect for."

Sometimes the producer's job is about production in the sense that people use the word most commonly. When someone says that a record has great production it can mean many things: they like the song (even though they didn't mention it), the arrangement feels right to them, the performances are appropriate and exciting, the whole thing sounds really good (clear, punchy, not harsh, not muddy or dull, good highs and lows), you can hear everything (especially the main melodies and lead vocals), everything seems to happen in the right place (the choruses, the little instrumental hooks, etc.) or simply that it's exciting or pleasing to them.

So how do you make a record sound great, balance it all up so you can hear everything, get everything in the right place and make it exciting as well? The first thing is to make the artist feel comfortable. No artist can perform well unless they are at ease and feel confident in themselves. They should be confident in the people they are working with and feel as though their collaborators have confidence in them.

Understanding the needs of the artist is paramount in production. Knowing when to push them, when to back off a little and when to stop altogether can be the key to getting that extra special performance. As Nashville veteran Barry Becket says, "I wish I had taken Psychology 101 in college instead of making music. It would have helped me out a great deal."

A little preparation can really lubricate the proceedings. An experienced engineer can pre-set the mic levels, EQ, reverbs and foldback (the mix of whatever music the singer will be singing to, either on headphones or speakers) before the singer arrives. If you've worked with the singer before, then you should know what they like to hear in the headphones and what levels they are likely to sing at. If you've never worked with them before, you can take an educated guess based on experience. It's relatively easy to make minor adjustments when the singer shows up. I've seen singers practically lose their voices (and certainly their patience) while the engineer "gets a sound". There's a bad joke that seems to have travelled round every studio in the world. It's always cracked at the end of a particularly brilliant take. Some bright spark will hit the talk-back button and say something like, "OK, we're ready – let's put one down." Sometimes, unfortunately for the performer, the 'bright spark' is not joking. An unrepeatable first take was lost because the engineer was not in record. Your first instinct is to brain the guy.

Lack of preparation can also cause unusable takes because levels or compression were not "in the ballpark" before the tape was rolled. Level, EQ and compression should all be set on the conservative side. You can always add more later but it's impossible to clean up distorted vocals and very difficult to expand over an over-compressed signal. Make sure you are always in record when a performance is happening. This cannot be stated often enough. You don't have to be a genius to get it right first time. You do have to be sensitive to the artist's needs. If you've ever been the victim of poor recording etiquette in the studio as a performer, when you're directing things in the control room you're likely to try harder.

Flood reinforces this. "You've got to make sure that, by experience, you know that even if you haven't heard the person open their mouth, that your mic level and your compressor level and your EQ is going to be OK so that it's not going to distort as soon as they start kicking in the first note they sing." He also points out that if you are always in record, with today's technology, if something's in the wrong place or a bit out of tune, you can fix so many things. "But that human spark – quite often after the first time you go for it – you never get it again."

So, rule number one in the studio should be: record everything. If you don't like the take you can always wipe it, delete it, or record over it. Bitter experience has shown that you cannot pluck a slice of pure genius back from the ether!

Good solid engineering practices will make sure that the instruments and vocals are recorded well in the first place. It's very difficult to make a great sounding record if the basic instruments are not recorded well. "Fix it in the mix" is a lousy philosophy. A lot of mixers complain about having to "rescue" records that are recorded badly. I always wonder how the producer knew that the recording was finished if he's intending to "fix it in the mix". It takes an immense amount of faith to say, "It sounds like a mess right now but when it's mixed it'll be fine." I like to be able to hear the way the finished record will sound as I go along. The mix is really an enhancement of what is recorded, not a complete re-think (apart from radical dance or club remixes).

Clever orchestration helps to maintain clarity when you come to do the mix. It ensures that each element of the record occupies its own space in the audio spectrum and does not compete with the other instruments. An exciting mix usually entails the use of equalisation, compression, limiting, expansion and gating to optimise the sounds, increase their impact and ensure they occupy their own space in the audio spectrum. (Very simply, equalisation or EQ affects the tone of a sound making it among other things, brighter, duller, harsher, smoother, fatter, richer, bigger, smaller etc. Compression, limiting, expansion and gating are generically referred to as dynamic control and they can be used in a number of different ways to affect the shape, the impact, the length or the apparent loudness of a sound or combination of sounds.)

An exciting mix is also a combination of careful balancing and panning of the instruments and vocals to focus the listener's attention on the most important things, and appropriate use of effects in order to give some front-back perspective, to put certain instruments or voices in relief and to create space between the different components of the mix. (Effects include reverb, delay, chorusing, phasing, flanging, distortion, ambience and combinations of the above.)

Mixing also involves riding the levels (changing levels relative to time and the other instruments) and panning of instruments and vocals. These techniques are both used to improve the dynamic flow of the track, to draw attention to different facets of the orchestration at different points in the song, and increase the overall excitement of the mix.

There are a handful of producers, George Martin, Phil Spector and Quincy Jones among them, who are as close as producers have gone, so far, to becoming household names. Jimmy Jam of Jam and Lewis says, "After *Thriller* everyone wanted to know, 'What exactly does a producer do?' The producer's not just a guy who simply sits in the studio and spends all the money. The producer can be a writer, an engineer – a self-contained entity. And Quincy's the man who proved that to the world."

One of the most influential and versatile producers who covered the entire rock and soul spectrum was Tom Dowd. Coming from an engineering background, he had a very wide brief when he was on the staff at Atlantic. He actually built and repaired the equipment on which he engineered and produced sessions. Speaking about a particularly intense and creative period in the Sixties he said, "All of a sudden I was commuting about 10 or 12 times a year to Memphis and five or six times a year to Muscle Shoals. I was going into Macon three or four times a year. I was seldom in New York. I'd be on the road, come home, listen to something, do this, that and the other thing, and go back out again. I was wearing different hats on all these missions; sometimes I was needed for updating facilities, or for engineering, suggesting arrangement changes or conducting, you name it. Whatever had to be done, had to be done."

George Martin said in an interview on the promotional site for *In My Life* (his all-star Beatles tribute album): "You've got to get on with people and you've got to lull them into a kind of sense of security and you've got to get rid of their fears. You've got to relate to people." This statement holds true for any type of producer. Whether you are getting a kick drum sound, suggesting an overdub, arranging a string part, trying to get the artist to consider an outside song, hiring a studio musician, recording a vocal or talking high concept with the artist they have to feel that they can trust you.

a) We Are Not Worthy

Aerosmith's lead guitarist Joe Perry says that every band has a different style and a different relationship with their producer. "Basically the way we work with Bruce Fairbairn, who did *Permanent Vacation*, *Pump* and *Get A Grip*, is that we will have our songs at a point where we all like them. Then Bruce will come in and listen for the rough spots. As part of the band, you get in the middle of the music, and you need someone with some distance from it. He comes in and listens with fresh ears and works with us to make it the best it can possibly be. If we had one part that we all thought was really smoking, and had something like two months away from it, maybe we would come back to it and see that it needed more. Unfortunately, we never get that luxury, so we get the next best thing: Bruce. Personally, I think that being a producer is such a harrowing experience that I'm glad I don't have to do it to make a living. 'Producer' is like a catch-all title. It's a very important position, but I don't want to get any closer to producing Aerosmith than I am right now. Everybody in the band has strong feelings about it too. I don't think it's wise for us to get to the point where we don't have someone to act as a mediator."

From only a few 'stage feet' away Steven Tyler has a slightly different perspective on it. He says, "I think it's more difficult to work with a producer. Everybody likes to come in and rework your stuff to validate their punch cards and say that they were part of something. It's like a bunch of people telling you what the sugar cone beneath a big ball of vanilla ice cream tastes like and, oddly enough, it would taste different to you from what everybody else described. Everybody has their own interpretation of things and you've got to decide whether you take a hard-nosed stand and say, ' No way, man, this is me and this is the way it stays,' or take chances. That's why we let people into our camp all the time. With each album it gets harder and harder to listen to other people, but every album gets better and better, so a producer is definitely necessary."

In those two points of view you can see one of the major dichotomies faced by producers. Artists very often don't want their ideas messed with. On the other hand the internal tensions and politics of the band and between the band and the label often necessitates a mediator. Acting as a peacemaker/intermediary is often a big part of the job. With a quality artist, very often there are more than enough good ideas flying around the studio to make a great record. The last thing they need is an outsider trying to force his way into the music. In this case the producer's role is to make sure that the very best ideas make it to the final mix while at the same time keeping the interpersonal relationships between the decision makers on an even keel. This tension is very common with artists who are groups but can also be true with solo artists where managers and label reps' opinions have to be accommodated.

The most fundamental conflict that happens when producing major label artists is the perceived tension between the commercial and artistic, which is sometimes cast as the need to be current versus allowing the artist to be themselves. In this case the pressure is usually coming from the A&R or marketing people at the label who are concerned about how radio, TV and the press are going to receive the work. Artists very often resent this pressure and consider it to be misguided. Some artists have a very true internal compass which guides them to exactly where they need to be artistically and commercially, and others, even among the most successful, do not, or at least not at certain points in their careers. Some of the worst music ever made is made in the name of bringing the artist up to date. Then again careers have been saved and enhanced by carefully reshaping the sound of a legend. The magic here is in matching the right producer with the right artist. Rick Rubin did an amazing job of revitalising Johnny Cash's sound very late in his career. This is a hard thing to do and it takes a good deal of flexibility and trust on the part of the artist as well as artistry, respect and sensitivity on the part of the producer. Without those qualities you get one of those late career horror albums that end up in the cutout bins six months after release. The right choice of a producer early on in a career can save a lot of heartache and a possible stalled career.

Beyond the practical actualities of day-to-day life in the studio and the commercial realities we all face, there can be a deeper inspiration and methodology for the producer. Jim Dickinson summed this up beautifully in his *Production Manifesto* in which he says, "Music has a spirit beyond notes and rhythm. To foster that spirit and to cause it to flourish – to capture it at its peak – is the producer's task." He elaborated on this by saying, "As a producer, I try to remain aware and attuned to the peculiar harmonic properties of the events as they unfold. This is not just musical. I'm talking about how the balance is gonna change in the room constantly during the process, just because of the process itself. It's in the life of the event where you find the soul, and that's what you are trying to capture. This becomes a moral responsibility for the producer. When you talk about records, what is the terminology that is used? This is a good record or this is a bad record. Well, that's basically the way I see it. There are enough bad records that get made, and you know it's your obligation during the process to try to make a good record. I think that in the case of many young bands, who can remain nameless, that the more they compromise, the more they eliminate the very thing that might have gotten them across." I say Amen to that.

"There are many different ways to produce," says Ros Earls. "The John Leckie type. Those that are surrounded by some sort of cool aura to do guitars. You almost associate them with sounds. People say 'That sounds like a Flood record.' He really hates the idea that people can tell that he produced something. I think that's a credit to [a producer's] attitude but inevitably you contribute something to the sound and it's visible, it's audible. I've never met a really good producer that admits it. Nonetheless it's there.

"If you're Brian Eno you can tell what he brought to *The Joshua Tree* for instance. He invented sounds and turned around a band's career. That's what you look for in a Brian Eno-type arrangement. The sounds are what we hear with a producer like that, but there are other things that we don't hear that form the whole really. It was quite frustrating for people working with Trevor Horn. Not in a bad sense. It was always felt that he could be at the end of a phone and tell what needs to happen. That's an extraordinary talent, I think. You've either got it or you haven't. Those that don't have it don't always see the value in it. It's equivalent to someone's name being on a record. You know if you've got Eno on, it's going to sound a certain way but you also know that the mere fact that he agreed to collaborate with you is almost enough in itself (because his name is going to be on the record)."

"The vast majority of records are driven by a very fearful thing of not doing something wrong rather than doing something right," says Andy Jackson. "We don't let things go. We're striving for perfection, which is actually just avoiding the possibility of someone saying 'Ooh, that's weird'".

It's true that you can construct an album painstakingly piece by piece or you can till the soil, sow the seed, and pray for rain.' (In some cases it's more like 'light the touch paper and retire to a safe distance' but the principle is the same.) The knack of 'letting that special thing happen' is a difficult to quantify, but highly desirable, production skill. Andy did an album a few years ago with Tony Visconti. "It was a really quick album," he says. "It only took about two and a half weeks. It was interesting to watch him function. What did he contribute? It mainly seemed that it was just a very easy atmosphere to work in. It seemed that things could happen very easily and quickly. It really struck me at the time."

As I said in Chapter One, the producer may also have to decide how and where the record will be recorded, who, if anyone, will help to make it, what technical equipment will be used, how the budget is going to be spent, and who will take care of the administration and paperwork.

Usually, in consultation with the record company and artist, the producer will choose the studio or studios that will be used. This may be one studio for the whole project or different studios for different phases of the recording. It is very common to use one place for the recording or tracking part and a different studio for mixing. There are several reasons for this. If an album stretches out over several months, both the artist and producer want a change of scenery. Budget can be a factor. Mixing rooms usually have large state-of-the-art computerised consoles (a.k.a. board or desk) and every piece of outboard signal processing equipment ever made. When you are recording a band or overdubbing you don't need the computerised console or that many channels on the desk, and you'll use only a few pieces of outboard equipment so to have it sitting around doing nothing for several months is a waste of money.

Some producers and their engineers have different preferences for recording than for mixing. In recent years old valve (tube) equipment and the older solid state (but usually with discreet Class A circuitry) has become very popular for recording. Some real audiophiles prefer to record and mix on the older equipment but generally the computerisation, greater number of channels, parametric equalisation, recall or reset and improved ergonomics of the new boards wins out over the older consoles for mixing. As we move deeper and deeper into random access digital workstations more and more projects are being recorded into a computer and will never leave the digital domain until the mix engineer burns the final mix onto whatever removable media he needs to send to either the mastering room or the manufacturing plant. Albums are being mixed or mixes tweaked on laptops. As long as the producer and engineer are confident about what they are hearing via their monitoring system I see this as an increasing trend. The idea that you can fix small problems without having to go back into the studio is very appealing.

Often bands like to record in a residential studio. It gets them away from their domestic problems. If they are a young band, it will probably seem like a luxurious experience where they get fed regularly (sometimes they have to slim down again before the tour). The producer has an easier time tracking down the bass player (when he suddenly needs him for an overdub at three in the afternoon) than he would in Los Angeles, London, or New York City. A trend that has been gaining momentum over the last 15 years or so is to put together a portable studio in a country house or even a house in a city that the band feels comfortable in. U2, Counting Crows and Sting have all recorded albums this way. The easy way to do this is to rent a mobile recording facility. The disadvantage is that the producer and engineer spend all day cramped in the back of a truck. So what usually happens is that all the equipment is flightcased, wheeled in and set up in the most suitable room in the house. Obviously it is much easier to set up a digital workstation in a house than a 48-channel analogue console with two-inch tape machines and all the attendant outboard equipment so the process has become much less complicated.

Whatever equipment you use the acoustics won't be perfect but the environment is pleasant and there is usually a lot of daylight, which for most people makes the whole experience more enjoyable. I say most people because I have worked with several artists and engineers who like their recording environment to be dark like a womb, a nightclub or a bordello. Depending on the type of producer and the kind of artist involved, there is usually some sort of team to be put together. The most compact situation is the engineer-producer working with a self-contained indie/alternative style band. Usually the only other person needed is the assistant engineer who is often supplied by the studio.

If a project is being put together entirely on computer, as most dance and hip-hop records are, the team could be just one person who does all of the engineering, playing and programming. The bigger the budget the more likely there will be a separate engineer, assistant engineer, a programmer and maybe some musicians. When you get into major, high-end productions involving well established pop artists, there will almost certainly be an engineer, assistant engineer, programmer, arranger, possibly the song writer and many musicians, all in addition to the producer. The artist may just show up when it is time to do the vocals and not even be there for the bulk of the recording. As far as the technical equipment is concerned producers tend to have their favourite ways of working. Some work only on digital equipment while others will not be swayed from the analogue stuff that's been around for much of the past 40 years.

In the late Seventies and the early Eighties the degree of standardisation in studios hit an all-time high. Most studios had one of about three or four consoles the same with 24-track tape machines, quarter or half inch mastering and monitor speakers. A tape recorded in a top-flight studio could be played back in any other high-end studio anywhere in the world without any conversion or major setup. Moving from studio to studio and country to country was extremely easy. These days the range of equipment is bewilderingly large. There are several professional digital formats, many semi-pro formats that are finding their way into pro studios in addition to all the standard analogue tape machines. Hard disk systems are proliferating at an alarming rate and compatibility and interchangeability of stored data is less than good. More producers are working out of their own facilities or at least carrying significant pieces of equipment with them so that they have some control over the technical formats they might have to deal with. Standards do exist for digital equipment but hardware and software plug-in setups vary so much that total 'plug-and-play' compatibility seems like a thing of the past.

In the Seventies and Eighties it was not uncommon to work on a project with no budgetary constraints, or at least the budget was so large that you didn't have to think about it. Those days are gone. Budgeting was always stricter in the USA than in England. The first overage clauses I ever saw were in American contracts (an overage clause is part of the producer contract which basically makes any expenditure over the initial agreed budget the producer's personal expense. It will either be taken out of his advance or future royalties). 'All-in' funds have become much more common. This is where the producer is allocated a fixed amount of money out of which he has to make the record and pay himself. This can work out very well for the producer, particularly where he is self-contained. In R'n'B, Rap and dance music, if the producer is a writer/programmer/musician who owns his own recording facility he can really control the costs. After the initial outlay for his studio has been recouped all he is accounting for is his time, and recording media (disks, tape, hard-drives etc). An engineer producer working on alternative bands can also do quite well out of an all-in recording budget. They can be pretty sure that they can record and mix the album in, say, five weeks. Their main costs are going to be studio time, recording media and, maybe, some equipment rentals.

When I first started producing, all costs were paid for by the record company. The producer was paid a fixed advance in two instalments, half at the beginning and half at the end. The budget would be submitted by the producer before starting the project and agreed by the company. Usually they would want to shave something off the proposed budget. Sometimes the company will tell you up-front how much they want to spend and it's up to you to figure out a way to make the money do everything you, the band, and the company want to do. In many ways I prefer the more traditional, separate recording budget with the bills paid by the company. The upside for the producer is not so good. On an all-in fund, if the producer can control the costs he can walk away with many times more than he would have on a fixed advance.

There are certain disadvantages, though. If costs get out of hand the producer can find himself working for nothing or even paying for the project to get finished. The producer may cut corners to save money. His interests may conflict with the artist's. The record company may not be so bothered how you go about making the record as long as you deliver something they like. The artist, however, may want real strings on three tracks. He may want to use a certain studio that is more expensive for part of the project. The producer might be inclined to discourage this because it reduces his profit. On a traditional costs-paid-by-the-company budget the producer may still have to limit spending. The difference is in how it affects the producer/artist relationship. On an all-in fund the artist will be aware that while his spending is being limited, the producer is lining his own pocket.

When the company is paying the costs, the producer and the artist are on the same side. They can jointly look at the budget to see whether they can squeeze the extra 'whatever' out of it or go back to the record company and ask for more money. An external budget limitation can increase the bond between producer and artist. An artist may not feel so good about his creative partner imposing limitations that maximise his own profit. This can be aggravated by the fact that an established producer usually lives much higher on the hog than a first-time recording artist. The tens of thousands that the producer is making out of the deal can seem particularly un-reasonable to someone who lives on a shoestring, especially when just a few of those thousands could finance the extra overdubs.

More bands are coming to realise that the recording budget is ulti-mately their money. If they spend it, they will have to pay it back out of their royalties. Many artists look at their advances like the person who hopes to die with his American Express card 'maxed out.' Bands signed to major labels eventually figure out that they will not see a penny of royalties until they have sold over a million copies of the album. Then they watch their label throw many times the album budget at a video production company for one three-minute video that takes no more than a day or two to shoot. It's no wonder they lose the incentive to penny pinch during the recording process. It's definitely fun to go nuts with the record company's money but there are a lot of ex-musicians out there who, if they had conserved a little of the good times, would be having a lot better time than they are right now. Overage clauses tend to inflate recording budgets. Producers don't want to get stuck with paying for part of the album out of their own pocket. Consequently they pad their initial budget projection.

Budgeting comes fairly naturally to some producers and others rely heavily on their management company. Peter Collins said that he will have a Q&A session on the phone with his management company. They ask him where he wants to work, how long it will take, any musician costs, rentals, etc. and then put the budget together for him. If you don't like playing with numbers, having a management company that offers this service is a very good idea.

b) Who Takes Care Of The Administration And Paperwork?

Doing this stuff is about as much fun as watching paint dry, not the reason why anyone wants to produce records. You can't even get started on most projects until you have submitted a budget. As discussed above if you are the delegating type you will have someone else put a budget together. Unless that person knows your working habits better than you do (long-time assistants very often do), you are at least going to have to answer a multiple choice quiz about studios, dates, times, tapes, discs, musicians, arrangers and equipment rental packages. Firstly your production contract has to be read (preferably by you as well as your lawyer and manager) to make sure that it reflects your understanding of what was agreed verbally or in the headings agreement deal memo. Once you are on the project there are studio bills, phone bills and rental bills to be signed and kept track of. Union forms and rights clearances have to be filled out, signed and submitted. And, if you don't want any horrible surprises, the budget has to be tracked as you go along by comparing actual expenditure to the original budget allocation. Some producers handle this themselves, some managers will take care of it, others hire production co-ordinators, the rest prefer not to think about it until the record company calls them in because their time (and money) is up.

If you own your own studio, are on an all-in budget and are pretty self-sufficient musically you don't have to worry too much about admin. The only other way I know to avoid paperwork is to cultivate a reputation for being an administrative imbecile and a creative genius. It's a fragile stance that takes some wild, abandoned upkeep but the music business loves to mythologise and protect a helpless prodigy.

c) Managing The Session From Day To Day

i) Pre-production

"If you don't know where you're going, you'll end up somewhere else." – Yogi Berra

Some albums are done completely without pre-production, which allows almost all the creative decisions to be made in the studio. It also makes the budget extremely hard to pin down. On other records virtually all the vital decisions, and in some cases a large part of the work, is done at the pre-production stage. Extensive pre-production makes costing more accurate and very often helps to keep the final price of the project down.

John Leckie (Simple Minds, The Human League, XTC, The Fall, The Stone Roses) says, "Usually the first decision I make is whether to use a live backing track or a computer and click [track]. The songs will shape themselves after making this fundamental choice. Also, your personal approach to a song may vary slightly or radically from inception to finish. It's an ongoing decision making process, all the way through to the final mix. You shouldn't decide that a song is going to be of a very specific nature before you begin piecing it together. But when it is good you'll feel it."

If it's going to be a live band recording together in the studio, pre-production is the time when the arrangements are finalised. Then the band rehearses all the songs to the point where they know them inside out. Arranging and rehearsing can be left till you get into the studio, but, if you do that, instead of going for great takes, you'll be wasting expensive studio time and the musicians' energies deciding whether the song is better with or without an extra two bars after the chorus. I'd rather work that out at a tenth of the price in a rehearsal room and save my expensive studio time for capturing great performances. The same methodology applies if the band members are going

69

to overdub to a click. Pre-production would be the band playing the songs through, figuring out the parts and making sure that everything works together so that there are no unpleasant surprises in the studio. With an inexperienced band it might be necessary to have them practice with a click so that they are not afraid of it when they get to the studio and so they get used to the song being played all at one tempo.

However, it's always a good idea to allow for flexibility in the studio. No matter how well prepared you are going in, once you get there and play that first take back on the big monitors your thinking and approach can completely change. Michael McDonald, ex-lead singer with The Doobie Brothers and now a solo artist says, "With the Doobies, no matter how much we rehearsed something out front, the minute we got into the studio, we ripped the thing apart and restructured it totally. That was really the moment that things started to come together." Even when that's the case I still think the increased familiarity that comes through pre-production will make the restructuring process faster. Pre-production is also a good, lower pressure time for the producer and the artist to get to know each other and to, inexpensively, feel each other out creatively.

"We were in pre-production for seven months, working on the material," said Rick Rubin of The Red Hot Chili Peppers. "Then we recorded the whole album in three or four weeks. So the process of getting the music on to tape is very simple, but getting the music to the point where it's even ready to be recorded is very tough." Referring to bands that like to write in the studio, he said, "I'm totally against that. The studio is not a place for writing. It's a place to make magic happen, not to think. I'm a huge fan of pre-production, and that should be done at home or in a rehearsal studio. So with this Chili Peppers album, I'd say we got the material to the point where if I'd left the project before we recorded, and they'd basically stuck to what we'd worked out over those seven months, I think the resulting album would have been the one I wanted."

If the record is going to have outside musicians playing on it, they can either be brought together as a band to rehearse all the arrangements and parts like a self-contained group or the basic arrangements can be worked out in pre-production and the details of the individual parts left until the musicians come in to record. This approach allows for some spontaneity in the studio.

In the case of a computer programmed album, not only can the arrangements be worked out in pre-production, but parts that may be used on the final recording can be played into the computer as they are created. Sounds and samples can also be decided on. The only reason a computer based project might have to go into a pro studio, these days, is either to record any live parts such as drums, guitars or vocals or to use a proper mix room with a large mixing console, comprehensive outboard equipment, and studio monitoring. Project studios with hard disk based workstations are sonically capable of handling a project entirely at home. Bob Ezrin produced the fourth Julian Lennon album *Help Yourself.* He didn't want to go into the studio until the material was absolutely brilliant, so the pre-production period became really intensive. "In fact it was the most intensive part of the whole project, and it was also the part when we made greatest use of the Akai A-DAM system (the first relatively inexpensive modular digital multi-track). It was during pre-production that I realised we needed to store all of our ideas on some sort of medium that wasn't too noisy, that was going to be relatively faithful, and that would also allow us, if necessary, to later use the demo material in a master recording context.

"We'd take a song, flesh it out on 12-track [analogue], do all the overdubs, add all the vocals and harmonies, and then step back and decide if the result was truly interesting. Meaning, are you going to carry on to the next refinement stage of recording, where you sequence out the song in terms of verse and chorus? We recorded several songs on analogue like I described, and then decided that many of the ideas we'd put on tape could be used if only they sounded better – less noisy and less distorted." At that point they switched over to the digital system. "Everything was laid down in a retrievable fashion, so if we recorded a killer guitar riff in a song that wasn't particularly successful, we could still salvage it because we also had SMPTE (synchronisation code)." The pre-production took six months in all but at the end of it they were able to transfer the digital tracks across to the Sony 3348 (48-track professional recorder). Some parts were re-recorded and some of the pre-production demo tracks were kept and used on the actual record.

The digital recording systems are invaluable for this purpose. They can save an immense amount of time and frustration by allowing the producer to use parts of the demos or pre-production work without any serious loss of quality.

Jack Douglas likes to have a good pre-production period of anything from a week to a month depending on the artist. "You have to get the artist ready for the studio, and I don't mean ready like there's not going to be any surprises, like they've learned it like robots. Sometimes I get a band and I have to go the opposite way in that respect, I have to say, 'Look, let's not lock in so much here'.

"Generally I like the band to know and understand the piece, and, for some reason, drummers usually have to work a little harder at this so they know where the shots are and what has to be emphasised. But for the most part I encourage bands to let go and try things. I always tell them that they're holding back even if they're not. Even if they're at rehearsal playing their absolute best, I will say, 'Well, when you get into the studio you can really let go'."

Talking about Aerosmith, Douglas says, "They would come into pre-production with these little guitar riff gems and we would work them into songs while Steven [Tyler] scattered phonetics over them. Then we would take cassettes back to my house and Steve and I would sit there and turn those phonetics into lyrics. They would always be the right phonetics for the song because they sounded good, so all you had to do was kinda get them to be words and they would automatically fit."

ii) Recording The Live Band

Any time there is a musician in the studio performing, the intensity level of the session goes up. You have to assume at all times that the current performance may be the best one they are capable of. In which case if you fail to record it well or at all, that performance may be lost forever.

It's bad enough if you forget to record a brilliant guitar overdub but the stakes rise when you have a group of musicians performing together. Suddenly you have multiple possibilities for mistakes, making the perfect performance even more precious. The chemistry that occurs between musicians playing together can create a whole performance which is significantly greater than the sum of the parts. When this chemistry happens, it is often dramatic and unrepeatable. It is a case of death to the producer or engineer who fails to properly record such moments.

"I like live recording, I think you get a better sound than with over-dubbing," says George Martin. "It doesn't take longer, it just takes a little more application – but you have to be in a studio that can handle it."

John Leckie: "I've always believed in recording a live backing track that holds some magical interaction between musicians. This is almost impossible to obtain when doing singular overdubs. So even today I'll start on some songs by getting the bass, drums, a rhythm instrument and the vocal all happening together. I'll choose the take that has this magical interaction or uplift or some spirited feeling that makes the song happen – you just have to feel it. When using a click track and starting with the drums, then bass and so on, you may never have more than one band member in the studio at the same time, and it's quite hard to keep a human essence or organic musical dialogue."

Mitchell Froom (producer of Crowded House, Richard Thompson and Jimmy Scott): "We don't really do what you call tracking (an American term for laying the basic rhythm tracks to which the vocals and overdubs or 'sweetening' will be added later). We just start working and oftentimes that's the end of the story. You get the sound of the record on the day you're working. We take it as far as we can and sometimes we'll go back to it later. Often it's finished but you may want a little more perspective, or if the singer isn't in good voice that day, we may go back. It seems that the most successful recording is done at the moment. If you have somebody sing on a track, and the engineer is working that sound into the track and everything works together, it's going to be much easier for the person to sing it at that moment. Much better than if you do overdubs without considering what the vocal may be. It can be difficult to have someone sing over some foreign sounds, conflicting frequencies and all that. In general, right at the moment people are really into it, they are not paranoid, they are relaxed. If they've sung the song through three or four times through the course of the day they are right there with it. And the same goes for the overdubs. People are into the real feeling of a track, and not coming back to it later, trying to remember. You tend to get the most done in the moment – if you stick with it.

"There's a few ways to approach working on a record. There are parts of a record which may do very well by being orchestrated, and then there are parts that don't. You have to make that decision, whether someone is going after a wild performance, where what they do may change throughout the song or whether it's more planned. Very often it's a combination, and it's not an easy thing to get that feeling of spontaneity but still have it sounding like a record, and not just a thrash." What he says makes a lot of sense but for various reasons a lot of records are not made this way. Sometimes the budget will dictate that the basic tracks will need to be recorded first. Maybe that's because the studio you needed for tracking was quite expensive, so, to stay within budget, you add the vocals and overdubs later, in a cheaper studio. You need a much larger, more sophisticated facility to record a whole band than you do to record one instrument at a time. Sometimes the tracks will be recorded piecemeal because it suits the producer or engineer. It is much easier to plough on and keep laying tracks once you have all the microphones set up and equalised, than it is to keep chopping and changing, backwards and forwards from band to vocals, to acoustic guitar to horns and so on.

With the advent of large inline recording consoles, and subsequently, digital workstations a lot of producers like to leave all the mikes and inputs set up at all times so that they can add, say, a lead vocal or acoustic guitar to any track at a moment's notice. This is a very musical way of building a track. You get to hear the song develop as you go. If you lay all the rhythm tracks first, then the guitar overdubs, then the keyboards and finally the vocals you are less likely to get varied and appropriate sounds and performances than if you do all the overdubs for each song as you come to them. The song-by-song way of working reduces the risk of the singer losing his voice. There are very few singers who can sing all day, every day, without some negative repercussions on their voice. Under pressure to deliver vocals, either because of nerves or physical overuse, less experienced singers can lose their voices completely. Even if they get through the intense day-in-day-out vocal sessions, the performance and vocal quality may be less than it could have been because of the psychological and physical pressure to perform.

Jack Douglas likes to track with the whole band live as often as he can. He doesn't even worry about too much separation, in fact he goes for a lot of leakage. "I like to hear guitars and bass in the drum track, and on one guitar track I like to hear a little bit of the other leaking in there. I love live vocals. You really get the excitement, and that's important. When you put it all together it just sounds so much bigger." He's not one for absolute perfection but neither does he like a really blatant mistake. Rather than try to patch it with an overdub and have all the leakage disappear he would sooner cut in a piece from another take.

Writing in the studio can be an expensive pastime but when it works the spontaneity and freshness can be unequalled. Daniel Lanois said that U2 is really about performance. "We generally try to get something on tape as a foundation and then add a lot of detail to that. Many studio compositions come about from jam sessions based upon a riff that they had prepared. That tiny riff provides the inspiration to come up with other chords, in a different type of arrangement. What we wind up with is very different from what was originally planned."

It's the result that is important and in the midst of agonising over every little detail week after week, it's always worth reminding ourselves that the first Beatles' album was recorded in a day and Jimi Hendrix's *Axis: Bold as Love* was completed in 72 hours. Many albums that have taken months or years to complete have disappeared without trace.

iii) Recording An Orchestra Or Big Band

Recording an orchestra or big band raises the stakes. The microphone techniques are somewhat different because to some extent you have to treat the group as a whole rather than a collection of individual players. The dynamic range is usually much greater than that of a rock group. Orchestral musicians will very often hold you to the letter of the Musicians Union rules. A two minute run-over at the end of the session can cost you a great deal of extra money. Preparation is the key. By the time the musicians arrive everything needs to be ready. The microphones must be set up, line checked, phase checked and rough levels set. The chairs and music stands need to be out, the coffee on and, with a little tweaking, you should be ready to roll. There's a lot of responsibility, the atmosphere is electric right before and during a take. It can be simultaneously an exhilarating and intimidating experience.

One of the great engineer/producers, Phil Ramone recalls the first time he engineered a session on his own. "Afterwards, there were stains on my pants. It was a Neil Sedaka record. I was about 17, and had never balanced a whole rhythm section before. It was like the first time that your Dad says, 'OK son, now you take the wheel.' It was incredibly exciting, and I still get that feeling. Consistently, over the years I have worked with big bands. A few years ago Quincy Jones called and asked, 'Will you do Sinatra with me with a big band?' And I was able to reproduce that experience recently while working with

Sinead O'Connor and a big band. You put your hands on the console, and suddenly you realise, 'Oh, my God. It all depends on me and if it falls apart, it's my ass'."

Another truly great engineer/producer is Bruce Swedien. Having been Quincy Jones' right-hand studio person and friend for four decades, he went on to produce tracks for Michael Jackson. Swedien has recorded the greats of the Fifties, Sixties, Seventies, Eighties, Nineties and is still doing the same now. He spoke about recording Count Basie at Universal Studios in Chicago during the Fifties. As was customary at the time the whole band was set up in the 80 x 60 x 30 foot high room. The singer, Joe Williams, was also in the room but gobo-ed off. (Gobos are acoustically treated, movable screens usually about eight feet high and four feet wide). At that time there were no second engineers, so Swedien had to set up the room, align the tape machines and everything. He says, "I would never get much of a chance to rehearse and get levels, but by that time I knew the band real well. There was a lot of carrying on and silliness and jokes and everything. Then Basie would raise his hand and say, 'Let's do it.' Dead silence, absolutely not a sound. It would make your skin crawl. And we would do a take."

iv) Overdubbing Live Musicians
This usually involves only one musician performing at a time over a pre-recorded backing track. The challenge is to get the overdubbed performance to blend with the pre-recorded track. If a band performs together in the studio, even if they can't see each other, they feel the natural dynamic and tempo fluctuations that happen as they play. Once a performance is recorded the signals that apparently emanate from a performing musician are not recorded with that performance and it becomes a matter of learning the idiosyncracies of the recorded performance – where it speeds up and slows down.

Overdubbing has worked fine ever since Les Paul invented the concept. Since the mid-Sixties overdubbing has become the standard way to make records outside of the jazz and classical fields. The process offers many advantages, not least the opportunity for one musician to play all the instruments or for different musicians in different locations and at different times to apparently play together on a record. You can change an arrangement or orchestration if instruments are overdubbed and the engineer's control over the sonic quality of each instrument is much greater. The downside is that the end result can sometimes be a little stiff or sterile.

The band that honed this way of working to perfection was Steely Dan. Walter Becker, a member of the band and part of the production team, recently said that it has always amazed him that you could create a tight, live-feeling groove entirely by overdubs. "You record all these little bits and pieces, layer upon layer, and then you play it back and it sounds like it happened at the same time. All I can say is to make that really work well, like so many other things, it depends on the choices you make as to what is a good overdub, or what the tracking needs." He also noted that "Back in the Seventies, our big problem was trying to get the tracks with live musicians to be steadier and more mechanically perfect and so on. Whereas now, the big problem is trying to get the machine tracks to be more natural sounding and have more of the feel and variation of tracks played by real musicians." Which leads us neatly to . . .

v) The Computer-Based Session

"The computer can't tell you the emotional story. It can give you the exact mathematical design, but what's missing is the eyebrows." (Frank Zappa)

If one single factor would distinguish the computer session from any kind of live performance recording it would be the absence of adrenalin. Things can always be modified, edited and corrected. The excitement of the performance disappears. Computers generally allow a great deal of procrastination and endless changing of minds. Sometimes this can be a lifesaving thing. Before computers, if the drum sound was not right, the key was wrong or the structure needed modifying, the only thing to do was to start from scratch again. It was very costly to make a mistake. Since computers, the arrangement, the parts and the sounds can all be changed right up until the mix is completed. Unfortunately the individuals who have difficulty making decisions seem to be the ones who are attracted to making records by computer. These people sometimes have great difficulty finishing a record. With everything in a permanent state of flux and no necessity to make a decision, the project can go on forever.

Walter Afanasieff, producer of Mariah Carey and Michael Bolton, talks about the way the sessions usually run. "I'm a big fan of sequencing technology. We usually programme for a couple of days first, get the arrangement down and then go to tape. Tape is the very last step, though, after the arrangement is exactly as I want it. Because sometimes I'll prepare arrangements for artists and if they decide to change keys, well ... if you're already on tape, you're cooked – no way to transpose without re-recording. I like computers and hard disks, the digital domain. No fuss, no muss, easy to transpose. No analogue punch-ins or razor blades."

Annie Lennox's producer, Steve Lipson, tries to avoid getting to the point with technology where you can do so much that you end up doing nothing, which, he says, is what happened a few years ago with the Synclavier. "We got up our own arses, big time. Trevor [Horn] bought it, and it sat in the room untouched for a while, so I just started fiddling about with it and ended up being the 'Synclavier Operator'. We both got quite excited by its possibilities and ended up investing loads of money in it. Every time an upgrade came out, we got it – but this would mean we'd do another version of a track just because there'd been an upgrade to the synclavier. Hi-hats would take a week – because it could be done. The lesson I learned from that was: *Use the gear – don't let the gear use you.*"

Interestingly, happy accidents still happen on a computer session. Lipson tells about one song on an Annie Lennox album, "When I'd mucked up in the computer, and one particular instrument was getting every sequence from all the other channels – drum patterns, everything. Whatever was in the sequencer was triggering this one peculiar noise. And it sounded fantastic. These things happen."

vi) The Vocals

Vocals and drums are often said to be the most difficult instruments to record. In fact, technically, vocals are relatively easy to record. Use a good microphone, Mic pre, compressor and cables and the less you do to them the better they sound. The aspect of vocal recording that seems to cause the most difficulty is capturing the magical performance. A great vocal may well be in time and in tune but there are plenty of in time and in tune vocals reorientating oxide or registering ones and zeros, that are less than great. Saying a vocal needs to be in time and in tune is like saying a car needs four wheels and an engine. Both the backing track and the singer's attitude need to be consistent with the content of the lyrics in order for the final result to be satisfying. With a good singer this stuff happens subconsciously, especially when the singer is also the writer of the song and has worked on the arrangement as part of the band.

A good production needs to be sensitive to the intention of the song, leaving space for the vocal and supporting it with the right musical attitude. It is a little worrying if you have to drastically modify the singer's interpretation of the song because it indicates a fundamental lack of sensitivity, which can be hard to rectify. Assuming you have the right singer for the job, then getting a good vocal is a matter of creating the right atmosphere and a comfortable environment for them. This includes setting up a foldback that is both enjoyable and workable. A workable foldback is one that allows that particular singer to immerse themselves in the atmosphere of the song whilst still being able to hear themselves enough to stay in time and in tune. Very often a novice singer will ask for the foldback to be set up in such a way that it sounds good to them but doesn't help them stay in time or in tune. The best indication that the foldback is unworkable is when a singer who normally sings in time and in tune (when singing live or on scratch vocals) starts having problems.

John Leckie's priority is to make the singer feel comfortable rather than worry about a technically perfect recording. "Some inexperienced singers cannot perform with headphones. So I see nothing wrong in tracking the vocal with an SM58 in the control room with the monitors cranked up. It's easy to freak out about the spill, but you can gate it out later. Sometimes, however, this spill can enhance the rest of the track. It's usually some high frequency rhythmic thing like a hi-hat that catches the effect on the vocal, and then during the mix this can add a mysterious touch that can work well for the song."

André Fischer, co-founder and member of the band Rufus, producer of great vocalists such as Anita Baker, Brenda Russell, Diane Schuur, Lalah Hathaway and his wife Natalie Cole, won a GRAMMY for his work on the album *Unforgettable*, a tribute to Natalie's father Nat King Cole. He said that when he works with a vocalist, two things he brings to the project as the producer are 'care and protection'. He elaborates, "Basically, most vocalists are scared of being judged before they think it's perfect, but there is no such thing as perfection. What we're doing on a record is creating an illusion; it's not real. It's capturing something that may have been spontaneous, maybe not. To me the truest art form in music is playing live, whether that's recorded or not. If you like to perform and express yourself, the studio should just be another place to play. But a lot of people are intimidated by studios. So my job is to make it conducive and be a catalyst to make things click. The care I give is letting the singers know I'm there to bring the best out of them and be objective, and not make judgments. I never tell a vocalist how to sing. I may make some suggestions: 'You're singing from your nose; you're not singing from your diaphragm, don't sing while sitting on a stool' – common sense things that don't get into judgments of someone's character or ability. As a producer I might not always get the performance that I want. The discrepancies might come in intonation or in timing or the emotional interpretation of the line – but you have to know how to pull back a little in dealing with that to get what you want in the long run."

The story can be very different when the producer is also the writer of the song and particularly if he is a good singer himself. Often the producer will have sung the demo and when it comes to making the record, he expects the vocalist to sing the melody note for note and inflection for inflection, exactly reproducing the demo. With an inexperienced singer this can work. The singer may deliver a vocal that is beyond what they could have come up with on his or her own. However, I have seen some pretty ugly situations develop where the artist has their own style and wants to give their own interpretation of the melody. The artist was simply not able to reproduce the inflections of the original demo or the producer was so dogmatic about each inflection and vocal styling that the singer becomes intimidated or offended, and the whole session descends into a major confrontation.

Even the great Jimi Hendrix had to be handled with kid gloves in the studio. Eddie Kramer, who engineered many of his classic records, says: "I also knew how to make Jimi feel comfortable in the studio. From the outset, he had strong reservations about his vocal ability – he never really liked the sound of his own voice. To help him overcome this discomfort, I would put partitions all around him when he placed the lead vocal overdubs. Jimi also asked that the lights be dimmed, so they were. After we recorded the track he would poke his head around the screen and ask, 'How was that? Was that OK? Was it all right?' And I would tell him it was fine because, when it came to his singing voice, Jimi needed all the confidence he could get."

"Nine times out of ten, the scratch vocals are better than the real thing because the artist doesn't have the pressure – that 'this is it' rolling round in his or her mind," says Jimmy Jam. "We used to give the artist a tape and say, 'Here's how it goes. Learn it and come back tomorrow.' We never do that anymore. You can catch gold (or platinum as the case may be) while an artist is in the process of learning a song and playing around with addictive new melodies."

He cites Janet Jackson's lead vocal on 'Escapade', one of the biggest singles from the *Rhythm Nation* album, as being a scratch vocal that made it all the way to the actual record.

Speaking from a singer's point of view, Steven Tyler of Aerosmith says, "When I record my vocal tracks, I don't like to go in and just throw them down. I like to do them at my own pace, which is pretty quick anyway. I prefer to have six or seven tracks and keep singing the same song with different voices and in different ways. I like after hours vocals. It's what I did on *Get A Grip* and it's what I did on *Pump*. I go in there after the band leaves – so it's just me and an engineer. That's when I can have the most fun. No-one's listening and there's no pressure. After hours is when I can get closest to a song and its real meaning. The emotions that come out of me then are always in sync with the song."

Many singers are uncomfortable singing in front of a control room full of people. Even if the singer is screened off and can't see into the control room, they might be that much more self-conscious and less likely to take risks. There's probably nothing more disconcerting than being in a darkened studio, exposing yourself vocally, only to hear a bunch of people talking, laughing, or worse, criticising what you just did when the talk-back button goes down.

There are those occasions when you are lucky enough to be in the studio with a truly great singer. Barry Beckett tells how, on a session with Joe Cocker, vocal genius turned out to be problem. "He broke into a vocal that was just amazingly good on the first take. I was so totally enthralled that I forgot the structure of the song. At one point he stopped singing and just stood there. The track was going on and I stopped the tape and said, 'Is there something that we can help you with? Is there something wrong?' He said, 'No, this is the instrumental part.' He couldn't punch in. Dylan was the same way. They are among a few who just can't punch in. They would have to do the vocal all the way from the top, good or bad.' He adds, 'I felt stupid as hell. What made matters worse is that I only had one remaining track when I got the tape. I was scared to death that we were going to pass up something else. I could have put it into 'input,' and done it all the way from the top, but I might have had something else just as good.

He ended up being maybe one per cent off what I was hoping for, but it was still good."

Barry Beckett touches on one of the all-time great production dilemmas when you are recording on linear tape systems either digital or analogue. When you are working on solos or vocals, very often you get down to the last available track on the multi-track tape. Even if you are working on an unlimited slave system (where you make up work reels with as many available tracks as you might need for overdubs) you can still run out of tracks. It's always possible to make up another slave or work reel, right then and there, but if the creative juices are flowing, by the time you've done that the moment will most likely have passed. Very often at these moments the singer (or soloist) will say, "I can do better than that." You, however, have been listening to this guy all afternoon and you know that the last performance was the best you have heard. You could, as Beckett said, roll the tape in input, which means that you don't record his next performance although the performer will think you are.

These are the potential scenarios:

You don't record the next pass. He reaches deep down inside, somewhere he hasn't been all day, possibly all week and does the vocal of his life. You didn't record it. He's going to know you didn't record it. Very ugly scene ensues.

You don't record the next pass. He doesn't do a great vocal. You breathe a sigh of relief. As you reach for the talkback button to tell him what a clever boy you've been, he says: "That was it. That was the one." A total silence from the control room.

You are stuck with the previous take which in his mind is utter crap compared to the one he just did. And he's going to like the one you have on tape even less when he finds out that the one he thought was it is now in magnetic heaven.

You do go into record. You wipe the best vocal of the project or, depending on the artist, the only decent vocal that he did all week. His performance is not quite as good or complete crap. You can't decide whether to shoot yourself, shoot the singer or kick the engineer.

You do go into record. He does the best vocal of the project. You break open the champagne and go to the beach for the rest of the day.

All of this stuff passes through your head in the time it takes the tape to roll back to the beginning of the track. That's about twenty or thirty seconds unless you are recording on a random access system in which case it's no time at all. Clearly if you are a person who has difficulty making decisions, producing may not be for you.

If you are working with a substantial, professional, artist, even if you wiped something irreplaceable they will more than likely say, "No problem, let's just go for another one." After all, everyone makes mistakes. Now ... if you did it twice, things might not stay quite so chummy. Since the quality of performance is a big factor in what makes a great production there are moments when it is hard to over-state the value of unlimited virtual tracks and multiple levels of undo.

There is probably no process as personal and individual as vocal recording. Great vocals are invariably done by great singers. There's no studio trickery that will turn an average or bad singer into a great singer. Sure, you can correct a multitude of sins such as tuning and timing but you cannot find a greatness button anywhere in the studio. As obvious as this may seem, it is, nonetheless, a point that more A&R people should bear in mind when they sign acts.

vii) Which Method Makes A Better Record – Live, Overdubbed or Computer?
T-Bone Burnett says that he still prefers using real musicians, and he does not like the overuse of computers in music. "It's good for things to speed up and slow down and be out of tune," he says. "Besides being conceptually correct, it's also emotionally true. People even try to program flaws into the music, but it's not the same. Once you program a flaw it's no longer a flaw; it's a program."

Manfred Mann, who nowadays records using a combination of live musicians and computers, said that when records ceased to be played live and started to be built up by overdubbing, a lot of the 'feel' got lost. "If you do live overdubs on a computer track, the musicians are playing to something that is known to be in time. Before computers, if the basic track was not solid you were layering discrepancy on top of discrepancy."

"When musicians physically play together, they get something off each other which you don't get when you're overdubbing. It's a clinical way of doing things," says George Martin. "You can be ultra-efficient, absolutely in tune and dead in time – and if you're not the machine will quantize it for you – but does it make good music? I don't think so. Music is what people do together, that's real good music."

For better or for worse, certain kinds of music would not have come into existence without computers. I was at the forefront of the application of computers to music. I can clearly remember the excitement of being able to program parts that would have been impossible to play, or being able to program all the instruments without having to learn how to play them. Computers have enabled us to separate technical proficiency from creativity. Nonetheless a bad computer track has very little to commend it. It may be in tune, in time and technically proficient but music is really about the communication of emotions or feelings.

We've all seen bands full of highly proficient musicians who have no ability to communicate. All instruments have varying degrees of expressive capabilities. The human voice is the most expressive instrument, partly because of its immense flexibility, partly because it's directly plugged into our mind and emotions and partly because it has the added dimension of language.

The guitar, trumpet, and saxophone have for a large part of this century been the most popular lead instruments because they are immensely responsive and expressive in the hands of a gifted player. Other instruments such as the Hammond organ (which is basically like a set of tuned on/off switches) and the vibraphone are inherently less expressive. Put those instruments in the hands of talented and sensitive musicians such as Jimmy Smith or Gary Burton and they generate emotionally charged and exciting music. A great musician can communicate with two pieces of wood.

Computers themselves do not communicate, they are tools just like the Hammond organ, or a paintbrush or a pen through which a musician, painter or writer can express themselves. The problem with computers is that they have made it possible for lesser artists to put together 'professional sounding' records. Great musicians and producers will continue to make great records, with or without computers.

In certain sectors of the music fraternity there has been a backlash against new technology. Mostly this has come from the younger musicians and producers who have rediscovered 'live' (in the studio) recording, analogue tape and tube equipment. It's very interesting to listen to the attitude of musicians, engineers and producers who come from the time when you had to do everything live. Miles Davis embraced computers, drum machines and synthesisers in his later years. Rudy Van Gelder, the premier jazz recording engineer of the Fifties and Sixties, loved digital recording from very early on.

Art Neville of the ultimate groove band, The Neville Brothers says, "In the past everything was cut right at the time. The musicians were playing all at one time. Now you can put things together in parts and still get the same, and even a better effect. Computers are great – it's a tool, that's all it is – just as long as you don't let it be the whole deal. The computer's nothing without what we're doing."

Herbie Hancock has been recording since he played piano with the groundbreaking Miles Davis groups of the Sixties. He is as well known for his cutting edge use of electronics (check out his Eighties album *Future Shock* containing the monster instrumental hit 'Rock-it') as he is for his acoustic piano artistry. There are very few musicians of his calibre at any one time on this planet. Currently he combines both live musicians and sequencers (computers) on his records.

"Overall, we record in a very old-fashioned way," says Jimmy Jam of Jam and Lewis. "We just turn on the tape and go for the gold. That's how you make those wonderful mistakes that give your song the unique touch you're looking for." But, of course, Jam and Lewis's sense of old fashioned does include the use of programmed drums on most of their recordings.

Clearly there is no right or wrong way to make records. There is definitely an appropriate way and an inappropriate way to make any specific record. The methodology that the producer employs will have an immense impact on not only the sound of the record but also on the attitude and emotion that will be communicated by it and the way the record will be perceived by the music business and by the public. The sound and attitude of the production needs to match the sound and attitude of the music. It's a gross over-simplification to say that a raw, edgy band shouldn't have slick production and a smooth, romantic ballad might miss the mark if the production was too rough around the edges. Nonetheless the general principle holds that the production should be totally consistent with the style of the artist and the content of the music and lyrics.

Brian Eno: "As more and more options have become available, and equipment more and more complex, the temptation can arise to forget the possibilities of simplicity. It's a question of balancing external influences and technologies with your own instincts and beliefs."

Many times a producer will be chosen because of the way their previous records sound or because they are known to be good at a certain style of recording. Obviously someone who spends all their time recording bands live in the studio is going to have honed those particular techniques to perfection. At the other end of the spectrum, the producer who likes to make records using computers, samplers and synthesisers will have developed the knowledge and skills to be able to construct a record in that way with great certainty. The artistry in production is in using whatever skills you can muster and whatever technology you can manipulate to record music so that it moves people emotionally. The skill might be management ability and the technology might be a guitar and a cassette recorder or a computer and some samples but if you can capture something that moves people (preferably not out of the room) you might just be a record producer.

d) What Are 'They' Going To Expect Of You?

"I don't know the key to success, but the key to failure is trying to please everybody." (Bill Cosby)

i) The Artist?

The artist wants the album of his or her life. If it reflects their every whim and indulgence, makes them look and sound good then they will love you forever from the day it's completed. They'll love you slightly longer than forever the day after the A&R person has given it his or her apparent stamp of approval by saying, "It's a real step forward from the demos (or the last album) and I need to live with it for a couple of weeks." (Interpretation: "I need to play it to everyone in the department and my bosses and if they like it then, and only then, will I come out with a qualified endorsement.").

All previous praise aside, it could become entirely your fault the day it fails to break all chart records. The blame may never be expressed in words but will be characterised by the fact that everyone else who worked on the album from A&R to promotions, marketing, artwork and management will survive. You will be replaced. If it is an indisputable hit you may get an occasional mention, by the artist, in the press as a helpful collaborator but, then again, probably not. If the album is not a major hit the chances of getting to produce the next album are less than even. If it is a hit the odds improve to about even. As far as the practical aspect of the recording goes, the expectations vary hugely. Alan Moulder believes that bands want someone to be their creative ally, to support what they want to do, try what they want to try and have some creative input.

Albhy Galuten, talking about the different role each member of the production team played during The Bee Gees incredibly productive Miami period says: "Technically, it was produced by Karl Richardson, me and The Bee Gees. The three people who were in the control room all the time were Karl, Barry [Gibb] and myself. Karl was primarily the engineer, making sure that everything was going well. Barry was the visionary, and I suppose I was the translator. I had an intuitive sense of what Barry was going for. He'd play me a song and I would hire musicians, work out parts, come up with some ideas, work on the arrangements. For many of those records there really was a band working together. It was certainly a collaborative effort with many talented people, but clearly it was the three of us in the studio, all day, every day."

Sometimes bands have a number of disparate influences and don't manage to pull them together into a coherent direction. This is an area where the producer's more objective viewpoint can really help. The late Michael Hutchence, of the Australian band INXS, spoke about producer Mark Opitz: "When we first met him we were scrambling for a style, and we were trying to mix together rock and funk. And he is the first guy to ever put that into some aural context, which was great. It was a revolution for us. The album *Shahooh Shahooh* was fantastic for us, and we made a giant leap forward. Suddenly it was, 'Ah! We see the light.' He really helped us with that, and he's always been a friend."

Jackson Browne, on working with Don Was (Bonnie Raitt, Was Not Was, The Rolling Stones) says, "It's like taking a recording seminar with one of your heroes before embarking again on a process that you are very familiar with. Part refresher course and part 'Oh, so that's what you do.' He's got great presence in the studio. He's got great instincts, and the standard he brings is something that he puts on the record immediately. I can't say that we agreed about everything we heard or wanted to try, but the process I am familiar with is a long one – it's more writing than anything. You continue to write when you overdub or when you work with someone who's going to solo on your record. What he brings to the process is something that I probably wouldn't even think of, like calling certain players. He made some very cool calls."

Rickie Lee Jones says that her relationship with a producer varies from record to record, and depends on the mood she's in for that piece of work. "The main criterion is that the producer provides

camaraderie more than technical expertise. I want them to relate to
the work, to dig it and help to bring an atmosphere of confidence. In
the future, I might like to have a producer like in the old days. You
know I would just walk in and sing, and the producer would do it all.
I'm getting tired of doing so much work, but I have the need to
control almost every aspect of what I am doing." The artist having
total control, as opposed to just walking in and doing vocals, involves
production styles that are at the opposite ends of the scale. But Rickie
is totally emphatic when she says: "If a producer always has a phone
in his hand at your session, you should fire him."

The producer needs to support the artist. That's not to say he can't
disagree with them or try to steer them in a different direction. But,
amidst all the anxieties, arguments and discussions that can be part
of making a record, the artist needs to feel that the producer has
their best interests at heart and that there is a supportive, creative
atmosphere within which they can work. Good performances cannot
come out of a hostile atmosphere. It would be better to hand the
project to someone else if a producer loses respect for the artist.

Bruce Fairbairn (Loverboy, Bon Jovi, Aerosmith, AC/DC) says, "I
think I'd be happiest if bands just said, 'We work with Fairbairn
because he lets us make our record the way we want to make it.'
That's the best advertisement for my work. Basically, I like to be
perceived as someone who facilitates the creative process. In a way
everything they get from me is something that they've taken from
themselves."

When Jack Douglas produced *Double Fantasy* for John Lennon he
was sworn to secrecy. Lennon sent him tapes of the songs with him
playing guitar or piano, recorded on a little Panasonic machine.
Douglas was told to hire musicians and book a studio; if he told
anyone who the artist was the project was off. Douglas arranged and
wrote out the tunes. The musicians he hired, Tony Levin, Andy
Newmark, Earl Slick, Hugh McCracken and George Small, were
around the same age as Lennon. Douglas sang the parts at the
rehearsals and the sessions were booked at The Hit Factory in New
York. The musicians did not find out till the night before the first
session.

As I said earlier the Merlin style producer may have nothing more
than a few conversations with the band and still pick up a full production credit. All-Singing, All-Dancing will make the entire record
with virtually no input from the artist apart from vocals. The sidekick

will be in the studio at all times with and without the artist but the artist is very much in charge. The collaborator will work more the way Jack Douglas did with John Lennon, although they usually don't have the secrecy factor to deal with. So the specific expectations will vary from situation to situation and from producer to producer.

ii) The Record Company?

You are their representative on the project. You will be required to read minds, including changing ones, and keep up with trends, including ones that change in the middle of the project. The budget is entirely your responsibility, even though you may not have control over the choice of studio or the amount of days the artist simply chooses not to show up. If you're working with an already successful artist, how many days will they have to fly out to New York to film an MTV special or Milan to stock up on clothes? How many TV film crews will show up to film them recording their new album? Of course, the singer won't be seen dead singing live on TV (he knows he sings out of tune and has to punch in or use the autotune for every other word).

The band's usual *modus operandi* is to painstakingly piece the album together overdub by overdub, so they decide to mime to a track you prepared earlier. This burns another precious day in the five-star studio of their choosing while you watch your budget rapidly approach overage. You sit up at night re-reading your contract to see whether your Rottweiler lawyer beat the record companies' pit bull on that overage liability clause. You spend more of your dwindling days debating with the label that this period should be paid for out of the band's promotional budget as opposed to the recording budget. You're starting to get concerned about the start date of the next project that you are scheduled to produce.

The genre of music in which you operate will affect the expectations the company has of the producer. Alan Moulder tends to work with (big selling) indie/alternative type bands. "They want a good sounding record and no problems. They don't really care how you got it," he says. "Some are more involved than others. Some of them are down there a lot and others stay completely away." He understands the importance of giving the company "something they can work with" and says that they like to hear a good progression from what the band's been doing, a good change or at least what they think the band should be doing.

He feels fortunate that A&R departments and managers don't get too creatively involved with the kinds of bands he works with. They give the bands a lot of freedom. "There is less commercial pressure," he says, "because the band is known to go its own way and do its own thing. When I've worked on more commercial projects there have been a lot more problems; a lot more A&R comment and a lot more pressure but generally not from the management."

The cycle never stops turning though and the indie/alternative rock genre has spawned some of the biggest selling albums of the last 15 years so the commercial pressures encroach on that area of music also. Unless you are making records that are never intended for airplay there will be lots of outside opinion and all the requisite pressures to deliver the sometimes elusive "hit single."

iii) The Artist's Manager?

Some managers are extremely hands-on. They spend a great deal of time with the artist and micro-manage every detail. Others call in once a week from an office located on another continent. Alan Moulder says, "If the manager has a close relationship with the band, then you tend to deal with him and have to deal with him more than if it's someone sitting in an office miles away." He adds, "They all expect you to make things go as smoothly as possible."

Most managers with whom I have come into contact want only success for their artist and a peaceful life. If there is a more difficult job than producing in the music business, it is undoubtedly artist management. Of necessity it is a political job and the support you can expect from the artist's manager will be strictly skin deep. The producer is a means to an end for the manager. If you keep the artist happy, produce a great album that satisfies the record company, which goes on to sell by the bucket load you will have an enthusiastic, albeit temporary, ally. When the time comes around to record the follow-up, expect the manager to be in the frontline with a clutch of alternatives to your faithful self. His artist cannot afford to be held back by growth-inhibiting behaviour patterns such as loyalty. The producer who put his reputation on the line and produced the first gold or platinum album is expendable.

Strong artist management is as important to the producer as it is to the artist. The artist's management can have a huge influence over the label's commitment to promoting and marketing the record. Don't expect too much in the way of enduring friendship.

Chapter Four

Will They Still Love You Tomorrow?

"As the camel falls, the knives that would stab it multiply." Arabic adage

a) What Is Your Working Life Expectancy?

Your working life expectancy can range from producing just one track to masterminding a lifetime of GRAMMY Awards. Manager, Katrina Sirdofsky points out that, "If you look at music history many producers have had careers that spanned several decades." If you are talented and successful the question may not be for how long will you be asked to continue to produce records but how long will you continue wanting to. The answer you come up with relates directly to how much control you have over your destiny and the destiny of the records you produce.

It is extremely frustrating to make good records and watch them disappear for lack of record company commitment. This fact alone drives some successful freelance producers into staff positions at labels. Their motivation is twofold. Firstly, it is easier to read the record company's commitment to a project from inside the company, thus enabling you to make a more informed judgment about which projects are likely to get the big push. Secondly, you may have slightly more influence over the future of the album if you are on the inside.

Other frustrated freelance record producers start up their own labels, the reality of which is often very different from the principle. If you don't mind flying a desk and a telephone more than a band and a studio, your own label will certainly give you more control. You still have to deal with the vagaries of promotion, marketing and distribution, which will most likely be done by one of the major labels anyway.

Some producers can't take it anymore and just get out of the business altogether. The first couple of years usually weed out the less resilient. If you survive those first few projects, the initial flush of success and the excitement of being the flavour of the month, chances are you will be in it for the long run. A 'long run' would be anything over five years.

George Martin once said: "I don't think I'm as good a producer now as I used to be. I think I suffer fools less and you have to suffer fools gladly to be a good producer. You must be patient, you must have great tact, and you must have that long view. You must know what you want and wait to get it – you can't rush it."

b) How's Your Health?

The music business attracts more than its fair share of people who treat their physical bits as if they live and (intend to) die by Pete Townshend's credo – before they get old. Rock 'n' roll will only make you deaf but nowadays both the sex and the drugs can kill you. Despite the abuse, most wind up facing a more down-to-earth reality; if they'd known they were going to live this long they'd have taken better care of themselves.

For the hands-on record producer, health can be a relevant issue. The hours can be very long for a number of reasons; studio time is expensive and is often sold on a daily (24-hour lockout) basis. If you're trying to stay within budget, the inclination is to take the fullest possible advantage and work in excess of 12-hour days. 14 to 16 hour days are not uncommon. In the remix world 48 and 72 hour days are sometimes the only way to get the job done at all. Residential studios lend themselves to ridiculously long working hours, which is one reason why record companies favour them. In most residentials you're confined by the sheer remoteness of the location. Since you eat, sleep and everything else there prevailing logic steers you towards the studio all day, *and* after dinner and after the pub if the band is so inclined.

A common residential studio syndrome is that of the 'turned around day.' On the first day, in the first flush of enthusiasm, you get to bed about two a.m. That becomes three a.m. the second day then four the next, etc. Breakfast gets later and later until eventually no-one is up until late afternoon and you're working right through the night until mid-morning again. This can be one of the quicker ways of exposing undesirable personality traits. I've seen more serious arguments break out at four in the morning when everybody's tired than at any other time. Most of us have had the experience of getting carried along on a creative high till six in the morning. More often than not, after one quick listen the next day we scrapped it all and wondered which influence we were under at the time. Unless I'm working with confirmed night owls I instigate a mutually agreed schedule that most accommodates all body clocks concerned. Exceptional circumstances aside, I stick pretty much to that schedule.

If you're in a hot phase, the projects come thick and fast. You hate to turn down anything good. After all, you love the job and you remember how the lean times really were. So the pressure is there to go straight from one project to another. This can be very exhausting. Starting a new album is really not much different from starting a new job: the personalities are all different and the music will be different from the last record. Your role will even be some-what different unless you're the All-Singing-All-Dancing type (described in Chapter One). You may even have to fly across multiple time zones to get to the next location. Your utilities may be about to get cut off at home and your personal life may be falling apart because you're never wherever it's supposed to be. Ideally, I take at least a month off between projects just to chill out and do normal things like going to the dentist. According to 'scientific' sources the most stressful things in life are getting divorced, changing jobs and moving house. In effect producers face all three prospects about once every other month.

Taking time off to recuperate and to listen to other kinds of music is important to Alan Moulder. "I still do a lot of small bands. Either their first or second record. If I like the band I'll do it and conversely if it's a big band and I don't like it I won't do it. I try to stick with what I like so I can give an honest day's work," he says. "On recording, the band sets the length of the day. Different bands have different burn-out periods. I've worked with some bands where they'll work almost a strict 12-hour day and at midnight even if they are in the middle of a guitar overdub they'll stop. I've done eight-hour days but some of the bands just don't get going until late at night. If you want to record them, you just have to be around until they are ready. Those days can be very long. I prefer a 12-hour day, and in an ideal world a 12-hour day and no work on weekends. When you get to the mix you tend to have more control over the hours and again that is usually a 12-hour day."

c) What Keeps A&R People Coming Right Back To You?

i) If You're Hot?

Absolutely no problem. If they can run their finger down the *Music Week* or *Billboard* chart and alight one or more times on your moniker, they love you to death. They will keep pushing your name forward to all of their acts (no matter how inappropriate). Until you cease to have a presence in the charts, you can rely on their publicly professed friendship and undying loyalty.

Producing is seen from the outside as a 'black art'. Producers often seem like they are selected by someone saying "OK, this guy has had some success, he seems like he might be compatible with the artist (they're both bipeds after all). Let's give it a shot." It often seems like there is not a lot of understanding of what the actual process is once producer and band are in the studio.

In a 1995 news group posting, Steve Albini said, "In the rock music realm, the 'producer' is often chosen by whim, based on whose name has been associated with popular records and sometimes with no regard for the competence of the individual so-chosen. If somebody told me Barney the dinosaur was the 'Producer' on the new Dimbulb Canopy album I'd believe him."

Many of the qualities that induce success in the music business are intangible. They may be related to, but are definitely not directly proportional to talent, hard work, experience, education or track record. At times a hazy pattern, a quasi-formula seems to appear and we all love to quote the quotes such as "you make your own luck" and "the harder I work at it, the luckier I get." Most of us have had the experience of making what we thought was a great record and seeing it fail miserably. Then the next effort, which we privately think is only average, inexplicably goes mega. You did nothing different from the other less successful projects but now success capriciously attaches itself to you and your production work. Appreciate it, wallow in it, try to understand it, but no matter what: capitalise on it. Make hay while the sun shines. Use your successes to climb the ladder in terms of the quality of artists you have access to, the suitability of the projects and the financial rewards available. When you are hot, no fee is too high, no royalty too unreasonable. After all, you have the Midas touch and everyone wants you to touch their project.

ii) If You're Not Quite There Yet?

Production careers, like most entertainment jobs, observe the laws of quantum physics … absolutely nothing, absolutely nothing, absolutely nothing, SOMETHING! You tend not to have gradually increasing good fortune – just endless, arduous, fruitless slog. Then one day you wake up to SUCCESS! I was very fortunate in that the first record I produced was a hit, no slog there. I can, however, draw from the rest of my career as a studio musician and artist. What worked for me was to be out and about working with as many interesting people as 24/7 would allow.

Obviously you have to be wise about it. I worked for several years in the areas of *avant garde* electronic music and free improvised jazz. I didn't for a moment think that it was going to lead to mega-success and life in the Hollywood Hills. I did it because it interested me. In the end success came, predictably enough, in commercial music through the normal major label route. But those years in non-commercial and *avant garde* groups paid off in that they gave me an edge, a lead, the drop, an insight, maybe. In my case it was an insight into the use of new technology that got my foot in the door and made me stand out from the crowd. You have to work with music that you like first and foremost. It's good to be realistic about its potential for success. I found a niche for myself that eventually expanded into the mainstream. A niche area of music can create an advantage for you, even if it is not unique. If there are less people chasing the same thing you have a better chance of becoming the expert at it.

To assess a niche, ask yourself why this apparent niche opportunity exists. Is it an unmined vein of gold? (In which case grab it with both hands.) Or is it fringe music that may never join the mainstream? (Almost every trend starts on the fringe and can be spotted months, if not years, in advance. Yesterday's alternative styles are often today's mainstream. Hip-hop has become huge, internationally, from very small beginnings more than 25 years ago. Alternative rock, which was on the margins in the Eighties, became mainstream pop in the US during the Nineties. But some fringe trends never make the transition. Washington D.C.'s Go-Go music has been on the edge for many years but has never made the leap to the international big time.)

Is the niche an old style that has faded into relative and maybe permanent obscurity? (It could still present an opportunity. Very few styles completely die out. They just morph a little.) The key element is belief – if you find an artist you believe in and you truly love their music, then chances are lots of other people will too. A very good example of someone, who got started because of his knowledge of what, at the time, was a niche market is Alan Moulder. He says, "I was very, very lucky that I fell into the alternative market in England at the time when hardly anyone else wanted to do it. Slick records were king at the time and alternative or indie records were almost like second rate music. Other engineers thought they sounded awful and trashy. So I didn't have a lot of competition. A lot of the producers that were doing those records were used to working in cheaper studios with assistants and they came to me because these records are quite difficult to polish up a bit without making them sound slick or smooth. So there weren't a lot of trained engineers who'd come up through the studio system from assistant to house engineer who wanted to make those records. I could co-produce [with bands] and they would only have to pay one person instead of both an engineer and a producer. Combined with the fact that I was not that expensive in the beginning, which helped since those records weren't selling in huge quantities at the time."

iii) If You Were Recently Hot?

This is possibly the most difficult position to be in. You are likely to get offered the second division projects, the ones that have been turned down by the truly hot, and, perhaps more significantly, the projects that are not earmarked for success. Labels will take success from any artist if it is handed to them on a plate but there are definitely 'priority' projects and 'the other kind'. If you happen to be working on 'the other kind' you may find the odds of winning the National Lottery are better.

The more of these second division projects you take on, the more failed projects you accumulate, the longer the gap since your last chart showing, the more you attract critical judgments about your success rate and the less recently you appear to have been hot at all.

iv) When The Night's Closing In?

In the music business most artists, musicians and producers struggle for several years to get their first break. Having arrived at the top of the mountain they often assume that the sunlight of success will continue to shine on them for the rest of their lives. As we know, there is only *one* way to go from the top. It should, theoretically, be easier to continue success than it is to create the first break. After all, you have developed all those musical, technical and people skills that enabled you to get there in the first place. The problem is the mountain is not stationary. While Mohammad is sunbathing on top of the, supposedly immovable, mountain, the mountain is quietly (and sometimes suddenly) eroding beneath him. All kinds of things can happen.

Musical fashions inevitably change and can leave you out in the cold. Many Seventies producers who were used to producing only live musicians were either unable, or perceived to be unable, to cope with the computerised, synthesised Eighties. In the Nineties the trend pendulum swung back the other way to live bands. A producer who made his name in the Eighties with highly-produced, computer-generated records may find himself, justifiably or not, sidelined. As the millennium drew to a close digital recording techniques became more widely accepted and producers once again needed to be more techno savvy in order to stay in tune.

Technical trends will surely change. If you don't keep up you may find yourself high and dry as an expert in old technology for which there may be much less, or no, demand. Equipment is also becoming much less expensive, to the point that solid studio experience is no longer the exclusive domain of the professional producer. For a few thousand bucks you can put together a home studio that can pretty well match and in some respects exceed the professional facilities of a few years ago. A talented beginner can not only train himself but also produce tracks, which he can use as a calling card to get work. These days there are records in the charts that came right out of an enterprising beginner's bedroom studio.

We all get older. Unlike, say the sciences where age and experience are regarded as positive attributes, for a record producer "over 40" can be unfairly equated to out-of-touch. There are notable examples of producers, such as Quincy Jones, who not only survive musical life beyond 40 but actually do their most successful work then. Nevertheless, if you are over 40 and the hits are getting thin on the ground, don't expect the same breaks that you got when you were 20. Your best shot is to find a project that you believe in and use your skill, experience and contacts to get back into the limelight.

You've tackled too many second division projects by now. You haven't had a name check in the *Music Week* or *Billboard* charts for a good few years. At best you are back at square one, looking for a way back in. Unfortunately several of the routes are no longer open to you because you are a known quantity – everyone has preconceived notions about what you can and cannot do – and you are probably a good bit older by now. Ageism is rife in the business, particularly in the UK and not least from the older executives. They tend to look for young talent, partly out of fear that they are losing touch themselves, partly to save money and partly to appear hip. Youth is apparently contagious – if you hang around it long enough you might catch some. Younger A&R staff can sometimes feel intimidated by older producers. Except if you produced a record that was a big favourite of theirs when they were still at school then they will jump at the chance to work with you. They will be extremely respectful to the point of being in awe of you – capitalise!!

By now you will need the money more than you did when you started out. You have a trophy wife, kids in private school and a frightening monthly nut to crack. Like a shark you keep swimming or you drown. Unfortunately you can no longer afford the time to develop unsigned projects the way you did when you were starting out. At this point you may want to consider your options both inside and outside the business. Anyone with a substantial track record as a producer has a lot of transferable skills but it is most likely going to be back to the old entrepreneurial enterprise and having to prove yourself all over again.

Personal experience has led me to believe that there is one thing and one thing only that will guarantee more, high quality, work: CURRENT COMMERCIAL SUCCESS. Danny Saber quite rightly points out that critical acceptance is a factor that can help early on in a career and that is supported by Andy Kipnes' comment to Peter Collins that being associated with cool projects can keep you in work. Nonetheless, Danny experienced a massive increase in interest once he had a successful record under his belt. He says, "Before I had commercial success I always had to talk them into why they should use me. There were a couple of guys who were really cool and would back me but there was always that doubt. Once you have a hit record you have that to stand on. They still have their doubts because they have their own insecurities. No matter what you did before, it's only going to do them any good if you do good for them." He doesn't think that A&R people pay much attention to what producers actually do. "I think they are more into what looks good on paper. They don't really know. They come in and scratch their balls and try to get out of taking you to dinner. One A&R guy said 'Right so you wrote six songs in four days, so you can write 12 songs in eight days and 24 in 16 days'. They look at it like it's a corporate memo."

v) What Prevents Them From Coming Back To You?
It can be as simple as habit. You get on a roll with a couple of A&R people and they keep coming back to you; break that roll and they find someone else. Although they didn't fall out with you or find fault with your work, you don't work with them again for years.

Not being the flavour of the month will immediately eliminate 85 per cent of your incoming phone calls. If you can't find your name in the top half of at least one current chart, the other 15 per cent may dry up too. Even being difficult to work with or, sin of sins, running over budget, will not create ugly, unwanted spaces in your schedule as quickly as a lack of a name check in at least one trade magazine.

Rule number one is that most people don't really know what you do and how you do it; rule number two is success is the primary measure of your ability as a producer. Exceptions to rule number two would be if you are very young, considered to be cutting edge hip, extremely inexpensive, managed by the A&R person's management company or by a company which has a loyal roster of artists who keep requesting you.

Chart positions are tangible evidence of success but they do not indicate the reasons for it. It is often difficult to define why certain projects are successful and others are not. In the trade press, hit projects are dissected like successful military campaigns. But 95 per cent of all releases that disappear without trace every year use very similar marketing and promotion techniques, A&R people and production crews.

The point is that failure is as difficult to attribute to tangible causes as success. Certainly, at the qualitative extremes, there are the 'truly incredible' and the 'really awful' records. In the middle, a significant number of releases qualify as OK, not bad or pretty good. The factors that tip the scale from failure to success are often difficult to define and unpredictable. If we could suspend the 'Emperor's New Clothes' mentality for a second we would see a good number of clunkers in the Top Ten and some undiscovered gems in the cut-out bins.

Lauren Christy of the Matrix has a collection of songs she likes, on her iPod, that were never hits. She says, "to me they were still hit songs but the person got fired at the label or the right indie promotion people weren't put on the job. There are a lot of things that are outside the control of the artist."

We like, or perhaps need, to sweep our failures under the carpet and in order to slide out from under any responsibility, the blame needs to be placed fairly and squarely on someone's shoulders. A&R, marketing, and promotion people all work for the company, the producer is freelance and can be terminated painlessly and at zero cost to artist or company.

Having said all this, it is not only possible to survive multiple failed records, it is absolutely essential especially if you intend to produce a lot of début albums. The first time one of your records fails, if you are the least bit sensitive, it really beats you up or knocks you for six depending whether you are American or English.

It's always good to analyse what exactly went wrong, what your level of responsibility was and what you can do to avoid the same problem in the future. Surviving failure comes down to your attitude, your belief in yourself and your relationships within the business. Having just fallen off the horse, you have to get right back on. Realistically and honestly acknowledging the extent of your responsibility to the artist and label is good. Carrying the can for someone else's failings is bad. Don't catch other people's 'hot potatoes'. If you know you've made a great album, which stiffed, kick the dust off your sandals and move on. The vast majority of major label releases fail and A&R, marketing and promotion aren't going to let a failed record blight their careers. Why should you?

vi) How Else Can You Get Work?
As Alan Moulder succinctly puts it, "Band requests and previous reputation." This is really the best way to get work. If your reputation is big enough that generation after generation of artists keep asking for you, it's quite possible that you can keep working until you get tired of it all and decide to retire to a Pacific island.

vii) What's The Best Way To Handle the Show Reel/Resumé/CV Tap Dance?
Personally I've always hated sending out CVs or resumes and show reels. My best work has come to me by word-of-mouth or personal recommendation. The artist or A&R person will have heard some-thing of mine they liked on the radio or maybe they knew someone I had worked with. Show reels can really be a problem if you're not there to explain the relevance or irrelevance of your previous

productions to the one under discussion. I prefer not to take on two similar projects. I like each production to be different from the previous ones. You would think that anyone with A&R or management skills could listen to your show reel and identify qualitative production factors that would benefit their own project. What generally happens is that people get hung up on the details of your previous productions (maybe they dislike the band or the singer's voice) rather than trying to understand what you brought to the project. None of this is surprising when you consider the large number of producers vying for a relatively small number of projects. With the market tipped heavily towards the supply side, why would the A&R person not go for what it perceived to be the safer choice. So, if you are lucky enough to be working regularly, it's very easy to get stuck in the genre in which you have most recently had success.

Some producers are not the least bit bothered by this. They are interested only in working within a fairly narrow field of music that conforms to their own range of taste. That's perfectly fine. If you really like one style of music, provided the market for that type of record never goes completely belly-up you can have a productive, happy career uncomplicated by heavy duty decision making. Personally, I like and listen to a very wide, constantly changing range of music and I would like my work to reflect that. All I can say is that, from my own experience, it takes a huge amount of personal effort, ingenuity, and constant commitment to escape this kind of type-casting.

"I'm very wary of sending out showreels," says Alan Moulder. "I try to tailor each showreel to each band. This can be difficult because very often bands come to you for different reasons than you thought."

I've often been surprised when some productions I've done appeal to artists in apparently completely different genres of music. Often the band might have heard something of yours when they were 10, and although they are strictly hard-core now, they still have fond childhood memories of that poppy little ditty you produced way back then.

The scenario I prefer goes like this: my name comes up for the production from whatever source – the band, the band's manager or the A&R person. If I don't survive their preliminary discussions I may never even know I was being considered. If I make it past that initial stage, then either the A&R person or the manager will call to set up a meeting. This first meeting could be with the A&R person, the band or all together. My objective is to find out whether I can work with the band and whether they can work with me. If we like each other, we're halfway there. My next goal is to find out how they think, what they listen to, what movies they watch, where they hang out, what books they read, what type of people they are, what makes them happy, what upsets them. I try to figure out what the power structure of the group is, who's likely to blow up on me, who's going to be the peacemaker, how their collective and individual sense of humour works (groups often develop their own, quirky, sense of humour and even their own language).

I also need to know what they think a producer does in general and what I in particular can do for them. In addition, I ask them what kind of record they want to make (it's amazing how many bands are not the least bit unified on this subject). I also want to talk to the A&R person and get his side of the story, find out what he is expecting from me and from the album. It's often truly mind boggling to behold the difference between the expectations of the A&R department and the band.

At this point they will go away and discuss it amongst themselves and come back with one of three options:

A) "Yes let's do it" – in which case you have to figure out whether you can fit them into your busy schedule. (Whatever they say about having to have the album out by Christmas, they'll start at least three months later than they're telling you now).

B) "The band have decided to go with someone else" – in this case it will be the A&R person or manager who calls and irrespective of whose decision it really was they will attribute it to the band.

C) "No response at all" – this is a music business special. After two weeks of five phone calls a day and Fedex's flying back and forth all over the planet, everybody suddenly forgets how to dial your number. Some people don't have the gonads to pick up the phone and recite option B. After about three months, when you're in the middle of another project, you suddenly wonder what happened to that such and such a project that everyone was so jazzed about. The very next day you read in the trades that they are working with the guy who produced the other five bands that they sound exactly like. Next week you run into them in a big studio complex in New York City. They're next door laying tracks (three months late remember). You're finishing up some overdubs. Of course you're 'real' friendly and so are they. You don't mention the fact that no one had the courtesy to call you back.

Chapter Five

Producer Managers

a) To Have A Manager or Not To Have A Manager?

If you're in the studio on a project, particularly if you are a hands-on producer, life is intensely focused on the record in hand. There is precious little time to pay your electricity bill, let alone find and negotiate your next project. Generally speaking, artists don't love producers who spend the entire project, head tucked under the console, finger in one ear, phone glued to the other, shouting over the playback to their lawyer about packaging deductions for their next project. Of course you could leave the room to talk to your lawyer but, depending on the kind of producer you are (see Chapter One) the session has a nasty habit of coming to a grinding halt when you are out of the room.

This is where managers come in very handy. They can take care of the nuts and bolts of the negotiations, line up the next 50 projects for you, do the budgets, help you find musicians in strange and exotic locations, book the flights and hotels, then summarise it all in a phone call, fax or e-mail. More than anything a good manager will keep your name in the minds of the A&R people. They may be able to persuade someone to take a creative leap of faith with you based on the manager's in-depth knowledge of what you do. A&R people have a lot on their plate and there are a lot of producers out there. If your manager has a good reputation and current roster of producers, an A&R person may even call them for advice. Ros Earls of 140dB has said that she will point them towards a producer she respects but doesn't represent if she doesn't feel she has the right person available for the job. That kind of attitude builds respect in the business and ultimately results in more work for her people.

Linda Perry's manager Katrina Sirdofsky says, "I believe it is important for most creative people to have someone else being the face of business on their behalf. For most people it's difficult to sell themselves and make their own deals. Most producers are locked away in the studio while the managers are out taking meetings and finding out what's new and in development thereby hearing things early and having an early shot at projects."

Danny Saber had a manager from Day One. "Until I had a manager I didn't have anything. The whole thing with managers is timing. If you have a manager that's too far ahead, they won't have time for you. If you've got someone who's too far behind then they're not going to be able to help you. My manager had all cutting edge alternative producers in the same vein that I'm in. When I played her my stuff she was totally blown away, but she could see what direction I needed to go in. Shannon O'Shea hooked me up with the Black Grape stuff. They had vision. They were able to put me with the right people and sell me to the A&R people on the back of their more established producers."

Lauren Christy of The Matrix can't speak highly enough of their manager Sandy Roberton. "Having a really great manager is the most important thing a producer can have. The three of us were feeling a bit like losers in the music business. Sandy said, 'I'm going to make you the most successful writing/production team in America,' and we thought 'yeah right.' And then when things started happening for us we were like 'wow this is fantastic, maybe he's right, maybe we could become big.' He just never stopped being enthusiastic."

Peter Collins has had several great managers during his career and says, "It helps having gurus around. In the rock world I had Cliff Burnstein and Peter Mensch from Q Prime. I was doing a lot of rock acts right through the Eighties and into the Nineties. I could always defer to Cliff Burnstein and Peter Mensch who managed Def Leppard and Metallica to name a few and they would give me the skinny (lowdown) as to what they thought of any rock bands I had been offered." Subsequently Peter moved to Advanced Alternative Media. Talking about the havoc that is wreaked during label mergers and when A&R people move on he said, "I've relied very heavily on my manager, Andy Kipnes, who's clued in to record company politics and has done a very good job of keeping me safe from those traps."

b) Do They Earn Their Percentage?

i) Is She Just Fielding Calls Or Is She Out There Pitching For You?
When you are truly HOT the over-riding temptation for a manager has to be to just field the calls. In actual fact this is when you really need the most active hands-on management. When you're at the top the only way to go is down. Every project, every deal has to be considered carefully. A couple of bad choices and you could find yourself staring down the slippery slope into the black hole called total obscurity. At a high-point in your career, your manager simply reaching out to catch the calls will still result in a substantial choice of projects, but a high proportion of these projects will be trying to ride on your name and reputation. They need you more than you need them. What you really need at this point is either a project that you believe in with your heart and soul, one that you want to donate your hard-won kudos to, or an artist who's even bigger than you. You've already converted lead into gold, now you need to convert that gold into kryptonite.

How your manager pitches you is a matter of their style. It's vital that you are comfortable with that. One manager will simply field calls while another will be a cold calling, telemarketing fool. Good connections can be crucial for a manager. Even with the best connections in the world, if the manager doesn't believe in you enough, is too busy or not really dedicated to your advancement, nothing much is going to happen. You may be better off with a manager who is not so well connected but is more enthusiastic and pro-active.

Ros Earls says, "It's important to have a general understanding of what's going on, to be in the general flow, so you know what new bands are coming up. So you know what bands are looking for producers, so that you've got a relationship with A&R men, and so you have constant information. You're also seeing the live bands. You're out and about. You present people with the facts, what your guys are up to and when they're available. If you hear about something that's brilliant, that you're absolutely sure that your guy's right for, then that would be the point that you would pitch for a job. My experience is that the pitching and the pushing isn't as important as the general PR that just trickles along on a daily basis, being in the traffic of people making records and looking for producers."

Recently I've seen a lot more new names producing a record here and there but not sustaining careers the way producers used to. Ros explains this by saying, "There are a lot more producer managers and a lot more people out there [producing]. A lot of bands are co-producing with young people. There is less of a selective process going on. It used to be that certain producer managers were known for certain types of producers. Now, I put up one producer against the whole roster of another manager. For the first five years we were known as being really indie but indie doesn't exist any more ... it's one big business arena. Everybody's up for everything. It's a very busy business now and a lot of people are settling for second best and not getting the jobs they'd like to get. It's partly a financial thing, partly there are so many people out there and, of course, studios can't afford to keep as many engineers on as they used to. So people that are inappropriate are out in the world competing. If they push hard enough they will get some gigs.

"There's definitely some undercutting going on but I don't see any point in worrying about that. It's not about how much you cost at the end of the day. As long as you are flexible enough to drop your rates occasionally for a project that you really want to do. You can be flexible about advances and you can prove to people that you're doing something as a trial or as an investment in something new. We're not out of business and we don't undercut people. I'm not interested in what other people can get. There's no one fixed rate. It's whatever you are worth. We have done projects for no advance and higher points. I'd rather not do that because everyone needs to earn a living. I've always thought it was worth getting involved in things that were interesting even if they didn't yield huge dividends immediately."

Sandy Roberton puts it plainly: "As producer managers, we always have to come up with new ideas. The days of sitting by the phone waiting for it to ring are over. It's not like the late Seventies and early Eighties when the labels were making hundreds of records. I visited London this week and two major labels each had only three or four acts. They have the established acts and they completely got rid of all the new acts and started over again. So they're not signing as many new acts as they used to. They are not in a financial position to spend two years to develop an act. They need the album in the marketplace to get returns quickly because their overheads are enormous."

So is it worth paying a manager the 10 to 20 per cent of your income that they charge? Sometimes in the music business it seems like everyone is taking a slice of the pie and there's not enough left for the person who created the pie in the first place. It's always good to bear in mind that 80 per cent of something is better than 100 per cent of nothing. Lauren Christy emphasised this when she said, "I moved to America when I was 20. I'd made two albums in America. If you were in LA and you were an artist and you hadn't cracked it after two albums, you were washed up. This is a town that wants fresh meat. I was like, 'Oh no . . . Sandy Roberton saved my career.'" It doesn't get any clearer than that. That's worth a management percentage.

ii) How Do You Avoid Getting Ripped Off By Your Manager?
The best insurance you have for not getting ripped off by your manager is to make sure that you are paid directly by the labels. The manager may invoice the record company but the payments can still come directly to the producer. The manager then bills the producer for their commission. If you have a contract with your manager make sure it spells this out. Not all managers will agree to direct payment. It increases their risk of not being paid. If they insist on this and the money goes to them first, make sure your contract with them is water tight and specific about how, when and how much you get paid. Your contract with the record label should be in your name or the name of your company, not in your manager's name or his company's name. Most managers are above board but if only for your own peace of mind it is wise to make sure that you have a clear understanding of how the money comes to you. It may be that payments are sent to your manager's office but your entitlement must be clearly spelt out in your contracts with labels and your manager. Either you or your independent attorney has to read the contract before you sign it. If you don't handle your own finances it is preferable to have a separate business manager who is not associated in anyway with your manager. Business managers have been known to go bad as well but at least you will have independent eyes on each part of your business. There is a lot of merit in the old adage 'sign your own cheques.' That way you see everything that is going out of your account. The only sure way to avoid getting ripped off, in any business, is to play an active role in the financial and contractual dealings.

iii) Does He Siphon Off Some Of Your Work To Other Producers In The Stable?
This can be as costly to you when you are just starting or when you are certified plutonium. I had two situations early on where already

established producers tried to poach projects from me. Once before the artist had even released anything (the pre-publicity and expectations for the group were huge) and the other when I had taken a début album to gold on the back of the first three hit singles. I didn't lose the project in either case because we were on a roll and a degree of, shall we say, 'functional' loyalty was in place. Maybe I would have had bigger problems had these raiders been part of the same management stable. I may not have known what happened had the other producer had more clout than I had with the manager. As it happened I owned my own producer management company at the time. It's a competitive business and other producers or their managers will play several innings of hardball to take your project away.

Once you hit the stellar levels, there are 15 viable offers for every project that you can or want to do. That leaves 14 available for other producers. Whether they admit it or not your manager would like to hang on to these for his or her other producers. One of the biggest and most successful producer management companies is World's End run by Sandy Roberton who says: "If a call comes in for a producer and he doesn't happen to be available, I very rarely let it escape. I try to get somebody else in my stable to get that project. Having a large roster like I do, it's a big magnet. You've got certain producers who are not that keen to work all the time, they want to be very choosy. If they get a call and they don't want to do it, I hang on like a terrier, I don't let go of it."

This may seem OK to you: you can't do the project, someone else in the organisation can, the record company is happy, the project stays close to home. The label will come back to your manager because she solved their problem for them. Management is happy, the producers, 'Big Shot' (you) and 'Medium Shot' are both working and maybe 'Small Fry' got one of the newer bands that had approached you. 'Medium Shot' and 'Small Fry' both got projects that they wouldn't have if 'Big Shot' hadn't been the bait on the hook. Three commissions instead of one, three chances of a hit instead of one, a possible step up the ladder for 'Medium Shot', and the first rung for 'Small Fry'.

The only potential downside for you is related entirely to the integrity of your manager. Say you are two months away from finishing your current project when a call comes in to your management company from 'Supercult's' A&R person who just signed them. She thinks you'd be perfect. Your manager thinks so too but unfortu-nately you're in the Mediterranean on a project and won't be back for at least two months and then you are supposed to go on a long awaited vacation. 'Supercult' have just come off of two relatively successful indie albums and want to get started on their first major label album a.s.a.p. They're stretching their budget to afford you because they really love your work. Your manager suggests your stablemate 'Medium Shot', an up-and-coming producer who used to be your engineer/programmer. He knows all your moves, is a lot cheaper, and has some good solid credits but hasn't hit the big one yet. He's available now so she e-mails his bio and discography and sends via Fedex a promo CD (which includes a bunch of tracks he engineered with you *not* clearly marked to distinguish between his own productions and the tracks he engineered with you).

'Supercult' call back the following afternoon to say they like the sound of 'Medium Shot's' work. If he could fly out to meet them this weekend and the chemistry seems good, could he start in two weeks' time in Colorado? The meeting goes fine, the chemistry is primordial and creation looks set to begin. Cue contract negotiations, enter lawyers stage left. Where's the problem? You couldn't do it, 'Medium Shot' is the perfect second choice. Although 'Supercult' had never heard of him, he worked closely with 'Big Shot', knows all his moves, commands a lower advance and royalty and is available now. Perfect. Well it may work out well for 'Supercult' and it could be the best thing that ever happened for 'Medium Shot'. In fact, 18 months later, when the album tops eight million sales he has leapfrogged over 'Big Shot' and transformed into 'Mega-mover'. By the end of that year, he has his own label deal with 'Supercult's' label, goes on to produce 'Supercult's' next eight multi-platinum albums (who by now have dropped the 'cult' and are just known as 'Super') and he is entering the realms of 'unreachable'. Apart from a few perfectly natural twinges of envy, what could you have to complain about? You were busy, couldn't be in two places at once, and whenever you pass on a project, there's always the possibility of missing the big one.

Let's re-examine that original phone call. 'Supercult' called your manager because they wanted you. They were not calling on speculation for suggestions or two or three alternatives. The manager with integrity would have immediately called and discussed it with you. You would have been able to tell her that 'Supercult' is your absolute favourite band, you bought both their first two albums on

Obscure Records and saw all their early gigs. You'd even drop your price and cancel your holiday, if necessary, to work with them. Your manager could have investigated the possibility of the band waiting for two months to start the project. As it happened the record company's lawyer went on holiday for three weeks anyway, holding up the contract negotiations so they didn't actually get started with 'Medium Shot' for six weeks. If you had started your contract negotiations rolling immediately they would have had to wait only an extra two weeks. There's no guarantee that you would have had the same success with them as 'Medium Shot'. Even though you're a lot more experienced (and 'Medium Shot' learned most of what he knows from you in the first place), successful chemistry is impossible to predict.

Perhaps, fortunately, you never really found out how 'Medium Shot' got to produce your favourite band, you assumed they'd called for him in the first place. You have a sneaking suspicion that your manager is spending a lot more time working your ex-engineer's career than yours. It's not long before you start looking for new management. There was nothing malicious about what your manager did, she was just trying to keep her roster working. Had she bothered to check with you first and found out how strongly you felt about the band, she would never have suggested 'Medium Shot' at all. But she knew you had plenty of good possibilities lined up and wouldn't be out of work whereas 'Medium Shot' was really just getting started. He had a lot of engineering work but his production CV was looking thin. No one was more surprised than her when what seemed like yet another indie/alternative flavour-of-the-week thing turned into the defining band of the decade. She'd never really understood that kind of music anyway.

Your next few projects went well; a couple of gold albums, a double platinum and one that should've been if the record company had got it right. You're fine but deep inside you wish that you could work on an album that you really loved, something that you would actually play at home for fun, a record that gets you excited about music the way it did when you were 16. Like 'Supercult's' third, for instance. It couldn't have happened to a nicer guy than 'Medium Shot' (as you used to know him). What a break that was, you put it down to the luck of the draw.

I have had first-hand experience of a manager (in this case also a lawyer) making what proved to be a critical, life-changing decision on my behalf, without consulting me and coming to a conclusion that was diametrically opposed to the one I would have arrived at. He turned down an album that I would've love to have done. Not to pass on to another producer in his stable (he was too stupid to realise the artist could be huge) so he let the project go to someone he didn't even know because he wanted me to produce an artist signed to his own label. The record I produced for him actually did extremely well but, given the choice, I would have picked the other artist.

The point here is not to say that managers are evil. I would say the truly devious manager is very rare. However, I have personally had situations where my rights, needs or ambitions have been compromised in order to line someone else's pocket. Unfortunately, in those situations where your manager's interests and your own are not entirely in sync, you are going to be dependent on their integrity. Be very comfortable with this person before you put your professional life in their hands.

In their defense every producer manager I have spoken to has assured me that not only do they not siphon off work but that the opportunity to do that rarely even comes up. I asked Sandy how he avoids a conflict of interest amongst his 60 or so producers and how he decides who gets what. "I tend not to have too many producers who are doing the same sort of thing. In the writer/producer category, unfortunately, they're all very much in the same category. But they are writing with the artist so it is slightly different. I don't have 20 rock producers so that situation has never really arisen. I can't imagine who you give it to if you have that problem. I have quite a varied selection of producers and very rarely has there been a situation where there are two or three people up for the same job and the band has wanted every one of them to do it."

Most artists will have a short list of producers that they are interested in and often they are not with the same Management Company. Ros Earls of 140dB, who manages Flood among others, says, "Flood is sitting at the top of his tree now but three years ago he wasn't quite there. Flood can't be everywhere at once. He can't do five albums a year. I'd love to clone him. I'd love him to always be able to do U2, Depeche Mode, Polly Harvey and Nine Inch Nails because they are the albums that sell and those are the artists he's most associated with. But he can't. Otherwise he'll never be able to 'dip his toe in' with any new, younger bands. He'd never be able to re-invent himself – which is necessary. So, inevitably, Flood will do half [an album]. He's involving Alan Moulder a lot now. Moulder's getting the gigs that were Flood's. After he'd done 'Some Kind Of Talking' for Jesus and Mary Chain he wasn't available, so he recommended Alan Moulder. So what's happened on Nine Inch Nails is he's brought Alan Moulder in to engineer the mixing. Now Alan's got the production gig which is interesting because I don't manage Alan Moulder."

Ros says that she has always found it really difficult to hand projects down to other producers on her roster. She says, "You end up feeling a bit like a door-to-door salesman." In her opinion there may be more than one man for the job but there aren't 30. What bothers her is that some managers have 15 people on the roster and they put every single producer up for every single project. Consequently, someone who has 20 years of experience is up against a guy who just got his first production gig.

Record companies do call up and ask for someone who would be suitable for a gig. There's an answer, "Yes, I have somebody and this is who I have in mind, or you could look at it another way, you could consider this other guy that I manage." There's a third answer: "I know who's right for the job and it's XYZ but ABC manages him." I think you have to be free to say that. Not to always try and manipulate things around your roster because you get a name for just filling jobs. Hopefully this attitude makes A&R people more likely to call in and ask a manager's advice. The more phone calls that come in, the more likely you are to find the right work for your producers. Relationships are very important in this business.

Personally, I like to have as much control over my own destiny as possible. I prefer to make my own decisions based on the best information to hand. If your manager does as Ros Earls does and makes you fully aware of all the options, if you then make the wrong choice (as most of us have at some point) you can at least be philosophical about it.

Obviously, in the story above, if you were 'Medium Shot' you'd be extremely happy. The system worked beautifully to your benefit. However, now you've been elevated the pretenders will be hovering round you like vultures. Your money moves up into the big league which makes you vulnerable to the same kind of manoeuvre that worked for you on 'Big Shot'. Record companies are always looking for ways to save money. If they think they might be able to get your ideas and techniques and as good a sounding record from your assistant for a lot less money, they just might not let their sense of ethics, integrity and fair play get in the way.

c) How Do You Define 'Best Manager' For You?

Simply, I suppose, the one who gets you exactly the productions you need exactly when you need them. Defining precisely what you need is not so easy. Finding and getting those exact projects can be even more elusive. A high degree of intuition, persuasiveness, creativity and determination are necessary to qualify as a great producer manager. The best manager for you is the one who believes that there is no-one out there who can do what you do as well as you can, has the ability to convey that to the appropriate decision makers, and can close the deal.

As I said before, when you're hot your manager doesn't really have to do very much to keep you working. That, however, is when they really should be selling you the hardest and trying to move you up into that 'unreachable' international league. When you're less than hot or when you are first starting out is when the manager's abilities are tested most. Belief is not enough to turn you into a mega-star otherwise most of us would be managed by our wives, our girlfriends, our mothers or ourselves.

Some producers don't rely on their managers to find work at all, they just like them to handle the business side of things. Alan Moulder says, "My manager doesn't get me work, she just discusses money and the terms of the contract, which I find incredibly difficult. I really like the way she represents me."

Like producers, managers tend to come in all shapes and sizes ranging from ex-lawyers to ex-studio managers to ex-record company executives to your basic street fighter (not necessarily in descending order). The perfect, 'made in heaven,' producer manager would know enough about the job to understand your individual strengths and weaknesses; know what's going on trend-wise (nationally, internationally, musically and technically); be very well connected in the business and be able to get to all the right people; be respected enough to be listened to when he gets there; always have an ear to the ground to find out who's being signed and who's changing producers for their fifth album; be able to find his way around a contract and know the obvious pitfalls to watch out for; be a tough negotiator; be able to pour oil on troubled waters (contractual, recording, financial or personal), have international contacts; treat you with respect; be discreet and hold any potentially sensitive information about you or their other clients in total confidence; all the while having complete confidence in you and your abilities.

d) How Can You Find Such A Person – If They Even Exist?

Unless providence has smiled on you in the most fortuitous of ways the only way I know is to do plenty of research and shop around. Managers, like producers, come in all varieties and it's probably unlikely you will find someone with all the above ingredients. What makes a producer-manager relationship work is as much about personal chemistry as ability. If you like the manager and the manager likes you, then assuming they have enough of the other ingredients to be able to function and you have talent, drive and determination, the relationship will most likely work.

If you already know A&R people, call them and ask them about the managers you are considering. See if they have any suggestions. It's probably not worth looking for a manager too early on. You need to build some sort of reputation or track record on your own, even if it's just on demos or remixes. Be realistic – it's difficult for a manager to convince an artist or an A&R person to trust you with a substantial budget if they haven't heard anything you've done.

e) How Do You Persuade Them To Take You On?

I remember a situation in Los Angeles where a producer, who had many multi-platinum albums under his belt but none in the last eight years, was looking for management. Several companies asked him for show reels (which I thought was insulting since if they didn't have most of his records on their shelves they shouldn't be in the business anyway). They all eventually passed on him, if not in so many words, perhaps more disrespectfully by just not calling him back.

He carried on working through his own connections in a low-key way until the inevitable happened and he had another multi-platinum album. Of course this kick-started his career again and the embarrassingly inelegant scramble for his time and attention started once more.

Unfortunately, you can get caught in that same old catch-22 where you can't get representation till you have produced something and you're going to have difficulty producing anything until you get representation. The same applies if you have a recent 'gap' in your résumé. You have to be enterprising, lucky, or an excellent salesperson to get your foot in the door.

The reasons why a manager would take you on are numerous. You are on an unbroken run of multi-platinum albums and your last manager retired to Tahiti.

You have some sort of reasonably current track record. You have something you can play them that will convince them that you might just have some ability (this only works when you are young, once you've been around or if you are starting at an older age, you will most likely have to prove yourself with actual success first).

They are not doing very well themselves and need to flesh out their numbers.

Manager Ros Earls came from a background of managing world-famous recording studios such as Trident and Sarm in London. She tends to specialise in engineer producers. The talents she looks for in an up-and-comer are particular musical talents, a mature approach to arrangements and someone who responds to bands very well. "There's something indefinable as well that virtually everybody at Trident had," she says. "Mark Stent's gone on, Steve Osborne's gone on, Paul Corkett's gone on, Flood's gone on and on, so has Alan Moulder. All the tea boys turned into engineers. They all had something else. There was the humility thing, but it was more knowing that you had to do your time and get as much information as you can, learn as much as you can as quickly as possible. There is an unquantifiable something that those people all had and I think it was because Flood was there with me in the early days that I was able to spot it. I do know now. There's an indefinable sort of cool as well. You want people to think of you as a creative person but not so much so that you overshadow them. You're a kind of catalyst but it's a very fine line because a lot of producers are very capable as musicians and writers in their own right. But the best producers don't jeopardise the chemistry by selling themselves too much as a creative person and know that instinctively.

"It's not just about the practical elements it's a lot to do with politics, diplomacy, the balancing of personalities in the studio and generally liaising with the record company. That kind of mature approach from an early stage would be what turns a manager on."

Obviously from the manager's point of view there are only so many hours in the day. The easier it is to find you work and the more hits you can generate, the more money they can make, more quickly. There are a great number of producer management companies around, all with varying styles, abilities and requirements. As important as anything else is the ability to relate to your manager and for them to believe in you and your particular set of skills.

Chapter Six

How Do You Deal With The Artist, The Record Company And The Artist's Manager?

a) What should your relationship with the artist be?

i) Best Friends?

> *I don't trust him, he's my friend.* (Bertolt Brecht)

I don't know of too many cases where a producer and an artist became truly best friends. Obviously it helps to be on friendly terms with the artist, and for the duration of the project you may even get quite close, but it is an intense relationship between people whose lifestyles and personality types are often quite different. Generally, once the album is over the artist will go on tour, the producer will move on to his next production and very often they won't meet up again until the next record or when they receive their GRAMMY awards.

Speaking of the bands he works with Jack Douglas says, "It's really important that we get along pretty well, so I like to hang out and socialise with them." Phil Ramone worked with Billy Joel for over 10 years and did three albums with Paul Simon. Of those relationships he said, "You do grow closer personally. Billy's my child's godfather. And Paul Simon and I are still close friends – I named a son after him. But there is a line when you are employed by someone. You keep yourself somewhat at a distance so that they have it clear in their minds that you didn't party the last two nights because you had work to do, maybe some editing at eight in the morning, that was more important. That's what I consider the proper relationship between an artist and a producer.

"I've always thought a producer's job is to be the objective director of action. You need to know what's going on with an artist because their emotional state may be reflected in their work, in the change of

117

a lyric, for instance. But you get enough intimacy working with them 10 and 12 hours a day in the studio. It's not always necessary to spend the weekend with them."

"The personal level comes out of the music anyway," says Quincy Jones, "but if you are closer than that, it gives you an advantage, because you get a chance to know what's underneath the personality. You can comfort that and soothe it and provoke it. You can make the arrangements a musical metaphor for what their personality is about."

Unfortunately the long-term friendships that are made in the line of fire are occasionally balanced out by the unnecessary difficulties that can be created by self-destructive, over-indulged individuals bent on making what should be an enjoyable, satisfying, creative experience into an island of hell, set in a place that probably looks like paradise.

ii) Able To Fit In?
Whether this is necessary or not really depends on the type of producer you are. The All-Singing-All-Dancing type has no need to fit in at all. If anything the artist may wish to try to fit in with them. The collaborator probably needs to fit in the most. A lot of the vibe of the session in this case comes from either being like-minded or comple-mentary personality types. Merlin will fit in only in the abstracted way that gurus can appear at home both on the mountain top and on Fifth Avenue.

Alan Moulder says he likes to hang around with the artist and get a personal relationship going. "Fitting in is very important. You want to make him feel as comfortable as possible. Singing in front of some-one can be embarrassing. Many singers aren't as extrovert in the studio as they appear on stage. In fact they can be quite vulnerable and insecure about singing one to one. It really helps if they can be comfortable with you. I've made some enduring friendships with people I've worked with. The relationship does change when you finish the record. On tour they may be pleased to see you, but it is a different mindset from the one-to-one relationship of recording."

iii) Hang After Hours, Between Albums, Party-Hearty and Laugh At The Jokes?
It all depends on your nature and the artist's but it is not inconceiv-able that you could find yourself in yet another club at four or five in

the morning surrounded by the artist's adoring posse, with a grin frozen on your face, listening to yet another shaggy dog story. Not to be unduly cynical but when half the civilised world gives its pocket money to an undereducated, demi-talent, some personalities may experience side effects. Ego may grow. Legitimate ability to sustain ego may shrink. Boring stories may be told. Of course the majority of artists are extremely nice people.

Wendy Page, speaking about the film *Laurel Canyon*, said, "In my experience, the drug-taking, excessive drinking and fraternising with the artists that the movie depicts is a complete rock and roll myth." For sure, the backstage passes and VIP access are nice benefits of being a successful producer but mostly not all they appear from the outside.

iv) Somewhat Aloof?
Not guaranteed to win you the next album but safe in the respect that you are not exposing your inner secrets to the artist. Aloofness reduces the risk of familiarity becoming a breeding ground for contempt.

Being aloof works when the producer is older than the artist, and has a more substantial track record. However, if the producer's track record is too much longer than the artist's, then the storytelling, ego reinforcing roles can be reversed and the artist might be the one who finds the rigor mortis setting in on his smile.

v) Professional?
Speaking about his work with Bob Dylan, Phil Ramone says, "Bob's a very nice man. He's not what you'd call a high intensity conversationalist, but you don't need that. You have your moments of privacy with somebody and you enjoy them. But my way of working is not to break that code of professionalism and privacy that the artist sets up, whatever that may be. Dylan treats the people he works with in a completely professional manner. Sometimes the doctor-patient thing is vital, so that you keep from getting too close. He shares what he needs to."

vi) How Do You Tell Them Something Is Not Working?
Every producer I have spoken to concurs on this subject. George Martin expresses it well: "You do it with tact. It's something I've always done. As a kid in my twenties, I would go up to an orchestra leader

and say 'I'd like to do another take, because I think the woodwind was slightly flat.' Generally, if you are right and you do it politely, without throwing your weight around, people actually like you for it. They recognise that you have a good ear and listen to you. And if you build up a reputation over the years and you're successful, eventually people will begin to ask you."

b) Where Does Your Responsibility Lie?

i) To The Artist?
The short answer to this is that every record producer's responsibility is to show the artist in the best possible light. In reality, it depends very much on the type of artist, the producer's style and the nature of their relationship.

In an ideal world I would always prefer to see the artist be centre stage and in charge of the artistic direction of the recording. This scenario sets the producer's responsibility toward the artist and the artist alone. The producer employs musical, technical and conceptual skills to protect, preserve and realise the artist's vision.

In the same rec.audio.pro news group posting that I mentioned earlier, Steve Albini referred to the necessity for the producer to respect the artist. "This goes beyond merely allowing the band to have a say in their album. It means that the social and artistic fabric of the band is its strength, and its defining characteristic. Take them away (by deconstructing the band with overdubs, click tracks and other Spielberg-ian techniques or by chopping up their arrangements because they weren't 'right', or by replacing members with session players or sequencers, or by over-accentuating one member as a 'star') and the band loses its identity, and in most cases, its reason to be. The band at hand, no matter how small in stature or weak aesthetically, deserves your respect. This also means you can't lie to them, or misrepresent them to the label or the listening public. Perhaps the guitar player wants his guitar to sound like that."

Albini does say earlier in the same posting that his experience has been almost exclusively with bands who operate as autonomous self-defining entities, not solo performers or dance music acts for whom 'production' in the classic sense is an unavoidable necessity. For a certain type of artist he is absolutely right.

The question also needs to be asked "What if the guitar player didn't really want their guitar to sound like that?" Maybe they just didn't have the expertise or the equipment to make it sound better. Maybe they would be grateful for the producer opening up some alternative possibilities for them. A lot of extremely popular records would never have been made if Mr. Albini's criteria were observed. Trevor Horn, Mutt Lange and even George Martin would've had difficulty making most of the records with which they are associated.

All too often, however, the producer is working to conceal serious flaws in the artist's musical, technical or conceptual abilities. The artist's vision may be "I want to be bigger than Madonna." Sadly, their musical and technical skills may be overshadowed by their visionary capabilities. Some producers prefer this mode of operation because it gives them control. Many pop records are made this way. The producer is in some ways more the artist than the artist. The weak artist enables the producer to, vicariously, realise artistic ambitions that may have been thwarted earlier in their own career.

In practice these producers are worth more than their weight in gold. They are the musical movers and shakers. These are the alchemists, the guys who can take nothing or not very much and turn it into, apparently – something. Lead into gold. This type of producer is the genuinely talented All-Singing-All-Dancing-King-Of-The-Hill. Generally speaking, the closer to 'live' a record is the more control the artist will have had. With most so-called alternative bands, what you see is what you get. If they can't sing, play or write good songs, there aren't many production techniques available to conceal the evidence. (This has changed with the increased acceptance of hard-disk recording systems which allow industrial strength, digital manipulation of the timing, tuning and overall sound of a live recording.) With heavily sampled dance-pop records, it's virtually impossible to tell whether the artist can sing, perform or write by listening to the record. Does it matter? Certainly not to the record company – sales are sales are sales.

When the artist is strong or already hugely successful, the responsibility is primarily to the artist and they will demand that the focus is on them. With a first time artist or someone not so strong on direction, your responsibility will be to deliver the right record based on a blend of information, starting with the record company brief, taking into account the artist's ideas and utilising your own judgment as to what will work for all concerned.

Talking about producers that will use any means to make the record, Jack Endino says, "I guess there is some value in that sort of sterile sort of produced music, and there must be a market for it, but it's not the way I work. Sometimes I've been asked to play a bass part or something on a record, usually for a very practical reason though, such as there's no bass player, or the bass player had to go home. If you're not technically the best that you can imagine, that's fine – you just have to work with them. I think, these days, people are valuing bands and respecting them as groups of people who have their own ideas and style of playing. What it all comes down to, and I think this is the most important thing, is you gotta let bands be bands."

Of course if you are the All-Singing-All-Dancing type you are not going to subscribe to this point of view. There would not be such different types of music being released without the different methods and styles of production. There are many ways to make a great record. The Nineties was a lot kinder to the more artist-oriented projects than the Eighties was. There seems to have been a trend back to the more manufactured sound again in the early part of the new millennium. It's always going to be a case of horses for courses, but at least not every record nowadays is highly produced and processed. For the moment you can pay your money and take your choice.

An artist may not be aware that they are stuck in a rut with their attitude towards studio recording techniques. The techniques they are using may be limiting the results they can get. Jim Dickinson talked about how he approached the production on the (initially unreleased) third Big Star album. "I was nailed for indulging Alex [Chilton] on *Big Star Third*, but I think it is important that the artist is enabled to perform with integrity. What I did for Alex was literally remove the yoke of oppressive production that he had been under since the first time he ever uttered a word into a microphone, for good or ill. I tried to show him how to use the studio, rather than be abused by it. And that's what I try to do with any artist who's interested in that. And if they're not interested in that, I try to eliminate the problems that are between them and a successful recording, which is something I learned from Tom Dowd, who is the great problem solver."

Tony Berg, producer of Michael Penn, Squeeze, Public Image Ltd and Edie Brickell and The New Bohemians, says, "The producer's dilemma is, who's in charge? I would say that the artist is in charge."

Alan Moulder agrees. "It's their career. The record company and management have other artists. If this one doesn't work out, there'll be others coming along that will. For the artist this is maybe their only crack at it. They may go on to other bands but it may be their only crack at being in this business. My allegiance goes definitely to the band."

As for accommodating artistic idiosyncracies, he says, "If the artist is just slow I'll try to find studios that are really cheap. Even down to doing each individual thing in different studios. I do the drums in one studio that's pretty good, then move to a really small cramped cheap studio to do the guitars and vocals." Even if the artist wants to do something that, in Moulder's opinion, most likely won't work, his approach would be to say, "OK, let's try one". The reason he gives for being so flexible is "because I've quite often been proved wrong and if I try [the idea] it covers my backside. I'll allocate a certain amount of time to it, almost demo it, I'll then point out the pitfalls but I get them to choose. If they want to go ahead with it I'll try to make it work. If it's a technical problem but it makes them feel comfortable and I think I'm going to get a good performance out of them then I'll really try to make it work."

ii) To The Record Company?
In the simplest of terms the producer's responsibility is to make sure that the record company makes money by creating an album or track that achieves the label's expectations. An indie label may be happy with an honest representation of the music that will sell a few thousand copies. In the case of a major label, expectations will mostly involve pulling a hit record out of the hat. How you perform the sleight of hand is not really an issue. If your style is to call in occasionally from the tennis court (just to see how things are going), unless the artist complains, you'll still get the credit and pick up the kudos since no-one really understands the mechanics of making a hit anyway.

The responsibility for maintaining the artistic direction will fall fairly and squarely on the producer's shoulders. He will have to look to the A&R person in the record company for the initial direction, the brief. After that it's up to the producer to make sure the project stays on track both artistically and financially.

Pete Ganbarg, veteran A&R person who's worked on major projects during his various tenures at SBK, Arista and Sony says, "I've always felt that if I hire a producer, they're working for me and we need to have a creative understanding between A&R person and producer. But certain guys don't feel that way, they're like, 'you're job is to find the band, my job is to make the record, leave me alone.'"

Peter Collins says his loyalties in the studio are "more to the artist actually. We're making a record for the artist. And if they're happy, chances are the record company will be happy. In most cases, though they always want the hit single. I always think my job is making the artist's album." On the surface these seem like two contradictory positions that could become a major area of tension. In reality my observation is that a seasoned hitmaker such as Peter will transparently maintain the balance so that both label and artist feel that their interests are being protected. This little juggling trick really comes down to maintaining good lines of communications and may involve a certain amount of mediation and diplomacy depending how confident you are in the end product. A major objective is to make sure there are no unpleasant surprises for the label along the way and especially at the end.

The producer's personal sense of fiscal responsibility towards the record company has been rendered much less necessary by the advent of the overage clause. The overage clause establishes that if the project goes over budget (sometimes it's more than 10 per cent over) the overage will be taken out of the producer's advance and/or royalties. This little kidney punch is guaranteed to deck even the most visionary record producer. There are plenty of variations on the theme, and if you have enough contractual clout you can get the clause deleted altogether. I can assure you that when it's in there you will be painfully aware of it and will not, really, relax until the last day of production, when you know that you made it on time and on budget.

iii) To Yourself?

The responsibility you have to yourself is to create the time, space and money to make the best production you can. Every time you make a record you potentially set a series of processes in motion.

Your work will be judged by the record company. If it's judged to be substandard the record may not be released or they may pull you off the project, have it finished by another producer or remixed with additional production. A remix with additional production does not necessarily imply that the producer's work was substandard. A&R departments have become so remix happy these days that the record is not considered complete unless a remixer or three has had a go at it. To be pulled off a project not only has repercussions within the business but unless you have an indomitable spirit and an uncrushable ego it can affect your ability to work no matter how clearly unfair it was.

Your relationship with the band will be tested. I can't think of an instance when a band decided not to use a producer again for spending too much of what is ultimately their money on a record that subsequently became a huge hit. Of course magnetic (and these days digital) heaven is littered with big budget records that didn't sell a single copy and in most instances the producer will, with some justification, be blamed for letting the budget get out of control. So don't think that you can spend your way out of a problem. Unless you are working on a limitless budget there is always a certain amount of pressure to compromise. You need to make sure that you've done your sums up front. Given the abilities, personalities and facilities involved in the project, you need to be confident you will have enough money to deliver the record everyone's expecting.

iv) To The Project
Unless you are vindictive, lunatic or just plain suicidal, I can't think of a situation where you wouldn't want to do the best possible job on every project you do. I have heard people talk about producers doing albums just for the money, implying that they are interested only in the advance and are not concerned with whether they make any royalties or not from record sales. The best producers won't do this. If you are a successful producer there is enough high quality work coming your way to be able to pick and choose the projects that really capture your imagination. If there should be a lull in the flow of work you can turn that into a well-earned break, an opportunity to pro-actively seek out new bands or a chance to get in the studio with a low budget project that you wouldn't normally be able to justify doing. If you do an inadequate job on a baby band project for a major label or an established indie, that will hurt your future chances of a good project from, at least, that label.

At the regional level where producers are not making beaucoup bucks from advances or royalties, there is an element of doing it for the money. Artists who work with this level of producer really need to examine why they chose this particular person. Even the local producer who takes on a project primarily to pay the rent usually takes a pride in doing the best job he can. If you are an artist looking to work with a local producer make sure that you do your homework. Listen to his previous work, talk to other bands that he has worked with and make sure that you have a clear understanding between you and the producer of what you are expecting to get for your money. The producer might sooner spend your budget producing higher quality demos that can show off his expertise in the best light, than use the same amount of time to produce a whole album. You don't want to spend all your hard-earned gig money for three label-demos when you really wanted a 12 track album to sell at shows. If possible put these conversations in writing, even it it's just an e-mail exchange. That way you have something to refer to if there is a disagreement later in the proceedings.

Producers don't get rich off advances – the real money comes from royalties off of sales. Every album or track that gets released with your name under the producer credit becomes your calling card and your passport to future work.

My philosophy has always been to make a record of which I can be personally proud. No producer can guarantee that every record he makes is going to be a hit. Even records that only achieve cult status can be very powerful advertisements for your production abilities. Often successful bands are quite hip in their listening habits and that underground cult band you just produced might well be the thing they listen to all the time on the tour bus or in the car. If your work's impressive enough and a band's thinking of changing producers you might well get the call for their next album. On the negative side, if you turn out poorly produced records you could get a practical lesson in how small the international record business really is.

c) What About The Drug And Alcohol Connection?

i) Should You Be Bathroom Buddies?
My experience is that even the most dissolute artist will be critical of their producer if they feel that his performance is in anyway being diluted by his indulgences. It's OK for the artist to screw up and be screwed up. It's not OK for the producer. You create the stability on the session, you set the pace, you make the running. Of course if you're a megastar whose name alone can guarantee success for the project (this may be a mythical creature like the unicorn), even if you were comatose for most of the album, the artist and record company will cut you some slack. We've all heard the apocryphal stories about

the rock'n'roll Einsteins who can produce a work of genius in any state of consciousness. Well, maybe once, maybe even occasionally but not consistently and certainly not over a long period of time. Reliable accounts have it that even Charlie Parker was crap when he was blasted.

Producing is less about isolated moments of inspiration and more about protracted periods of concentrated, determined, and single minded, focus. Unless you're a nominal name, or a buddy who went to school with the artist, I doubt you can survive constant over-indulgence, personally or professionally. In the days when rock 'n' roll was more about fun than money, Jefferson Airplane took the matter into their own hands with engineer *extraordinaire* Al Schmitt who was producing the band. Referring to LSD, he said: "I didn't take it every day [laughs] although they did try to spike us every day! I got spiked when we were doing the first Hot Tuna album. I was nailed. The engineer was Allen Zentz and I thought I was drinking apple juice. I was working in a remote truck, and I had my pad out, ready to go, and all of a sudden the sides of the truck started to breathe. I looked at Allen and said, 'Buddy, you are on your own tonight.' I rarely did any drugs while I was working. Some engineers could smoke joints and keep working, but I couldn't. I didn't drink on the job either, but afterwards we all got into it pretty hot and heavy."

Andy Jackson thinks that generally drugs in the studio are unhelp-ful. "If nothing else, in terms of efficiency, they make you much slower," he says. "You make more mistakes of judgment. You end up re-doing things, doing crazy hours, which is very counter-productive."

An apparently innocuous practice which triggers the crazy hours syndrome is going to the pub or a bar after dinner until 10 or 11 p.m. Everybody gets back to the studio fully juiced and ready to roll. Judgment, however, is seriously impaired or suspended. Once every-one gets lubricated, it's usually best to can the session for the day. The likelihood of getting anything amazing is very slim. Occasionally an altered state of consciousness works for a certain type of perform-ance but mostly not.

I have never met a single producer who has said that an artist performed better because they were using a drug or alcohol on a session. Nonetheless there are producers and artists who don't seem to be able to function, in or out of the studio, without using one drug or another. Andy Jackson thinks this is a wider issue. "You are dealing with someone's entire life. There is an arguable case that marijuana use can be good for inspiration. There's a very clear case that it's not good for work. There's the rub. Making a record is a combination of the two things. Maybe you can divide the two things. The truth of making a record is the 99 per cent perspiration thing. There's a degree of inspiration but really that mostly happens at an earlier stage; the writing, arranging and rehearsing. Maybe there's the divide. What qualifies as work and what qualifies as creative? It's, arguably, helpful for one and destructive for the other. It's not a black and white case. It's shades of grey."

ii) Is It OK If It Happens Outside Of Working Hours?

It may be OK for the producer to indulge after hours. If you're close friends with the artist, but if your habits translate into diminished performances, your career will eventually diminish too. There are no best friends in hell. Some of the biggest druggies I've had the misfortune to fall over really love to run other people's reputations into the ground. Generating gossip that focuses on their alleged drug use seems to be a popular way to do that. I know of one situation where the producer and the artist had been sniping at each other for several years (through several highly successful albums) about their respective drug abuse and how it was affecting their work. Eventually the producer did get the big push. Interestingly he went on to have more success with other bands – whereas the artist has seemed to be in a 'resting phase' ever since.

Tony Visconti talking about this subject said, "I'll be perfectly honest with you, because David [Bowie] is honest about it. I witnessed David taking a lot of drugs around *Young Americans*, and I was no angel myself, though I'd usually limit my drug taking until after the session in a very recreational way. And I must go down on record as saying I haven't taken any drugs at all for about 10 years now."

iii) What Do You Do If The Artist Does And You Don't?

Depending on your relationship with the artist, if it's his sixth album and you're the new kid on the block you could try pontificating. You'll probably get fired. If it's their first album and your 51st, you could try the friendly 'voice-of-experience' routine wrapped up with a health warning and encompassing the 'road-to-success-is-littered-with-the-carcasses-of-talented-people-who-screwed-up' scenario but if their eyes are firmly fixed on Aerosmith, even if they have reformed, your words will surely fall on deaf ears. I'm totally amazed how many artists have a Kurt Cobain/Jim Morrison/Jimi Hendrix/Janis Joplin/Elvis Presley fixation (usually all at once). Check the posters in their room: if they have three or more of the above, clear the studio of guns, fast cars, baths, alcohol and drugs. Try to get the album done real quick.

None of this has ever been a problem for Bruce Fairbairn who is known for his work with heavy metal bands, some of whom have excessive lifestyles. He takes a hard line against drugs. "The proof's in the pudding when it comes to drugs and alcohol in the studio. There are bands out there that are smart enough to stay sober and make good music. Those bands are the ones that I've found have the best people in them, are the most successful and are the most genuine, sincere people to work with. All I ask when a band does an album and I'm involved, is to try and do it the right way. It can only help. What they do after they finish the record is their business. But if they feel they can't make a good record unless they're high, I tell them to find somebody else to get high with and make the record with."

d) What Do You Do When The Artist Freaks?

Notice I said when *not* if. It doesn't necessarily happen on every project but it does happen. Second albums are the worst for this. For the first album they're a bunch of sweet kids who sit humbly at your feet and shyly ask if they can borrow the bus fare to get home (or money to gas up their car/get it out of the car park). By the second album it's "Where's the fucking limo/why isn't there any Bollinger/Cristal in the fucking limo?" etc. All from the exact same bunch of formerly unassuming kids. Fortunately limos are not the producer's responsibility but the attitude gives a clue as to the philo-sophical orientation of the group – slightly to the right of self-centred.

This business feeds egos with various permutations of adulation, sex, alcohol, drugs and money. Sooner or later this ego is going to freak. There are, of course, artists who remain completely down to earth and unaffected. You do grow to love those people. It's hard to survive the extremes and excesses of rock'n'roll and it usually takes a few career peaks and valleys to give them some perspective on the whole thing. A studio freak-out can be as mild as throwing headphones across the room because the foldback is not to someone's liking. On the other hand it can be a full blown verbal and/or physical attack. The only solution that has ever worked for me at that point is to walk right out the door. In my personal all-time favourite studio incident, I wrote out a cheque for the advance I had been paid to date, handed it to the still freaking artist and headed for the hills. I was back at work with a greatly subdued and much more respectful artist within 24 hours.

Walking out is, obviously, an absolute last resort and I would never walk out for effect. You need the patience of Job to even get started as a record producer. If someone can annoy me enough to make me give them back their money and walk out the door, at that moment in time I have zero intention of going back. Walk out for effect and there is a serious possibility they will call your bluff. If that happens you have either lost the record or, worse, lost control of the record.

e) What Do You Do When The Record Company Freaks?

One might assume, if one hasn't spent much time in the music business, that the record company would never freak. After all, we're all professionals chasing the same dream, seeking the same objective – a hit record. Orson Wells once said something along the lines of "Hollywood is not, as people think, about sex and money – but power". The music business is not much different. When you get into the higher echelons of the business, egos run as rife as they do among the stars themselves. The difference is that a rampaging star is ultimately going to cause the worst damage to himself. A stampeding executive ego can destroy careers.

When I first started in the music business I thought that the major objective was to have hits and make money. This is largely true but there are a great number of sub-plots and hidden agendas that influence the overall picture. Personal likes and dislikes can be the fuel that rockets an artist to either mega-stardom or oblivion. Obviously talent and the quality of the records are very important factors. A bad singer without good songs is probably not going to make it even with the Managing Director's total support. However, with the head of A&R or MD's (senior vice president and president in the US) goodwill, the company will hang in for much longer with an artist. They would be inclined to set up co-writing situations with successful songwriters, pull in outside material for the singles, hire the best producers to add some name clout and to cover up the problems. They will be inclined to spend more on promotion and marketing, not to mention artwork and videos. With the will of the company and the co-operation of both artist and management, stars can be created from empty space. Unhappily, a good artist can be lost forever if the goodwill is not there. What the artist regards as integrity or an unwillingness to be manipulated can be written off by the record company as a lack of co-operation.

I've seen both edits of this video. There are many times when an artist truly does not know what's best for them. The basic talent may be there but the material is not strong, the video concept is all wrong for their market, they won't tour or they insist on touring when there is no point, and they're paranoid and confrontational. All these problems are traceable back to over-inflated ego and lack of experience.

On the other side is the situation in which a talented artist gets pushed through the sausage machine by an uncreative A&R/marketing team who think only in terms of 'what's happening' right now. They are market led rather than talent led. Chasing the market/trend/fad is a perfectly viable and well established way to achieve success, and for an artist who's not concerned about breaking new ground it may pose no moral dilemma. It creates a clone-like scene but a trend wouldn't be a trend without clones, and sometimes the clones prove to be more enduring than the originators.

The point of all this is that you need the co-operation of the company. By the time the record company does freak out, it is way too late. You need to see the early warning signs, you need to keep the lines of communication open. Generally it is up to the producer to make sure that the company is happy and up to speed with what is going on in the studio. The A&R person usually has more than one project in production at the same time, along with many other company commitments. Often the first time they really get to focus on your project is when you deliver the finished mixes. By then most of the budget has been spent. If the record has gone off the rails or down a different track from what the A&R person had visualised, recovery can be both difficult and expensive. Maybe you or your management can rescue the situation using extreme diplomacy, clout, or your own money but it should never get to this point. The best way to prevent things from falling apart is to communicate with the label. If all else fails, you can fall back on your relationship with the artist and his management. But, no matter what the artist is saying to you privately, you are the most expendable link in the chain. You will most likely survive through to the next album only if this one sells well and proves your point.

It's also worth remembering that if the record company does freak on you and you can't recover from it, you haven't just smashed some golden eggs, you've killed one of the geese that lays them. The question is how many golden geese do you have? (Clue: there are four major labels and that may become three!)

Depending on your personality there may be a limit as to how much garbage you will take in the name of diplomacy and peace-keeping. There is a point at which you might be better off leaving the project rather than see an album get completely screwed up. As I've said before, much of what producing is about is having an opinion. If a project is being pushed in a direction that your experience tells you is wrong and you don't feel like going along for the ride then you either have to regain control or leave.

Only once in my life have I kicked an A&R person out of the studio. He was making uninformed, irrelevant comments and we clashed on nearly every point and at every level. He was not the A&R person who brought me the project and his vision was different than the briefing I had been given at the beginning. I began to realise that I was not his first choice to mix the album and that it was the artist who had insisted on having me mix as well as produce it. I realised in retrospect that he had a hidden agenda. He had always intended to get someone else to remix the project, even before we started recording. I later found out that this was his standard MO. So he was nit-picking me to death, primarily to provoke a reaction and justify his position.

After that I was a lot more careful about vetting the situation. It's important to make sure that everybody concerned wants you on the project including the A&R person, management and artist. You need to know that you can get on with all the various players and that you are capable of delivering what they are expecting. Watch out for A&R people with aspirations to produce. They have a tendency to rework the hit from the album and stick their name on it. If you hate having your work remixed, check the mix credits on the last few albums the A&R person has been involved with.

It's important to make sure that everyone involved is clear about what they want. I learned this lesson the hard way. I had been warned about a particular artist's mental stability by my attorney. I later remem-bered that even the A&R man had a look on his face that is only seen on kamikaze pilots about to embark on their final mission. To make matters worse I agreed to record residentially in a foreign country. I might as well have suggested Alcatraz. I obviously loved this girl's music. I asked her what she wanted and she assured me the full, live band. The next 10 days were as close as one could imagine hell to be.

We were holed up in a beautiful but significantly non-English speaking country prison. I somehow toughed it through the recording and we took a couple of days off before mixing. The two days turned out to be more akin to the silence between drops in Chinese water torture than a rest. In a spirit of desperation I managed to finagle it so the mixing would be done in a city, I mumbled something about equipment and the rental situation. The city was still non-English speaking but, according to all the horror movies I've seen, a safer place to be than the country if there's a crazy person loose. Nothing in any life I can remember could have prepared me for what was about to happen. Bear in mind that the artist had been present every day, every step of the way so far. Nothing had gone down, on this physical plane, without her knowledge. She let me set up the mix in the morning as is customary and said she would come down to the studio at three in the afternoon. By two-forty-five I was starting to feel better about the whole project, yes she really can sing, I was starting to see that it was worth all the pain she'd put me through. Despite the odds, the tracks were sounding great.

She walked in, cordial hello's all round – everyone's relaxed and happy. I played the track for her while she sat at the console and I moved to the back of the room (a little trick I learned from old Clint Eastwood and Al Pacino movies: keep your back to the wall). The track sounded great. Often when someone else comes into the room, strangely, you hear things filtered through their attitude. The tape stopped, there was a moment's silence and then she hissed in serpent-like tones that I had tried desperately to love: "vhere iss da drum machine". About 20 minutes of utterly pointless negotiation ensued. I reminded her of all the many discussions we'd had, the fact that she'd been there the whole time, her insistence on making a record with live musicians. And not only was there not a drum machine on the track but that we hadn't even been graced by the presence of one during the whole recording. Absolutely no luck. I'd finally had enough. I made my one phone call to the A&R person at home. He had also had enough and was, fortunately, sympathetic. I grabbed my stuff and made a run for the border.

133

f) What Do You Do When The Artist's Manager Is A Freak?

I saw Danny Saber (Black Grape) live through a situation (not with Black Grape I hasten to add) where he was away from home working on a record for a well-known artist. Initially the manager tried to put him in an apartment with mould growing on the walls. Having got somewhat of a negative reaction from Danny they eventually got him a nice place in a nice part of town. All was well. The project went smoothly and Danny's stay was extended. He called the management company not once or twice but three times to remind them to renew the apartment lease. They didn't make the call until the last day when it was too late. In the middle of recording an album he had to move all his stuff to a hotel. His reaction was "I could have spent this energy on the fucking record instead of moving my shit around town."

Now I know Danny and I know there is no way he would let something dumb like this damage his attitude towards the artist or the record. Nonetheless, you have to wonder what planet the manager was on at the time. The hotel was about four times the price of the apartment so the artist got stuck with a much bigger bill. Producers are human. It's unrealistic to expect someone to put in 18-hour days, seven-day weeks and then disrupt their life like that without breaking their stride and without affecting their ability to do a good job.

It may be a pre-requisite for artists' managers to be freaks. Nobody in their right mind would take the job on. As a producer you are bonded to the artist for the duration of the project, as a manager you are fused for many years. Anything that goes wrong is perceived as the manager's fault. It's easy to understand why they can be heavy-handed at times. A manager has to have clout with the record company and be able to play the political games that get thrown at them by the label and radio people. They have to deal with agents, attorneys and business managers as well as the street fighters like club owners, promoters and merchandisers. For an unknown manager with a 'no-count band' only superhuman acts of willpower and great force of personality can achieve this. Since they are ultimately held responsible for every mishap and failure along the way, a little crankiness is forgivable. Certifiable as they may be, managers have been known to save an album from a certain death when all on board the good ship 'Record Company' have taken to the lifeboats.

Chapter Seven

Lawyers

"It's like going across the river on the back of an alligator." (Tom Waits about the music business)

Hiring a music business lawyer is like trying to retrieve your ball from a patch of thorns – you have to reach in if you want to keep playing but you know it's going to hurt.

Ros Earls nailed it when she said, "Lawyers are a necessary evil really. I'd rather not use them and for the most part we take the contract as far as we can. There's only so many things that you expect to see on a contract and you could write the whole thing yourself. You do need to involve a lawyer at some stage because most of the contracts aren't binding unless you have independent legal advice. You can set up a regular deal so that you ask for the same terms as last time but they always try to change things so you have to pay through the nose again, although everybody knows, there's only a limited number of things they are going to repair." Katrina Sirdofsky said similarly, "We do the initial negotiations and the deal memos and let the lawyers handle the long forms."

No matter how much it costs, somewhere along the line you will need a good lawyer. As I mentioned, some producer managers are also lawyers. This can be a convenient arrangement and very economical for the producer. For a producer the downside of your manager being your lawyer too is that it leaves you in a vulnerable position. One of the two times in my career that I have been seriously ripped off was when my lawyer was also acting as my manager. You know the saying 'power corrupts, absolute power corrupts absolutely.' If somebody has a creative sense of ethics, giving them that kind of power can be bad for your financial well being.

You're safer having an independent attorney who is paid by you. A manager may have a hidden agenda. Your lawyer can give you an objective opinion about legal issues connected with your contract negotiations.

Music business lawyers see deals and contracts cross their desks all day long. They have a very good idea of what the going rates are. They also know what is regarded as standard practice for the time and what is not. This translates, in practical terms, to contractual points you can win and points you cannot. You have to have substantial clout as a producer to go against the norm, especially if you want better terms than the artist is getting. A good lawyer can actually save you money by advising you on which points you should stand your ground.

Don't, whatever you do, make the mistake that my first band did of using a non-music business lawyer to negotiate a contract. The music business, like most others, has its idiosyncrasies. We spent nearly a year negotiating a contract, which in the end was still awful. It could have been done in about two months by a music business lawyer and would have been a much better deal all round.

a) How Much Will They Cost You?

A lot – but a lot less than if you get ripped off or sign a dumb deal. Different lawyers operate in very different ways. Most will work for an hourly rate. Around £250 ($375–$450) per hour is not un-common. If you have a constant flow of contracts, some firms try to get you on a monthly retainer. I've done this and I didn't like it. The theory is you can get as much advice as you need for a fixed monthly cost. I always felt they were trying to do as little as possible for the retainer. It seemed like they wanted to bang out my contracts as quickly as they could and get me off the phone in the shortest possible time. The company invariably has a big name, come-on, lawyer who is one of the partners who you will meet with initially. Once you've agreed to go with the firm on a retainer, a very junior lawyer will do all of your contract work. I found it frustrating and at least one of my contracts got royally screwed up. If you opt to pay by the hour, your attorney will talk to you for as long as you like.

There are a lot of multi-producer records being made and albums where you're asked to do one or two tracks before they commit to doing the whole album with you. This has the unfortunate side effect of creating even more contractual work for the lawyers. It is just as complicated to negotiate a contract for one track as it is for an album. It takes just as long. The producer will usually be paid about ten times the advance for an album as he is for one track. His lawyer's bill will be pretty much the same for a one-track contract as for a 10-track agreement. In the case of a low to mid-price producer this could result in him paying out 50 per cent or more of the single-track advance in legal fees.

There are a few possible solutions. Negotiate a fixed fee per contract preferably either prorated per track or stepped with one price up to say three tracks and another for full album agreements so you know how much you are going to pay. Pay a percentage of what you make, just remember that they'll hold you to this percentage when you hit the big bucks. Pay a monthly retainer. The only way to tell what is the better deal for you is to calculate a rough average of how many hours they would spend on contracts in a month. Multiply that by their hourly rate and see if you're better off on the retainer. Lawyers are not the slowest people in the cosmos when it comes to finances, so you can bet your Nikes if you find you are winning slightly it'll be calculators at dawn. He's quicker on the draw than you are so as the notion of how much money you will save flashes across your synapses, his assistant is calling you on your cell phone, checking your schedule to see when she can slot you in to discuss fee arrangements.

Some producer managers have a lawyer in captivity as it were, someone that they try to get most people to work with. Sandy Roberton has this kind of arrangement which he points out has two advantages, "I've been able to get him to give us a really good blanket deal for each project so the clients get a really good deal and I don't have to speak to 60 lawyers." Of course the producers have to pay the fees still but they get the economies of scale.

b) How Much Should You Depend On Them?

You're the one that gets hurt if they screw up so . . . find someone you trust and keep an eye on things. Dealing with lawyers gives you some insight into how Daniel might have felt in the lions' den. If the lawyer's feeling hungry he can take a big bite out of your bank account and there's not a whole lot you can do about it. Not depending too much on your lawyer means spending time reading contracts and emails referring to clause 13 (i) (ii) and (iii). It's boring but so is looking left and right when you cross the road. If you enjoy having money I strongly recommend learning a bit about contracts.

c) How Much Do You Really Need Them?

Sadly, quite a lot. Producing can be an international experience and the laws of each country are somewhat different from each other. Even if you get pretty knowledgeable about the laws in your own country you will, undoubtedly, be in over your head when it comes to another territory. As much as I hate to admit it, a good music business lawyer can ultimately save you a lot of money. Because they are seeing contracts all day long and dealing with all the record companies all of the time, they are in a good position to know about trends and standard conditions in production contracts.

d) What Happens When They Get It Wrong?

Truthfully, it's your problem. For all the money you've spent on this person, if he makes a mistake you may never realise it. He could really screw up. Unless you go through your statements very carefully and double check against other agreements you may never know that anything's amiss. Meanwhile your precious royalties will be leaking back into the record company pot.

In one of my earliest contracts, my then-lawyer agreed a TV advertising clause that I would never have agreed to in subsequent years. I didn't realise he'd done this (I don't generally spend my Sundays re-reading old contracts) until about eight years later when the group's greatest hits album was TV advertised and went multi-platinum. I did some calculations and knew pretty much what I was expecting to get. The group's manager even called me and suggested that I might want to think through the tax implications of this huge cheque I would get in about six months. When the cheque showed up it was for less than half the amount my calculations had suggested. I double checked my calculations, they were right, I went to the contract and sure enough, tucked away on page thirty-three, there was this vicious little clause which took away 50 per cent of my well-deserved royalties.

I called the original lawyer who negotiated the contract. I expressed dismay at the fact that he had allowed me to sign the agreement with this royalty-eating virus in it. I also pointed out that in subsequent contracts I had never had to agree to this pernicious little nasty. His self-serving response was that if I wanted to retain (read pay him) again he would take a look at the problem for me.

What an amazing job! They charge you a fortune based on their expertise. Then when it turns out that they weren't such experts they want to charge you again to sort the problem out. You could sue them but what kind of nightmare scenario is that employing one tricky dicky lawyer to sue another.

e) What Tricks Do They Get Up To?

As Carol Crabtree of Solar Management said "Music business lawyers are a minefield. They can cost you a fortune by dreaming up ridiculous things to argue over." She cited the example of the lawyer who she caught faxing himself to death (at her expense of course) over the size of the producer's credits and whether they could be seen on the outside of the packaging or not. A legitimate enough subject for discussion. Credits are, after all, an essential part of our livelihood. A missed or wrong credit on a huge hit album can cost you future work. I didn't get paid for a project once but I did get my producer credit. The record turned out to be a big, influential hit from which I picked up a lot of work. The credit compensated for the lost income.

But to get back to Carol's lawyer who's arguing over credit sizing and positioning. What he omitted to take into account was that the record had been released several months ago so it was a moot point anyway. I have long suspected that in the induction lecture at law school they make each student turn to the student next to them, give them a big hug and promise on their mother's life to drag out every negotiation to the max. The lawyer's code of practice must require them never to get back to the other guy in less than a week or be fair and reasonable with each other despite the fact that they will be playing golf together on Friday. They both know at the outset what the final result is going to be because they just agreed six identical contracts in the past two months.

Sandy Roberton tracks each of his projects in his computer so that he knows where they are on each project . . . if it's a mark up or not. He said, "The lawyer that I have is not one of the lawyers that rushes around clubs trying to get bands signed. He's a contract guy and he comes in the morning and he works all day on contracts and goes home at night. You won't bump into him at Don Hills or some other club. I've had a lawyer like that before and umpteen contracts didn't get completed." He also identified a problem that happens in the States where the band's lawyer does the producer agreement. The band pays the lawyer for doing the record deal and if you don't get the producer deal done quickly, the band's lawyer doesn't want to do it because the band won't be in a position to pay him. As Sandy says, "you get into a situation where you can't get the producer contract signed." Without that you can't get the letter of direction signed where the band is giving the label permission to pay you. No letter of direction and "the label won't pay the backend. If it's a new band, you have to get the paperwork done very quickly once the producer selection has been done. We have a standard producer agreement and it's been seen by so many people they can mark it up very quickly and we can close it very quickly."

Sandy thinks part of the problem is that, "US music lawyers invented this shopping thing. Quite a few law firms survive by doing these deals for bands to be signed with labels, charging anything from 20 to 30,000 dollars a pop to do their record contract. In the heydays they were churning these out every single day. But now they are suffering a bit more and they're having to reinvent themselves because there aren't that many deals."

f) And That's Just *Your* Lawyer. How Much Damage Can The Other Guy Do?

The way negotiations usually run is that you, your manager or your lawyer will discuss the basic terms such as your advance, royalty percentage (commonly known as points), number of tracks and any other deal breaking points with the A&R person or the business/legal affairs person. They may at that stage send you a deal memo outlining those terms. The label now sends you their standard producer contract with your basic terms supposedly incorporated. Invariably, the original terms you thought you had already agreed, and that may be stated in the deal memo will be seriously eroded by the rest of the contract. There may also be a couple of mistakes or misunderstandings in the label's favour.

Basically the first couple of pages will give you what you wanted. The next 32 pages will take most of it back again via, what are euphemistically, known as, deductions and reductions. Your lawyer will send it back to them with the modifications and corrections that you and he want. There will be a bit of to-ing and fro-ing and eventually there will be a red-line or marked-up version of the contract with the amendments underlined. If this version is agreeable the final contracts will be sent. Supposedly the final contract should be identical to the red-line or underlined agreement. Mostly this will be the case. But, in two cases, I have found alterations to the agreed terms in the final contract. When these alterations were brought to the record company's attention, in both cases, business affairs claimed they were typo's or computer mistakes. In both cases the mistakes were significantly in the company's favour. It's basically the same scam that the London barrow boys run: you pay for something with a 20 pound note they hand you change for 10. If you notice they say "Oh, sorry mate" and give you the extra. If you walk away without noticing they just boosted their profit margin by several hundred per cent.

I have spoken to prominent lawyers who have had exactly the same experience. Whilst it would be wrong to imply that record companies are unethical, it's obvious that there are some individuals who will try to diminish your terms by any means. The moral of this tale is that it is wise to check, or have your lawyer check, the signature copies before you sign and return them. The next time you will read the contract will be if you have a major dispute with the label in a few years over royalty payments, rights or credits. That is not a good time to find out that you signed off on things you should not have.

It's not uncommon for the record producer to be in the studio making the record before his contract is complete. This is rarely to the advantage of the producer. Once you set foot in the studio or pre-production room you have, in practice, conceded the rest of the un-negotiated points. Ros Earls says, "I've never had a situation where the producer would pull out of the studio because the contract was not in place. It leaves such a bad taste in any creative kind of situation. What you want to do is to avoid that at all costs. You have to agree things before pre-production starts. So the business politics is not interfering with the other politics and the producer can be the good guy."

My experience is that record company legal departments go slow on the contract. Obviously it kills your negotiating position if you have significant outstanding points and you are already in the studio.

This lawyer business is a love-hate thing. You need them. They need you. I've had some very successful working relationships with lawyers and then again I lost a lot of money to one who went bad. The very best law firms tend to take a long-term view when it comes to money. They don't kill you early on or on the small deals, they'll wait until your career develops and then make up the difference.

Chapter Eight

Difficulties And Pitfalls

"The ultimate measure of a man is not where he stands in moments of comfort and convenience, but where he stands at times of challenge and controversy." (Martin Luther King, Jr.)

a) Studio Nightmares

"The difference between stupidity and genius is that genius has its limits." (Albert Einstein)

Bad personality traits become highly magnified by the enforced closeness and the creative pressures of the studio. Add any amount of drugs and alcohol, sprinkle a little success on top and you have an explosive mixture. Always remember things are never so bad that they can't get worse.

b) Serious Differences Of Opinion

Tony Visconti related a difficult time that he experienced with The Boomtown Rats, "It was a nightmare. It was like a Stephen King novel – it starts out in an innocent little village somewhere. Then there's that little touch of evil that starts to grow . . ." Speaking about Bob Geldof, Tony says, "He's difficult, and he knows it. He's a good performer, a great songwriter, but you have to keep him out of the mixing room. Apparently, he wants everything to sound very sizzly and trebly, so I used to mix a really fizzy top just for him. I used to put this glistening sound on the cymbals, and he loves to hear his sibilance, which was very hard to get on a vinyl record. Then I said, 'Bob, there's a limit. We can't put too much of this on tape.' His drummer told me, 'You think that's bad, he goes home and he takes all the bass off his hi-fi set, and he adds more treble!' It was then I realised I must be dealing with a deaf person!"

Being at real loggerheads with the artist is Andy Jackson's worst nightmare. "Or worse," he says, "different members of the band being at loggerheads with each other." He's never seen a situation where the band has completely broken down. But he has seen disagreements where one person gets pretty upset. "You can usually deal with it," he says. "You just have to take the time and try to make them feel that their concerns are being listened to. Generally, if they feel that they are being listened to they will back down from their stance. If they become very entrenched and you can't find any compromise you have to get them to feel that their opinions are valid."

Bands often have very complex personality interactions going on. A minor issue over a guitar part can turn into a major psychological field study of interpersonal relationships. Childhood stuff can be dug up and thrown along with any other psychological missiles, the "when I was six you did this to me" type of thing.

c) The Endless Album

They may not qualify as nightmares but interminable album projects can be mentally, emotionally and physically exhausting. Unless you are seriously into job security and on a daily rate the endless project is a killer. The problem used to be confined to the ultra-rich artists with their own studios. At least you could console yourself with the knowledge that you were working on a record that was definitely chart bound. Now almost anyone can own their own studio and the problem is becoming epidemic. When the artist owns the studio the budget versus studio time part of the equation is removed. You don't have to finish. Andy Jackson is a veteran of the endless album. "After six months you think 'I want to go into a studio where they have to pay for it, I want to get this damn thing finished'." The discipline imposed by having to pay for studio time can be a good thing and a creative stimulus in itself. Unfortunately it seems like the artists who are most inclined to want to work in their own studios are the ones who have the most difficulty making decisions.

d) Lack Of Vision

Andy went on to say, "I think a lot of records are made and nobody's sat down beforehand and said 'OK what are we trying to achieve here, what record are we really trying to make.' I remember when I was a house engineer, sometimes you would wonder why you were on the session. You would feel so inappropriate. You were starting to develop a sound that was yours and the project you're working on is just not what you do. Obviously nobody had a clear idea in advance of what they were trying to do. They just said, 'Oh this is a good studio so we'll book it. It comes with an engineer.' End of story. Nobody really knew what they were trying to achieve in the first place. You get it, as well, in the actual working practices. 48-tracks crammed full of stuff. Then you attempt to make an arrangement in the mix. It seems like a bizarre way to work to me. They don't really know what record they are trying to make."

e) Micro-Vision

When most people listen to a great track they don't necessarily hear all the complexities of the arrangement, how different parts come in at different times helping the song to develop as it goes along, the whole thing just works. Very often it's a surprise to first time recording artists how much deconstruction and detailed reconstruction goes into making a three minute hit. Every now and then this process triggers a latent obsessive-compulsive nature. You find yourself spending endless hours adjusting the length of every third sixteenth note in the first violin part that happens during the third verse or doing 32 overdubs on the two-beat acoustic guitar part that leads into the bridge. The old studio musicians would often say of these kinds of overdubs, "will it help sell anymore records."

These days those guys are rarely around to pass on their wisdom so the producer and the artist stare at the computer screen for another day adjusting this and tweaking that. As Andy says, "Obsessive artists are very often the problem. You spend hours and hours and hours punching in little bits that won't make any audible difference to the finished track and probably won't make the mix anyway." When you feel the micro-vision setting in you really have to try to pull back and look at the overall picture rather than the details. Details can be very important in adding the finishing touches to a great track or album but if you don't maintain macro-vision they can become the proverbial lipstick on the pig.

f) Panic Stations

i) The Singer Can't Sing In Tune/Time

Nine times out of ten, if a singer who didn't seem to have problems with tuning in a live situation has problems in the studio it's going to be something to do with his foldback. Number one suggestion is to rework his headphone balance to try to give him more harmonic support. Make sure he can hear enough of himself but not so much that his own voice is drowning out the track. Headphone mixes are a very personal phenomenon. Some singers like them insanely loud, with very little of themselves in the mix, others like to hear a little bit of the track with their voice obliterating everything else. I worked with one singer who wouldn't allow even a smidgen of reverb on their vocal in the final mix. In the studio he couldn't sing without Phil Spector-style vocal reverb in the headphones. Who knew?

Some singers can survive with almost any mix as long as they have one side of the headphones on and the other side off. Failing all else you can bring her into the control room, turn the monitors up like a live show and she'll probably bag it in one take.

For my sins I was once locked in a residential studio for over a month with a band that had an original sense of time and a singer who couldn't manage more than one syllable out of three in tune. Sadly the one, which was in tune, was out of time. I tried every trick that I knew. It was out of the question to hope for whole words to be in tune and whole lines were things I dreamt about at night. This was pre auto-tune but, thank God, I had a very early prototype digital editing system. Fortunately I was able to compile (out of an average of 12 takes on each song) the most in-tune set of syllables that she had sung. From there I had to set about tuning each word digitally by hand. It was painstaking but in the end I got the lead vocal part to sound good. Then, she said she wanted to sing the harmony parts. I tactfully suggested that it might be nice to have the contrast of a different singer on the harmony lines.

Certain styles of music are more forgiving. Alan Moulder takes the view that, "With vocals, if the attitude is there, you can stand a certain amount of timing and tuning problems. I'm not averse to a bit of sampling and adjusting with the pitch wheel. Generally I just try to get the best performance I can."

As much as it has become a part of the sound of some styles of music and as much as I can't stand the synthetic sound of over auto-tuned vocals, I have to say that, from a producer's point of view auto-tune can save a lot of agony. When you have captured a great overall vocal performance that has a few little sharp or flat words a little bit of inaudible auto-tune can be a great blessing. You don't have to make the singer keep going over the same line, you don't have to make choices between pitch and performance. For those times when you make a fundamental error of judgment and you find yourself in the studio with a complete non-singer – pay homage to the wonderful people of Antares.

ii) The Band Can't Play In Tune/Time
What Jerry Harrison says is, "We can work around someone, if that someone is not the most proficient guitar player, but if he has a style, we'll work around that. That's what the studio now offers. I can use the studio to help draw out the performances from the people that they maybe can't just do one take after another."

Hopefully you will have figured this out before you get in the studio. Unfortunately, if the demos were made at home on a computer or using a drum machine you have no idea how good the musicians are until you start working with them. Even if you've seen the band live it's still hard to assess how they are going to respond in a studio situation.

A couple of things can happen when you get into the studio. One is that you hear a great deal more detail. Listening to something on studio monitors is a bit like looking at a poster size enlargement of a photo. You see a lot more than you did even when you were taking the picture. You notice that someone's shoes are dirty, a tie's not straight and the girl has a huge zit on her chin. Same with bands in studios, now there's no audience distracting your attention and you have control of the volume. The other possibility is that the band can fall to pieces. Sometimes less experienced musicians get intimidated by the studio environment and especially by the self-imposed psychological pressure of this being their long-awaited opportunity.

So it's the first day in the studio and you find out that the tempos are all over the place. The first thing to do is apply a bit of analytical thinking. Were the demos like this? Did they speed up and slow down when you saw them live? If the demos or the live show had timing issues then you are looking at a re-education process and may have to deconstruct the arrangements and build the track from the drums up by overdubbing. You may have to use a click. You could straighten things out in Pro Tools but major digital surgery on the timing of a whole track doesn't usually sound that great.

If the demos and the live show were in time then the problem could be studio nerves? A little encouragement, some practice takes and some bad jokes can sometimes solve that problem. It could be the headphone mix. Make sure that you have listened on head-phones (don't just send the headphone mix to the monitors) to hear exactly what the musicians are hearing. Sometimes it's obvious what is wrong with the headphone mix to a producer or engineer where an inexperienced artist might not identify the problem. So if the tempo is moving around you can try taking different things out of the drummer's mix and watch how he responds to that. Does the drummer gradually speed up or slow down, does his time shift dramatically before or after a fill or in different sections of the song? It's a process of elimination. Could be that just one of the musicians is rushing or dragging and pulling the drummer along with him. In this case you have to identify who the culprit is and either reduce the level of his instrument in everyone else's head-phone mix or get him to sit out the initial takes. When I was a studio drummer, I often found that an overzealous musician on the session would push the tempo. My solution was to discreetly ask the engineer to take that musician out of my headphone mix. Then I could hold the tempo steady and it was up to the other musician to play to me.

If the music calls for a very strict tempo, a click may be essential. If someone has never played with a click before, this is guaranteed to freak him out. Never drop that on a drummer for the first time in the studio. This is where pre-production time is invaluable. You might realise in rehearsal that the drummer's timing is suspect, that the live stuff is going to be synched to computer generated tracks or that there may be a lot of editing between takes. In any of these cases it would be wise to have the drummer practice playing to a click long before you get to the studio.

OK, so removing things from the headphones didn't work. You've checked the live demo tapes and found them to be fine. Could be the nerves I mentioned, otherwise known as 'red light fever'. Nothing to do with the studio being in a bad neighbourhood, just the pressure of knowing that 'this is it'. What happens today will be preserved for posterity. Everything the band has dreamed about is coming to fruition and it's scary. In this case it's really a matter of making them feel comfortable, letting them know that they can take risks and if they screw up there is enough time for them to come back to the track and have another crack at it. It's always valuable to record all the run-throughs since they will invariably play better if they don't think they are being recorded. So forget turning the record light on. Push the talk back button and say "Let's run through it to get some levels." Hit record, and pray!

If it proves to be totally impossible to get the band to play in time, thanks again to digital technology it is now possible to quantize (correct the timing of) recorded audio. There are still limitations within which this will work and maintain signal quality. Many producers feel that too much timing correction leads to sterile tracks. Often it is better to edit parts that were originally played in time from another take or from another part of the same take. This can be done either on analogue tape by cutting and splicing the tape, by copying from machine to machine or by using the cut and paste function on a digital system, just as you would cut and paste text on any word processor.

Of course nothing to do with technology is as simple as it sounds, and nothing ever works exactly the way it is supposed to. Sometimes when you have to go through all this stuff you can't help but think that it would have been easier if the musicians just got it right in the first place. Other times you can use this studio trickery to rescue something very special that otherwise would have been unusable because of tuning or timing discrepancies.

Probably one of the most soul destroying things for a band member is to be replaced by a studio musician. Most band members will be OK with a bit of sampling and digital manipulation or even having their part programmed. But, when another human being comes in to play their part it's generally very uncomfortable. Alan Moulder says, "If the drummer can't play, I'll try tape-edit comping. I wouldn't ever get someone in to replace him unless the band suggested it. I might suggest programming the drums but if they're against it I'll work with what I've got. I try to find what works for them. It may be a time of night or keeping on going back to it. Some people like to keep working on it, punching in until they've got it. Very often it's a matter of working on it in frequent short bursts. The hard part is remaining objective. Once you've gone in with the micro-scope your perspective is completely lost."

Tuning is potentially less of a problem than it used to be. I can't believe it these days when I hear demos that are out of tune. Even with a cheap electronic tuner someone who's completely tone deaf can get a guitar in tune. It's a good idea to record an A440 tone right at the beginning of the project. All the tuners can be referenced to that tone no matter how many studios, countries or altered states we are in. There are quite a few tricks in stringing up guitars that help prevent them from going out of tune. With a first time band it's a good idea to have the guitars and bass set up professionally right before recording starts so that intonation is consistent all the way up the neck. Experienced bands have guitar techs, drum techs and key-board techs who obsess over their instruments which is a wonderful thing. Check tuning before every take.

If something does get recorded which you later realise is out of tune with the rest of the track, there are now plenty of devices and plug-ins that will change the pitch of an instrument without chang-ing the speed or vice versa. Depending on how much correction you are applying, there is a signal quality trade off. It's possible to conceal a certain amount of out-of-tuneness on an instrument that is out of tune with itself with a heavy harmoniser/chorus/ phase/flange FX. Ultimately the best solution is to redo the part with an in-tune instrument. This is one of the advantages with computer-controlled Midi parts. Should a part that was recorded via Midi to a computer be out of tune, you can simply retrigger an in-tune part by running the program again. Any computer generated part currently needs to be referenced to either a code, a click track or a device that can analyse tempo from the already recorded track.

iii) One Of The Musicians Is Screwing Up Every Take
Tony Brown, president of MCA Records, Nashville, and one of the most successful country music producers of all time, says, "I've seen one person completely start shutting down a tracking session. The artist needs to be creative and shouldn't have to worry about that problem. It's the producer's responsibility, and how he does it is as important as deciding to do it. You can pull the person out of the room, or have him sit in the control room, but you have to give him a reason. If things start getting weird, then I take him outside to talk. Nine times out of ten, depending on his ego control, he will usually

say, 'Have I got time to run an errand?' That means, 'I'm embar-rassed. I'm out of here.' I find that even great musicians know when they are not cutting it."

It's even worse when the musician is a permanent member of the band. I had a situation early in my producing career where a band had changed its drummer since they had made the demos that got them the deal. They had a very good reason. As good as the original guy was, he was a complete screw-up as a person. He had just about every problem a musician can have. I went into the project really excited about the whole thing based on what I had heard on the demos, only to find that the new drummer did not cut it. He didn't have the style, the feel or the timing of the original guy. For me it really goes against the grain to replace somebody on a session. When I was a studio musician, I had often been the drummer brought in to replace a guy in a band. I saw how badly they took it, but more importantly I was aware that, in many cases if the producer had been a little more sensitive, he could have made the guy comfortable and could have got a great performance out of him.

Anyway, here I was first day in the studio hoping and praying that a miracle was going to happen and my fears that had developed during pre-production would not come to pass. No such luck, he was even shakier in the studio than he had been in rehearsals. I was faced with no attractive options. I could play the part, I could get another drummer to play the part, do it with a drum machine or persevere with this guy. Drum machine was out. It would have destroyed every-thing the band stood for. Being the supersensitive wimp that I am I chose to stick with this guy. Out of about 20 takes I did 32, two-inch multi-track edits, cutting a bar here and a bar there. I finally got my three minutes and 20 seconds to make up the song. I did two songs like that and came to the inevitable realisation that for my sanity and the future of the band, I would have to have a chat with them. By this time they had realised that something was seriously amiss. The drummer was fired from the band. Not my favourite situation but the band could not have had any kind of success with this drummer. The album went on to be a hit and launched a substantial career with a couple of gold albums and multiple hit singles.

Later in my career I would have dealt with the situation sooner. It wouldn't have been right to let the band make less of a record than they deserved to. Obviously, when they chose this drummer they didn't have enough time, enough money or enough good players in their hometown to choose from. I prefer it when the band makes the decision to change a player. Sometimes a musician is really not up to the recording process but the band decides that they want to make the record with him no matter what. In those instances the producer has to decide whether it's even possible to make a good enough record with that musician or whether he should bow out of the project gracefully.

I'm not suggesting that you immediately discard any musician that is having some difficulties. I made a couple of very successful records with a band that was quite inexperienced but improving fast. We decided to go our separate ways on the third album. They went off and used another successful producer. Right at the beginning of the recording sessions the new producer decided that the drummer wasn't good enough and would have to be replaced. When the band told me about it later, I realised that the producer had simply intimidated the drummer with his attitude. He was used to recording either with machines or studio musicians with rhinoceros skins. Band members, for all their bravado, often have more fragile egos. In fact one of the last singles I did with this band, which had been a worldwide hit, had been a first take. In the end the band decided to bail out on the producer and went with some-one else. They were able to carry on recording as a group, having hits.

iv) You're Calmly Cruising Up To The End Of The Album, Bang On Budget, And The Artist Decides Half Of It Is Crap
This reaction is usually attributable to 'Buyer's Remorse' or 'Post Purchase Dissonance' very often brought on by studio burnout. Logic dictates that if someone liked something over a substantial period of time they'll probably come around to liking it again. Then again where is logic when you need it. Sometimes it can be very hard to get people to take a break from recording and almost impossible to stop them from listening over and over to the roughs or the mixes. If you work long hours and long weeks without breaks, burnout will happen, without question. People will get confused and unhappiness will set in. Producer panic at this point will burn whatever budget is left. You may go into a dive that you can't pull out of. This may be a very good time to take a week off or at the very least bring the A&R person into the debate.

v) The A&R Person Hates The Mixes: Stay Calm And Survive

Once upon a time I delivered an album that the artist and A&R person had monitored all the way through the recording and mixing process right up to the last day. They had been in and out of the studio, from the laying of the basic tracks to the final overdubs and mixing. Not a negative word had been spoken. Enthusiasm abounded. I delivered the album and started a well-deserved break. Day one of break at 10:01 am I received a phone call from the A&R person saying, in not so many words, that she hates the album, it's all wrong. Hmmm! Check I am awake, check drinks for hallucinogenics. All clear? Panic? Being of logical disposition, I was dumfounded. How, I puzzled, can you rave about something right up to the day it was completed and then hate it less than 24 hours later.

I hadn't learned how to deal with a classic case of 'Buyer's Remorse' or 'Post Purchase Dissonance.' This was a big budget project with a lot riding on it and now she was going to have to champion it at the label. Foolishly believing in my sanity, my ability and the project, I stood my ground and argued the case, succeeding only in painting myself into a corner. An older wiser me would have asked for a specific, blow by blow, critique. I would have listened sympathetically to the gripes and grievances. I would have read between the lines and realised that she was getting pressure from someone else, most likely the artist, who was not a fun person even on a good day. I should have then suggested a meeting between all the concerned parties (all those who had a stake in the project and who had any influence over its outcome) to figure out how to fix the problem. Subsequent experience taught me that 'sympathetic ear defuses many fraught situations.' By defending the album instead of listening I lit the fuse for them.

This one blew up in my face and it took me a couple more projects to figure out how to deal with this type of situation. What seem like "major problems" in the mind of a non-expert (many A&R people, some artists and everybody else) are mostly able to be resolved by making minor changes, usually in the mix, sometimes by fixing some overdubs and very occasionally by re-recording a track. Emotionally charged, harshly critical words make it difficult to interpret what people really mean. It's amazing how upset people can get about a reverb or delay they don't like or the fact that something might seem too loud or too quiet in the mix to them. It's even worse when they don't realise that these things only require minor adjustments. If they don't have the expertise to express their concerns in a way the producer can understand what would come across as a couple of helpful suggestions winds up sounding like they hate everything you did. What we should have done was to set up a listening session in the studio with all the stakeholders and try to pinpoint what the problems were.

It's not often that an A&R person will say anything really negative in the studio. This is partly because very few record company decisions are made by one person. The A&R person will come in and say all the right things or at least something along the lines of "I'd like to spend some time with the mixes" or "I need to hear the mixes on my own system." Very often that means they want to take it back to the office and get their bosses opinion as well as the marketing and promotion person's. Neither the boss nor the marketing and promotion departments may have even heard the demos. They will comment based on what they perceive as the difficulty of getting the album played on the radio or reviewed in the press. A couple of days later you get a phone call indicating that there are problems.

In order to avoid getting this phone call you need to ask a lot of questions before you take on the project and certainly before you get into the studio. Before taking on the project it is useful to figure out who was involved in signing the band. If it came through the president or managing director of the label even though you may never see them in the course of making the album it will be their opinion that you will be dealing with at the end. It's very rare for a producer to talk to marketing and promotion people regarding the direction of a particular project. Since the marketing and promotion department is where the rubber meets the road in the music business it's important to understand how the label anticipates promoting and marketing the project. If they see the album as something to satisfy the huge base of fans created by endless touring this will require a very different type of album than an unknown artist who has never toured or an established artist who hasn't had much success on their last couple of releases.

There are many reasons why albums can be rejected. Andy Jackson says, "I have worked on records where at the end of the day, the record company says 'Hmm . . . no, we'll pass on this,' having spent a hundred grand on it. As much as we despair about it, they are making a commercial decision. They don't want to spend another $200,000 promoting and marketing a record they don't believe in.

Unfortunately, in most instances that this happens, it is not because a sound commercial decision was rightly or wrongly taken but because the A&R guy has either left the company or been fired. No one has any personal mileage in promoting the record. It's not their project. They won't get points on it or a promotion if the album is a big hit."

This has become a bigger problem with the increasing amount of corporate mergers that have taken place over the past few years. There's not a lot you can do to insulate yourself against a label being folded by its corporate owner apart from keeping your ear to the ground and not taking projects from companies when too many rumours abound. Having said that, you wouldn't have worked a lot if you did that over the past three or four years because all major music groups have either merged or been rumoured to merge at some point in that time. What you can do, if you are in the position of being able to be picky is to figure out what the standing of the artist and the person who signed them is at the label. If either looks shaky and you have other choices, consider them.

g) What Makes It Seem Like Hard Work?

"Some scientists claim that hydrogen, because it is so plentiful, is the basic building block of the universe. I dispute that. I say that there is plenty more stupidity than hydrogen, and that is the basic building block of the universe." (Frank Zappa)

"The hardest part about being an engineer/producer (because they both fall into the same category) is to be willing to give of yourself to the project," says engineer/producer Bruce Swedien (producer on Michael Jackson's *Dangerous*). "To commit totally to what you are doing. And there are things you have to give up, like free time. But you get out of it what you put into it."

"The hardest thing is the pressure to come up with a strong single," says Steve Lipson. "It makes it easier when you're making a whole album, because your chances of finding and nurturing a single within it are that much greater. You have so much more time and facilities at your disposal and over time, things become clearer."

The anti-social hours would have to be one of the major negatives. I know several producers who insist on working eight-hour days, 10 to six, 11 to seven or whatever. This makes complete sense. You stay fresh and don't get burned out. Unfortunately most artists do not keep those hours, especially the younger ones who tour. They are used to getting up late and may not feel like singing until at least eight in the evening. Studio days can be as long as 18 or 20 hours. Working seven days a week is not uncommon. Trying to hang onto a relationship or bring up kids (they get up early no matter what) under these conditions is tough.

Obviously, it all depends very much on what type of producer you are and what type of artists you usually work with. The All-Singing-All-Dancing type defines his own hours. Merlin drifts in and out as he pleases. The sidekick is definitely locked into the artist's working schedule. The Collaborator may be able to influence the hours some-what but very often the producer will change his working pattern to suit the artist. Since one of the major objectives is to get the best out of the artist, it doesn't pay to have them trying to sing lead vocals at 10 a.m. on a Sunday morning.

h) How Much Loyalty Can You Expect Within the Business?

i) From The Artist?

Most of my work originated from the artist, usually because they'd heard one of my records on the radio or in a club, liked it and wanted to work with me. Once or twice I have known an artist long before the subject of production has been discussed. We get a chance to find out about each other, which helps if we do work together. Sometimes I have met the artist 'cold' on a recommendation. If we hit it off well enough and they like my work, we get to make an album together. Where the loyalty comes in is after the first batch of work, either an album or a couple of tracks.

Let's assume what you did together was successful musically, artistically and/or commercially. Does the artist come back to you because you did a good job – or does he use his newfound success, visibility and increased budget to attract another big name producer. Do they go for an even bigger name? Worst of all, do they figure that they can get the same results at a tenth of the price by getting your assistant to co-produce the next record?

I doubt that there are many artists who will use a producer again out of pure loyalty. They may come back because they thought you did a great job and don't want to change the formula (i.e. if you have success so don't change a thing – not the studio, the engineer, the assistant – don't even change the ashtrays). They may carry on working with you because it's a comfortable working relationship. Obviously it's easier to use the same producer than it is to change and have to strike up a new relationship. On the other hand there's the first girlfriend syndrome (see below), where you are the first producer an artist has worked with. No matter how good a job you did and no matter how much success you brought to the party, sooner or later, they are going to wonder how it would be to work with producer XYZ.

One producer who has engendered a great deal of loyalty from his artists is Tony Visconti. He produced nine albums with David Bowie (after a hiatus they worked together again) and nine with Marc Bolan. Asked what he gained from such an extended partnership he says, "Well, obviously there's real team work going on. We were a damn good team. You pick up where you left off, and hopefully it gets better, as long as the artist is making a commitment to improving and going forward, like David used to."

"When the producer or artist makes a change, the work they did together remains," notes Phil Ramone. "The tragedy of it is, the record business demands that you have hits almost every time out. And if a producer has a relationship with someone over a number of years, at some point the time will come where someone, be it the artist or the producer, will say, 'I think I'd better go make a move somewhere else.' Nothing lasts for ever. Every time somebody calls me up and says, 'I'd like to make another album with you,' I'm like, 'Oh! Well great!'"

"I've done two or three records with bands and then thought I don't think they are going to come back to me again because it's time for them to move on," says Alan Moulder. "I try never to expect to be asked back and that way I'm not disappointed. Whilst I'm generally tart for hire if you like, it's the band's career and they have to work with who they think can keep it going. You can't really take it personally." But, he adds, "It can hurt a bit sometimes."

For whatever reason, artists will move on to the next producer. Watching a band go off with another producer can be like watching your girlfriend leave with another guy. Sometimes you're happy (she's his problem now) and sometimes it hurts. Ros Earls says, "Everybody feels that way. If you don't feel like that then I suppose your heart's not really in it. Or the band and you were not ideal partners. People present different fronts but to a man everybody finds that the hardest thing. You are invested emotionally not just technically. You've invested huge amounts of time. Some albums take years."

ii) From The A&R Person?

If you are generating hits and you are easy enough to work with, you will get asked back but you can't expect an A&R person to put his job on the line for you. A&R is a precarious enough occupation as it is. An A&R person who values work you've done for them is in a very good position to put your name forward for upcoming projects. A loyal A&R person, by offering you a project that's a little bit different, can keep you from getting stuck in a rut. Very often they have the casting vote in a close competition for a coveted project.

Do they look out for you very often? Sadly no, in fact it seems that rather than building close working relationships with a small group of producers, many A&R people are either chasing the latest, hottest, most expensive model or trying to find a young engineer who can do the job as cheaply as possible. When I was the flavour-of-the-month I would get the most ludicrous calls for projects. If anyone had looked beyond the fact that I had a current Top Ten hit they could have seen that I was not the best person for the job. Getting good results is partly to do with the correct matching of the producer's creative and technical skills with the artist's needs. It's partly to do with how well the various relationships work. And it's partly to do with the ability of the artist and label to convey to the producer exactly what it is that all parties are expecting.

When 'Hot Dude' is being hired, the general assumption is that he will figure it out and get it right, after all he's 'hot'. The fact is that no matter how much you pay someone and no matter how big their last record was, some of their projects will fail. Most label people play the odds and choose not to notice the failures that hot producers sweep under the carpet. A multi-platinum album or a huge hit single can overshadow a great number of failures.

There are two major labels, for each of which I have produced only three albums. Each of these six albums had high chart placements, all of them were either gold, platinum or multi-platinum, all came in under budget and made substantial profits, four were début albums that broke the artists. No misses at all. In both cases, whenever I worked for those labels again, it was at the request of the artist not the label. The gap between projects was often more than five years. So record company – and specifically A&R – loyalty has never been the cornerstone of my career.

When I asked Ros Earls how much loyalty a producer can expect, she said without hesitation, "None whatsoever. Once you've made a record you have to try and move on. For a lot of producers it's like leaving their firstborn child."

Not being asked to make the next record is one thing, but having the record you have just made changed or taken out of your hands is another. Ros says, "[It's terrible] if the A&R person wants to come in and tamper with their work. It has happened that a new A&R guy has come into the frame and wants to change the tracks that the previous A&R guy absolutely adored. [The producer] felt like he'd reached perfection and for the radio promotion guy to say 'Can't get it on the radio', it's heartbreaking. This is something that nobody I have ever met has accepted – but you have to move on."

iii) Final Word On Loyalty
When times are tough you don't get a lot of help. In hard times, all the favours you did don't count for much. You have to pull yourself up by your own bootstraps. The goodwill you may have generated may be the key to the door at the top of the stairs, but somehow you have to drag yourself up those stairs. As far as just getting a call out of the blue – it's unlikely to happen.

It's very frustrating to make the first two, career-building records, and then have the artist go off and do the third 'mega' album with someone else. You don't reap the financial rewards and, to the rest of the industry, it can look as if your earlier records weren't up to scratch. In fact many bands (especially in America) don't hit their stride until the third album. The consolation is that the back catalogue will be, pretty much, guaranteed to sell. If it's an ego boost you need, there are always the hard-core fans who prefer the lesser-known early albums. It sure is nice to reap the rewards on the big sellers though.

Jim Dickinson (producer of The Replacements, Ry Cooder and Big Star) says, "In this business, rejection and humiliation are literally a daily occurrence. You can't ask an artist to not be sensitive, but if you take it too personally, it will kill you and your art. I had a coach in high school who told me, 'You've got to remember, Dickinson, they are not doing it to you, they are just doing it.' I apply that to the record business: they are just doing it. It is happening, and it is falling on you and your art, but you can't take it personally."

The bottom line is; aim low to avoid disappointment. Don't expect loyalty from too many sources.

i) First Girlfriend Syndrome

This is a very common situation that occurs when you produce a band's début album. I have done many first and second albums and it is inevitable that the band will eventually get itchy feet and think about playing the (producer) field. No matter how good you are, no matter how well you get on with the band and no matter how much success you create for them, eventually their thoughts turn to other producers. What would it be like to work with so-and-so who did that amazing record by such-and-such. Other people's cooking always tastes better than your own.

Most producers I speak to, if they are being open and honest, find it hard – maybe even painful – to watch a band they nurtured go off with another producer. The first producer a band has, the one who introduces them to the mysteries and intricacies of the studio world, the one who breaks them through into the limousine and champagne lifestyle, is really like the high school sweetheart. No matter how much you like her, there are other girls out there and the grass is always greener. There are several ways to look at it. Some bands are not the least bit interested in the nuts and bolts of how the record is made. When they manage to strike a successful working relationship with a producer on their début album, they are inclined to continue working with that producer for a very long time. The longer they work together the easier and more comfortable it becomes. On the down-side too many hours together in the studio or a wrong thing said in an interview can cause the relationship to deteriorate. So can a drop in sales (don't forget it's always the producer's fault) or a change in musical direction.

If the artist has self-production aspirations they may immediately want to produce themselves after their first album or two or they may, consciously or subconsciously, decide to go to 'producing school.' The quickest way to find out how to do anything is to work with the best people in the business. If you want to learn what to do and what not to do, it really makes sense to work with as many good producers as possible.

Mitchell Froom, talking about why Chrissie Hynde stopped working with Chris Thomas after three albums, says, "It's inevitable that after you do three records with somebody, you tend to want to see if you can do it with somebody else, or how it would change the formula. Recording's a constant process of wanting things to be fresh. I think she did it to shake up the formula, to try things differently, that sort of thing. Chrissie Hynde speaks very highly of Chris. I think at that point she just wanted to see what would happen."

If you produce début albums you will almost certainly experience 'first girlfriend syndrome'.

Chapter Nine

Success And Money

a) How Much Can You Make?

Potential earnings range from the dirt-eating end of the scale to extreme wealth. Initially the income may not be so great. If you are a complete unknown, even working for a major label, you probably won't get a big advance to start with. Until you have a hit or get yourself established in a niche, you may not make enough to live on, unless you live in a mud hut. Prior to producing I was a signed artist who worked as a studio musician on the side. The first project I produced outside my own band was Spandau Ballet's first album. The advance was respectable for an unproved producer but until the royalties kicked in I was still making less than I did working as a studio drummer. The sacrifice turned out to be worthwhile because that album went gold, launched my producing career and I still earn royalties from them today.

The rule of thumb as to how much you could make from producer royalties is, GB £50,000 to £65,000 or US $75,000 to $100,000 income per one per cent royalty rate per million sales. There's no way to calculate an accurate number because some labels base their points on suggested retail price and some on wholesale or dealer price. Retail and dealer prices change, the infamous deductions and reductions change and the changes are never to the benefit of the artist or producer. Royalties are calculated in one of three ways: as a percentage of the retail price of the album, as a percentage of the wholesale price (published price to dealer which is also known as PPD), or as a percentage of the money actually received by the label. Generally it is a combination of two of those methods with royalties from sales being calculated as a percentage of retail or PPD and the producer's share of licenses to film or commercials being calculated as a percentage of the label's receipts. There are some small labels that just pay on a percentage of their receipts. You have to be clear in your contract how they define receipts. There are lots of clever ways that a label's accountants can jig with that number. Whichever way they define them it will invariably be the least favourable to the artist and producer.

One per cent of the retail price of an album that retails for £14.99 amounts to 14.99 pence. This, theoretically, translates to £149,900 per million units. That wouldn't be too bad. But the £50,000 per 1% per million units is closer to the mark by the time you factor in all the packaging deductions, free goods, reductions on foreign sales, TV advertising promotions and the other wild and wonderful ways in which labels giveth and taketh away.

Producers command anything from no royalty at all to around three per cent of retail. Four per cent is not uncommon for a very successful producer and above that it's negotiable depending on your leverage. Using a retail price of £14.99, a three per cent producer will make somewhere between £150,000 and £449,700 on a million units. A four per cent producer's range will be from £200,000 to £599,600. Whether you are at the top or bottom of the range depends on how well your contract was negotiated and how good the artist's contract is. When it comes to the way royalties are calculated and the reductions and deductions, the producer rarely gets more favourable terms than the artist.

The countries and companies that calculate royalties using the wholesale price or PPD adjust the producer's and artist's percentages using a formula so the income works out roughly the same as it would have if you used the percentage of retail calculation. The kind of royalty rate you can command is not simply a function of your reputation and track record but also the stature of the artist you are negotiating with. It may be that generally you are a four point producer but that a major world power wants you to produce their next album for no royalty at all. Now this might not sound like a good deal at all except for the fact that the fee they are prepared to pay exceeds what you could reasonably expect to make from a good royalty on most other projects. Not only that, but the addition of the world power's name to your résumé/CV/bio is going to up the ante for future projects and make you into 'desirable dude.'

As Ros Earls says, a good producer can earn millions. "Ideally you want to have several albums that go on selling forever." Peter Collins commented that you are much better off if an artist does well after they leave you than if they disappear without trace. As much as your ego may want them to fall off the map when they move on to another producer your bank account will be happier if they have a long healthy career. Each time another album penetrates the charts the back catalogue increases in sales as well.

Not to drive you crazy with numbers but let's put these potential millions you can make into some sort of overall perspective. In 2003, major labels released over 7000 new titles but depending on whose figures you believe there may have been as many as 100,000 titles including releases by artists and small independents in the US, 60 per cent of which are not counted by Soundscan. Most of these 'invisible' releases will be at the lower end of the sales spectrum, big selling releases are going to show up on Soundscan. In fact, Nielson Soundscan reports that more than 38,000 albums registered with them were released in the US in 2003. Not surprisingly only 40 of those 38,000 sold more than one million copies. These days a major label act that doesn't sell one million units is an act that will most likely be dropped.

The real bucket of iced water is that only 10,500 of those 38,000 releases sold more than 100 copies, 1,200 exceeded 2000 units, just over 500 titles each sold more than 10,000. To give an extremely rough idea of what these numbers represent in cash to the labels, artists and producers, if the CD is retailing for around $14.98, the price to the store will be about $9.75 not including discounts and incentive programs. The cost of physical distribution will be approximately $2.75 so the label is getting roughly $7. Out of that $7 they will pay $0.85c in mechanical royalties for a ten-track album (at full rate) and, depending on contractual terms, somewhere in the $0.60c to $1 in artist royalties.

Manufacturing costs will be just under or over $1 depending on the packaging. This leaves about $4 out of which the label has to cover their salaries, rent and other overhead costs. At 10,000 units sold this means the label is at best netting $40,000 before their costs and, without unduly creative accounting, the artist's royalty statement could show around $7,500 earned. This is allowing for a 3% producer royalty. Recording costs, any advances, tour support and marketing costs would, in most cases, come out of this $7,500 in which case, at this level of sales, the artist will receive no royalties. A three point producer would earn about $2,500 but that would be offset or recouped against his advance and even when his advance is recouped he won't see any more money until the label has recouped their recording costs out of the artists' royalty. At that point he will get paid from record one, meaning that he gets his royalty on every record sold less his advance once the artist has recouped costs agreed in the producer contract. There are tons of variables and these are very, very approximate numbers but the point is that 98 per cent of releases registered with Soundscan sold less than 10,000 units and nobody is getting rich at or below the 10,000 unit level of sales.

b) Where else does the money come from?

Certain genres of music such as hip-hop, R'n'B and pop are more likely to use multiple producers on one album. In these genres, the producer is very often also the songwriter. Writing the material ups the potential income hugely. Not only do you get paid as the producer but you also get paid a mechanical royalty for every record sold and a performance royalty every time your song gets played on the radio. The mechanical royalty amounts to $0.085c per track in the USA. In the UK, they work it out a different way: distributed labels pay writers 8.5% of the dealer price (the wholesale price that dealers pay) and non-distributed labels pay 6.5% of the retail price (excluding VAT). It's worth noting that you get this money via MCPS in the UK and Harry Fox in the US. MCPS does not collect for non-members so if you wrote a song on an album you need to register it with a mechanical copyright collection organisation such as MCPS or Harry Fox as well a performing rights organisation such as PRS (UK) or ASCAP, BMI or SESAC in the US. Most major collection societies have reciprocal agreements with each other so, for instance, MCPS and PRS both collect from the other agencies all over the world. You generally join the societies in the country where you live – you don't have to join up in every territory.

But wait a minute – surprise, surprise – the labels want to reduce the amount of money they pay you yet again. If you write one of the songs you are producing, in the US, the label slips what is called a controlled composition clause in the producer contract which usually says that you get 75% of your statutory mechanical copyright royalty of the songs that you wrote. Hmmm – isn't a statute a law? So instead of getting $0.085c per track you get $0.06375c. This may not sound like much of a difference but if you have just one track on a million selling album this amounts to a difference of over $20,000 that will go to the label instead of the writers. Well, I guess the labels need it to pay for lunch or something!

Pretty much everywhere in the civilised world, with the notable exception of the USA, radio stations pay a performance royalty to the copyright owner of the actual recording (as distinct from the composition) every time they play a track on the air. In the UK this royalty gets channeled through PPL. 50 per cent goes to the label or copyright owner and 50 per cent goes to the performers either directly from PPL or via AURA or PAMRA. The money comes from a negotiated payment per play from the non-commercial stations such as the BBC and from a portion of advertising revenue on commercial stations. The performer's 50 per cent of the royalty is split. 65 goes to the featured artist and 35 per cent goes to non-featured performers such as studio musicians. So a featured performer such as Kylie Minogue would get 65 per cent of this performance money and the remaining 35 per cent would be split between the musicians who worked on the track.

You can only get a piece of the 35 per cent if you are categorised as making a musical contribution to the track. Until recently producers were categorised as not making a musical contribution unless they played an instrument on the recording. Hello, gotta love that! Tell that to George Martin! Thankfully AURA has been successful in lobbying for producers to get paid on the same basis as conductors of orchestras in that they make a non-audible musical contribution. Go figure! Even then you are only entitled to this money if you either recorded in the UK, or are a citizen or UK resident. Other territories have their own agreements and collection agencies with reciprocal agreements but US producers (and performers) are excluded because of the lack of a terrestrial right in the US. This is a problem that needs to be rectified in US intellectual property law.

Commercial radio stations with a music format base their business on playing music, that's how they sell advertising. They play songs from their chosen format that market research shows will attract listeners. The number of listeners the station attracts determines the station's ratings. Stations use that rating to put a price tag on the airtime they sell to commercial advertisers. The argument goes that airplay is promotion that helps sell records thus making the artist and producer money. Airplay definitely promotes sales on new releases. It also promotes advertising sales for the station. Believe it or not stations don't play music to help artists, musicians and producers – they use it to sell advertising. In case you think that's my paranoia showing, Lowry Mays – the founder of Clearchannel, the largest single owner of radio stations in the US – said to *Fortune* magazine in 2003, "We're not in the business of providing well researched music. We're simply in the business of selling our customers products."

Oldies or classic stations play older music to target a certain type of listener, in order to attract advertisers who want to appeal to this demographic. The advertising money that the station pulls in is directly due to the music they are playing and yet the producer and performers of that music will receive nothing from the airplay unless they wrote the song. The "we promote your record" argument falls down because the performers and producers receive very little from sales when recordings are not well distributed, and deep catalogue material rarely is. They will get nothing at all if the album is deleted from the label's catalogue. Simply put – performers and producers should get paid for the use of their work particularly when large, rich, corporations are being supported by the exploitation of their work.

The US Digital Millenium Copyright Act (DMCA) ensures that a performance royalty gets paid on digital broadcasts in the US. Although this doesn't affect FM and AM airplay it covers all non-interactive digital performances such as cable music services, satellite radio and Internet radio stations. Non-interactive just means that you choose the channel rather than the song and you can't fast forward, rewind or download a song. This royalty is administered by the non-profit organisation Soundexchange and is split 50/50 between the copyright holder (usually the label) and the performers. The performer's share is split once more with 45 per cent going to the featured artist and five per cent going to non-featured performers such as background singers and musicians which gets paid via the unions, AFTRA and AFM. If you play or sing on the record you can receive a portion of the five per cent from AFTRA or AFM. Otherwise the only way producers get a piece of the digital performance royalties is by contractual agreement with the artist. The producer engineer wing of the Recording Academy does supply a boilerplate letter of direction for producers that, when signed by the artist, will direct Soundexchange to pay the agreed percentage of digital performance royalties directly to the producer. You can also have your attorneys draw up a letter of direction at the time they are drawing up the producer contract.

Digital download royalties are now happening and once again the producer's share of digital download income will depend on having a contractual agreement with the artist. New producer contracts are being written with this in mind. The older ones are being interpreted to include digital downloads as an income stream along with regular sales and licences. The labels are all treating downloads as a sale (not a license) so the artist gets paid some permutation of their normal royalty against retail or wholesale price (in the case of iTunes retail is $0.99c and wholesale $0.65c per track). If downloads were deemed to be a license then the artist would be paid under that contractual provision which is usually a 50/50 split of receipts. This would generally be better for artists and producers and worse for labels.

The subject of royalties is a book in itself when you start to look at the various entitlements in different countries. But this is how producers make their living, so suffice it to say that as a producer you should take the time to make yourself aware of the various royalties that may be due to you. All of the collection agencies are online and are extremely helpful. Make sure your contract covers all non-statutory income streams.

c) Do Producers Earn Their Percentage?

Producer royalties are almost invariably taken out of the artist's royalty (as is almost everything else) so if the artist will jump for it, generally speaking, the record company will too. Mostly the deal is struck between the producer and the artist although you want the record label to pay you directly. As downright dishonest as major labels can be you will most likely be able to track them or their new owners down in twenty years time. That may not be true for the artist, manager or production company. The label will want creative approval of the producer and budget approval for the recording costs and producer advance. All recording costs are ultimately paid out of the artist's royalty so if it's a follow up to a hugely successful album the label will not be as careful about the budget or the producer advance. They know the artist has the money in the pipeline so the label is really only spending the artist's money.

With a solo artist it's not such a big struggle for them to pay a third or sometimes more of their royalty to the record producer. When there are five members in the band sharing, say, a royalty of 14 per cent if the producer commands a royalty of, say, four per cent that leaves each band member with two per cent each. The drummer will be making less than the producer. True, the songwriters will participate in the performance and mechanical copyright income. Bands can also make a fortune from touring and merchandise sales. Nevertheless, that producer royalty can look like a huge bite out of the future pie to a non-writing band member.

So How Do We Justify Our Percentage? Steve Albini says we can't. "Paying points to a producer is a standard industry practice, and it's one of the reasons why bands go broke. They have to give a lion's share of their income to other people in the music industry, and everybody ends up making money off them, except them. I think it's criminal for a producer to take a royalty on a record that he produces – especially before the band itself has recouped."

Recoupment works like this: producers are traditionally paid from record one which is the first record sold but they don't actually get any royalties until the amount of royalties earned exceeds the amount of the advance they were paid. Although the royalty may be calculated from the first record sold the producer usually doesn't get his first royalty check until after the recording costs for the tracks he or she produced are recouped. Artists on the other hand have to pay for the recording costs, advances, packaging, promotion, marketing, tour support and often videos out of their royalties before they see a penny. Steve Albini goes on to say, "Royalties are for producers who say people are buying this album because I worked on it, it has my signature sound on it, and so I deserve a cut from every record that's sold. With the points system, the producer has a personal financial stake in making sure the record is commercially successful. The money he makes for himself and his family is more important than the band sounding like itself."

Mostly this is a true statement regarding the commercial producer. The label has seen the band live and heard the demos that they produced themselves. They hire a producer precisely because they want to create hit singles and a big selling album. Oftentimes that does involve modification of the band's sound. When the label or the act really wants the band's sound to remain unchanged they either release the demos or put them in the studio with an engineer and let them produce themselves. Many independent labels do this but in most cases a major label will not. In some genres of music some producers, particularly the All-Singing-All-Dancing songwriting producers are as important, or more important, than the artist. By the time a producer earns royalties the artist is well on their way to establishing their career and becoming famous enough to up their touring and merchandising income as well.

So the decision to pay a producer to modify the act's sound depends on the artist's and the label's priorities. If a band is totally confident of their direction and sound, and has the ability to go into the studio and record a great album without help, then they should do it themselves or just use an engineer and avoid paying points. If the artist needs help in shaping the record then the person who helps shape it should get compensated when the record sells. Many bands are simply not capable of making records without help. For others it is just not what they want. Part of the vision for many aspiring artists is to sign with a major label, be produced by a well-known producer and make a record that is far beyond what they could achieve on their own. These decisions are all part of the pros and cons of signing with a major or remaining independent. Signing with a major is a lot like buying a lottery ticket; you have a shot at the big-time but it's an all or nothing game. The winners win big and everybody else loses. Not many artists sustain a modest, midlevel career via a major label. The majors are not interested in playing a midlevel game they need to hit the jackpot on a regular basis. They spend so much money and miss so many times that the deal is now set up so that the artist won't make money until they go platinum. These days a new artist gets one real shot at a single on their first album and they will only move to the second single if the first is a hit. Unless they have a hit even with a guaranteed two album deal they often won't even get to make the second album. This is why having a producer who can deliver a hit single becomes important. Going the independent route is more like having a day job. There's no jackpot, the act works to get paid. The label won't pump huge amounts of money into creating a hit but the artist will see royalties at a much lower sales threshold. Success comes incrementally.

Even artists who break at a very young age such as Britney Spears or Christina Aguilera have five or more years of hard work and development behind them. Overnight success usually takes five to ten years in the music industry, however you slice it, and the independent artist might take longer. With very few exceptions the ultimate rewards are much more modest than with a major label but the independent artist has more control over their career and their music than a baby major label act. An astute, hardworking independent artist can sustain a midlevel career for decades. Very often independent artists make most of their income from touring. Consequently producers who specialise in midlevel or indie artists often don't get the big royalty checks but they don't have the same commercial pressures either.

So the big bucks are mostly made via the majors but the statistical probability of having a hit record is very low. The RIAA website states that fewer than 10 per cent [of releases] are profitable. They point out that releasing an album with major distribution costs a label at least $1 million and that the overall sales volume is lower than it was in 2000. This doom and gloom led to the consolidation of the major record labels down from six a few years ago to four at the time of writing. Some believe that soon there will be only three major labels worldwide giving each a roughly 25 per cent market share leaving the independent sector with the remaining quarter. The consequence of all this merging and acquiring is the dropping of many acts, reduced numbers of signings and cutbacks on new releases. It is significantly harder to get an act signed to a major label today than it was ten or 20 years ago and much harder to get them on the radio. This all adds up to less major label work for producers.

Of course producing one hit that makes some money and continuing to produce hits in order to sustain a living are two very different things. This is a 'winner takes all' business and 'success breeds success' so, at any point in time, a relatively small group of proven producers are being offered the acts the major labels have earmarked for 'priority' treatment. Once you manage to produce a hit that will generate new work for a reasonable period of time.

Despite the RIAA's optimistic figure of 10 per cent, the rule of thumb in the music business since the Seventies has been that one in 20 acts signed to major labels recoup their costs. It's these acts along with the back catalogues of previously successful artists that sustain the entire industry. The record producers who can consistently increase an act's chances of having a hit are definitely earning their keep.

A successful commercial record producer is, by definition, someone who has had multiple hits, often with multiple artists. He or she understands the process involved in making a hit. Many people can (and will) tell you whether a record is likely to be a hit when it's finished. Very, very few can consistently take the raw materials and construct one with any degree of certainty.

On a less stellar level a good producer can earn his bed and breakfast just by good organisational and project management skills. Groups who produce themselves are notorious for spending years and (sometimes literally) millions attempting to materialise their collective dream. The right producer can gently steer the confused, placate the warring, and motivate the unmotivated. Practical organisation of the sessions and musicians can save the label and, ultimately, the artist, thousands, tens of thousands and sometimes hundreds of thousands – offsetting part if not all of the producer's advance and royalty.

The world of freelance record production is a free market economy. The laws of supply and demand apply. If producers didn't pay for themselves many times over, nobody would hire them. Producer advances and royalties can amount to a big chunk out of the artist's income. But the producer does not participate in the future spoils of victory such as merchandise sales, touring, publishing, sponsorships and endorsements or royalties from future albums that he doesn't produce – even though his work may have been a key element in elevating the act to the position where they can capitalise on these income streams.

Unless the artist is signed to the producer's own production company, they usually have no obligation to use him or her to produce subsequent albums. Breaking an artist or giving them their first hit is like launching a rocket into space. It's hard to get up there but once you're there you can float for a bit. If a producer gives an artist a hit début album, he has helped create a platform of success upon which the artist can continue to build.

Others involved in the hit making process such as the record company and manager have multi-year, multi-album contracts that protect them and guarantee them continued income. Producer contracts are album by album. Producers can be replaced at any time. In times that are more about creating artists than just developing them, the producer's role comes more to the forefront. Producer manager Katrina Sirdofsky said, "As producers have once again become the driving force of the music business, the deals have gotten better. Lately it seems most producers are infinitely more talented than a lot of the artists they are creating careers for so it has certainly tipped the scales."

Taking into consideration the talent, experience and hard work required, the insecurity of the job, the difficulty of getting started, the traveling, the long hours and the positive consequences great production can have, there is no doubt that good producers earn their keep.

d) How Can You Increase Your Chances Of Success?

Is there a direct relationship between ability and success? Or is success purely down to good luck? Andy Jackson thinks there is some connection. "You can be lucky for an album or two but I don't think you can stay lucky. People that stay doing well do so because they are good. It doesn't necessarily mean that just because you are good you will get there either. You've got to be lucky to get there in the first place. If you can be successful and stay successful then you are most likely good. Some people do apparently next to nothing but their contribution is valuable. Other people do everything and there's every possibility in-between."

It's called the music business for a reason so if you happen to be somewhere where you can't study production, I strongly recommend studying music and business. It's also called the music industry and I suggest that the other meaning of the word industry – diligent and energetic devotion to a task or endeavour directed to some purpose – is a good indicator of what is required to shorten the odds in your favour. Know your history. I don't know anyone who is good who doesn't know where the music they like came from and how it evolved.

So, "if you are good you will make it" is not necessarily a true state-ment. Everyone needs a lucky break. Although as the saying goes "the harder I work, the better my luck gets." What constitutes 'good' in context of being successful as a producer is complex. Whatever your specific ducks are they will need to be in a row. If you know you have missing ingredients concentrate on acquiring those skills or form a team with someone who has them. Important qualities include having a good ear for music that has mass appeal or at least a large niche audience, an instinct for being in the right place at the right time, patience and persistence, enthusiasm and energy, connections and confidence, musical, technical and people skills, business abilities and some common sense. It helps to be a problem solver – to have the knack of being able to make diverse situations 'work' and an ability to work with the details and at the same time rise above them, keeping the overall objective in sight. Producers succeed with very few of these qualities. If you happen to be gifted in most or all of these areas I would think it unlikely that you could fail.

e) What Is The Secret Of Longevity?

Arif Mardin may be the greatest example of a long and continuously successful production career. In the Sixties and Seventies he was working with the greats of the time including Aretha Franklin, The Young Rascals and The Bee Gees, he continued to produce massive hits through the Eighties and Nineties for artists such as Chaka Khan and Bette Midler. In his seventies, he helmed the phenomenally successful Norah Jones debut album *Come Away With Me*. Looking at his career you can say he pretty much did everything right. He had the talent in the first place – he won the first Quincy Jones scholarship to Berklee College of Music in the Fifties. He went on to graduate from Berklee and hitched his wagon to Atlantic Records for over 30 years. He has a degree in economics from Istanbul University and studied at the London School of Economics which I'm sure helped in his years at Atlantic. He said before he went to Berklee, "the level of my musicianship was actually high. At Berklee I learned to formalise it and learned new techniques, it opened up new horizons."

Arif is a very gracious person who has obvious people skills along with his formidable musical talents. He has a deep love of many kinds of music, an open mind to new ideas along with an appreciation for the importance of lyrics and the emotional connection that the right combination of lyrics and music can make. Three of the most successful and enduring producers Arif, Quincy Jones and George Martin share a lot of common factors in their careers. Each one of them was a musician, had a formal music education, developed impressive arranging and orchestration skills prior to their production work and worked at a label for at least some part of their career.

Russ Titelman's career also spans from the Sixties to the present. He started out in a group with Phil Spector while still in high school, wrote songs with Barry Mann and Cynthia Weil, Carole King and Gerry Goffin, played guitar on the internationally successful Sixties US pop TV show *Shindig!* and worked with Randy Newman, James Taylor, Paul Simon, Chaka Khan, Steve Winwood and Eric Clapton. Russ worked in the legendary A&R department at Warner Bros throughout that company's incredibly successful and creative heyday with Mo Ostin and Lenny Waronker. His modest comment on this incredible run of success was that "being in the right place at the right time is part of it."

You need to be the right person with the right skills in the right place at the right time in order to enjoy that level of success. In Russ Titelman's case he was able to use his musicianship to unlock the inner doors of the business. On *Shindig!* he says: "We played behind Jerry Lee Lewis, Jackie Wilson, on and on. I got to see everybody and play music behind these great artists. I used to hang out at Metric Music with Lenny Waronker (who went on to become president of Warner Bros and subsequently moved to Dreamworks), go over to Screen Gems where Brian Wilson would be working. I started taking sitar lessons at the Ravi Shankar Institute where I met Lowell George (Little Feat)."

This is the other kind of music business education that you can't get in school. To be able to observe and work with the great artists of the time is both inspiring and challenging. You have to be born with the talent, you need some luck for sure, but you also need the determination to rise to the highest levels and stay there.

Ros Earls thinks that the secret of longevity is to restrict your work to projects that you have your heart in. "That's my personal golden rule," she says. "If you look to the money all the time, something's bound to go wrong. It's a negative way to approach any kind of creative project. If you've got your eye on the record you want to make rather than the dollars, the chances are, if you're good enough, you'll make good albums and people will recognise that, particularly in England. The British attitude is that money is vulgar. If you can be associated with a particular style of music and keep on reinventing yourself that's the most likely way to achieve longevity."

f) Hitting The Jackpot

Sometimes, very occasionally, a producer can find himself in a position where business savvy, the right act and circumstances can result in a truly gigantic payout.

In the music industry, the term 'production-company' indicates a company with which artists sign an agreement, often guaranteeing them only *a chance to record,* possibly even *at their own expense.* The production-company then endeavours to sign an agreement with a label or distributor to release records by the artist. The artist is not signed directly to the label. Sometimes artists sign with a production company as a last resort after approaching all the majors and the bigger independents. Increasingly, signing to a production company is becoming the only first option for many artists as the majors retreat further and further from artist development. Usually the master recordings remain the property of the production company creating long term value in the company. An established production company often has very good connections with at least one major label. As Sandy Roberton pointed out, "Urban producers were in control of acts long before rock producers were. The producers were signing acts, making deals and writing songs." He thinks that, especially in the pop arena, more acts will be signing to production companies to make their albums. He said, "The Matrix, who I represent, have just formed a label and signed their first act. They're going to make a finished album and I'm going to make a distribution deal for the label. They found the act, signed them. They are being very proactive in that area. They are not going to be just producers for hire they're creating a brand name." He went on to say that these deals are better than 50/50 splits between artist and production company. "They are very fair deals. Some investment from the producers, but it's mainly a spec situation. Major labels are not trying to get nine or 10 albums anymore. More like six albums."

In order to protect their investment most production companies will try to sign the artist for as many albums as the subsequent major label deal will require. Sandy points out, "If you have signed an act and you haven't got them to so many [albums] you can always adjust it later on. You can sign them direct to the label for the last two records or the act will alter your deal before you sign the major label deal." If the major label wants to sign the act but only as a direct signing he says, "Part of the deal the producer strikes is that [the label] either hires the producer for the second record or [the producer] gets an override." So the way this works is, "The producer has got his own studio. He goes in and develops the act, works on spec, we have an arrangement with the act. We get the act a deal and the producer gets his advance and royalty. The acts are happy because they get a record deal." If it should happen that the label wants the act, but wants to remake the album with another producer. Sandy gets a kill fee for his producer so that the producer has not wasted his time, "if the record scores, he makes out."

Anyone can own a production company and it doesn't even have to be a real company. Lawyers, managers and producers are in the prime position to profit from these kinds of deals. The scenario goes like this: 'Wizard Productions' discovers a band called 'The Young Hopefuls'. The band may not have any connections in the business or they may have been seen by many labels and still have no deal. Most hugely successful artists have been turned down by more than one major before they finally get signed. Major labels are not that interested in artist development. So 'Wizard' sees potential in the band and figures they can either produce a great album or find someone to produce a great album. The production deal is signed guaranteeing the artist either a fixed percentage of retail/wholesale price (with all the complex reductions and deductions) or a percentage of the production company's receipts. 'Wizard' then produces some demos, a few masters or a full album and shops the deal to the majors and larger independent labels. 'Wizard' pockets the difference between what they are able to get from the major and what they have to pay to the artist. As with a direct signing to a label the production costs, and varying percentages of video, marketing, promotion and tour support costs all come out of the artist's royalties. In some instances, the production company will be getting as much as 50 per cent of the income stream and the artist will get the other 50 per cent. It might be that 'Wizard Productions' is just one person. 'The Young Hopefuls' might be a five-piece with a manager taking 20 per cent off the top. In that case, the individual band members could be earning less than one per cent each even after recoupment whereas the production company could make substantially more although they have their costs and the risk of the time and money they initially invested in the project.

Production companies go in and out of favour. Many production companies fill a gaping need for artist development in the business. Sometimes, however, the artist's naiveté and desire to succeed can be taken advantage of. With success, artists learn more about the business, realise what is going on and rebel, as was the case of Bruce Springsteen with his first manager/producer Mike Appel. Springsteen had signed to Appel's company Laurel Canyon Ltd., and Appel signed Laurel Canyon to CBS. After two and a half albums, Springsteen and Appel fell out over money and production methods. When it came to court, Springsteen was eventually free to go with his succeeding manager/producer Jon Landau but not without conceding a substantial payout to Appel who argued, not without justification, that he had discovered Springsteen, nurtured him and supported him before the megabucks beckoned.

Sometimes the production company will refer to itself as a label but if the artist is not signing directly with the major or distributing label the deal is, in effect, a production deal. The press and VH1's *Behind The Music* has documented many of these situations that occasionally lead to bankruptcy for one reason or another, as was the case with the group TLC.

Perhaps the biggest jackpot of all went to American producer Shel Talmy, who in the early Sixties, was resident in London producing several bands that followed in the wake of The Beatles. One of them was The Who whom Talmy signed to a six-year production deal in 1964, giving them a 2.5 per cent royalty. He took their records to American Decca who released them in the UK on the Brunswick label, and who doubtless gave Talmy a royalty substantially in excess of 2.5 per cent. The Who's management soon realised how little they were earning and persuaded Talmy to increase their royalty to 4 per cent, but this was probably still far less than Talmy was getting. Worse was to come.

After three singles and one album The Who wanted out. They reckoned they could make better records and still more money without Talmy but he wouldn't budge. To force Talmy's hand, Who manager Kit Lambert took the group's next single, 'Substitute', to Robert Stigwood who put it out on his Reaction label (distributed through Polydor). Talmy sued, and in an out of court settlement was granted a five per cent royalty on all of The Who's records and singles for the next six years, up to and including *Who's Next* in 1971, i.e. much of their best selling work. He thus earned considerably more in royalties from The Who's record sales than the individual members of the band did. Even now, 30 years later, Talmy still collects pro rata royalties on every track The Who recorded up to 1971.

Many legendary artists have been through situations such as these. In some cases they can buy their way out of an unfavourable deal. There are fair and unfair production deals. Once success happens the points of view usually become polarised and the disagreements begin. The artist usually doesn't like getting paid less than they would if they were signed directly. They often come to think that the original producer or production company should just fade out of the picture after the first couple of albums and every artist eventually gets to a point where they would like to own their masters. The producer or production company owner who took the initial risk, often by pumping substantial amounts of time, money and expertise into breaking the project, feels justified in continuing to make money long after their direct involvement in the artist's career. Undoubtedly there are deals that are simply opportunistic in that the production company was in the right place at the right time to sign a naïve and talented artist to a long and parasitical deal. More often the artist would not have had the connections and expertise to traverse their way through the maze that is the music business without the production company.

The hip-hop scene is particularly adept at using the success of one artist to piggyback newcomers via production deals, producer or artist labels. These relationships vary greatly in their financial fairness but many artists are broken by using the smart marketing strategy of having the newcomer guest on the label's most successful artist's tracks or vice versa.

Chapter Ten

What Are the Timeless Ingredients in a Hit?

a) The Label

In previous editions of this book I started this list with "the song." I asked Lauren Christy of The Matrix this question and the first thing she said was "the right label, (and) the right president at the label. With Avril, we had the right label [Arista], L.A. Reid was totally ready to kick ass with her. He heard 'Complicated' and said 'Oh my goodness this is amazing'"

Lauren is the first producer I have spoken to who has mentioned these vital ingredients. Her comment was both insightful and an unfortunate sign of the times. With the increasing consolidation in the industry and constant buying, selling and merging of labels the chances of losing your A&R person, label or entire international music group, mid-production, has increased to the point of being a major obstacle in generating hits. Having said that, Lauren went on to say "I think you get into a very dangerous guessing game when you start trying to analyse if you should do a project because it's this person at this label. I never do that. All we try to do is concentrate on the creative side of it. Everyday, go to work, be creative, love what you do, put 100 per cent into it, and hope the stars align. I've had my heart broken before over records when I was younger. Now I'll never be attached to anything because, it's out of your control. It's down to the label and the president and the promotion department and whether that artist is going to press the self-destruct button. If I turn on MTV and see it, then I regain enthusiasm and think 'yeah it's happening.' But most of the time I think 'I've done my best, there's nothing I can do now."

This is also true. A good manager will help a producer to steer clear of volatile corporate situations but sometimes you just can't predict them so you have to focus on factors you can control and that brings me back to . . .

b) The Song

The next item on Lauren's list was "The right melody, the right lyric that's emotional – to me it has to be an emotional lyric – it has to be the right artist, the voice is very important."

T-Bone Burnett is pretty clear about this issue also. "I'm attracted to good songs and good singers and I don't want to distract too much from that. The way records used to be made is you'd hire an arranger, the first thing you'd write down was the melody line, and then everything would be voiced around the melody. We started going backward with multi-track recording. We'd put down a rhythm track and a hundred overdubs, get two 24-tracks filled in with music and then try to stick the vocal in the middle of all this sound. Jerry Wexler (the legendary Atlantic Records producer) called it 'track happy'. For me, it's gotta start with the song and the vocal performance."

Rick Rubin is just as emphatic when he says, "I think the most important thing a producer can do is spend time getting the songs into shape before recording. The material is so much more important than the sounds."

L.A. Reid, who went on to helm the labels Arista and then Island Def Jam said during his time with the incredibly successful L.A. and Babyface writing and production team, "The reason we're not that into high tech is because we try to concentrate on great lyrics and awesome grooves. If we spent all our time paying attention to technical tricks, then we'd never get around to the melody, which is the most important aspect of a song. After all, the melody is what we pick up on when we're listening to a song. And isn't that what loving music is all about – being a good listener?"

Ron Fair, A&M president says, "The most absolutely critical production move that you are going to make is, 'What is the song?' That is the most important thing. Everything else is secondary to me."*

Producer *extraordinaire* Jerry Wexler was responsible for many of the classic Sixties soul hits on Atlantic Records. Wexler states it very simply, "To me, a record comes down to a singer and a song; other elements must be subordinate."

---

* Doug Minnick, interview for Taxi, http://www.taxi.com/faq/av/fair.html

c) The Vocal

A great vocal is an undeniable essential on any record. After the song itself, the vocal performance is the next most significant factor that will make people pluck out their credit cards. Greatness in a vocal is very little to do with technical performance or recorded quality; these are the tangibles. A great performance is an intangible that is connected with the interpretation of the emotional content of the song. If you can get the tangibles and the intangibles on tape you're really flying. But focus on the tangibles too much and the intangible will fly right out of the window.

Barry Beckett, of the influential Muscle Shoals Rhythm section, produced an award winning vocal on a Bob Dylan album which he says was cut live. "He had been singing those songs over and over to himself, so he had them down backward and forward. He would just get it on the first pass, which blew me away. I did insist on trying to punch him in on one line, but we couldn't match the voice, so we just let it go. He later won the award for Best Vocal on that song, which was 'Slow Train Coming'. Beckett laughed, saying, "I went up to him later and said, 'I give up'. He just laughed."

"What I do is only as good as the vocal, particularly when I'm doing a remix," says Danny Saber. "If there's a good vocal then it's easy. A good vocal is not necessarily something that's sung really well. It's when the lyric goes with the voice that it's coming out of. When the whole thing clicks then that's special. You can't teach that to anybody, they've either got it or they haven't."

d) The Arrangement

When it comes to hit singles, after the song and the vocal perform-ance, the arrangement is paramount. It's often assumed that the arrangement is part of the songwriting process. Sometimes it is. But, very often the melodies, the chord sequences and the lyrics can all be in place, yet it isn't until the arrangement comes together that the song has that compelling, "I want to hear it again," quality.

"You nurture every song to make it as good as possible, but a single has to be attractive in a more obvious way," says Steve Lipson. "You don't always need a gimmick. The arrangement has to be exactly right, unquestionably. I learned a lot about that from Trevor [Horn]."

There are two parts to an arrangement. They are the orchestration and the structure. The orchestration is the instrumentation that you choose and the way those instruments work together in harmony, unison or counterpoint. Orchestration also covers the dynamic development or ebb and flow of the track such as extra parts coming in as the song develops, a bigger sound in the choruses, stops and starts, things dropping out such as in a breakdown section. Even the addition of reverb, delay, panning or other effects can be considered part of the orchestration.

No matter how beautiful the orchestration is if the structure of the song is less than optimum, you probably won't have a hit. Good structure is a vitally important part of a successful arrangement. The structure of a song is the order in which the different sections of the song are played, and the way they are joined together. If you think of a song as being a museum or art gallery full of amazing things the structure is like the guided tour. If you wandered around the museum on your own you could get lost and confused, even miss the best parts. Good song structure gives the song maximum impact on the first listen, helping the listener to learn the song as they discover it. At the same time a good structure is not so repetitive that the song doesn't bear repeated listens.

It's relatively rare that you come across a potential hit song in a bunch of demos where the structure and the orchestration are exactly right. If an artist can do that they might not need a producer at all. Usually the best you get is a few parts that are good such as a verse and chorus that make you think that the song could be a hit if it got the right treatment. It's not uncommon for a producer to have to generate new sections for a song. Typically that would include intros and outros and sometime bridges or, as they are called in the UK, middle-eights (even if they are not eight bars long).

Intros and outros rarely involve additional writing because you can usually co-opt a part from somewhere else in the song and with some manipulation of the orchestration make an attention grabbing intro and an unforgettable outro that demands to be heard again and again. Bridges are tricky. Often a bridge is a permutation of chords and or melodic ideas that already occur in the song but sometimes a bridge can go to a completely different harmonic and melodic place. Not all songs have bridges but a great one can make a song complete. Writing a brand new bridge constitutes a co-write. More often than not the producer has to change the order of the sections as they occur in the song – sometimes the lengths of sections and sometimes the way sections make the change to other sections. A few tweaks of this nature can make all the difference.

Common problems with demo arrangements are that the first verse or all the verses are too long. It's usually not good to take two minutes to get to the first chorus. Choruses are sometimes too long or too short. Lame intros really hurt your chances, you have to grab the listener's attention and a strong intro can make the difference between a radio program director jumping to the next track or listening through to the first chorus. Exiting the song on anything less than a great hook even if it's not the chorus is usually not smart. You can almost measure the quality of the writer by the quality of their bridges (in genres that use bridges). Probably the hardest thing to do when you are assessing a song is to maintain objectivity. If you find that you like a song the more often you listen to it that can point to a structural problem. A good structure helps the listener to appreciate a song more easily on the first few listens. A great song pretty much teaches itself to you. The intro says, listen up. The verse sets the scene and pulls you in, there might be a B section or channel that lifts you from the verse to the chorus and then the chorus drills right into your brain melodically, harmonically and with excitement or whatever emotion the song is trying to communicate.

Bridges are often a respite from the choruses and verses after the rest of the song has been stated and reiterated and they are often a lyrical variation or conclusion as well. The outro might simply repeat choruses, mix and match content from the body of the song or be a completely new section that nails you to the wall with its hook. Instrumental sections can be used as well as and sometimes instead of bridges and can also serve as a respite from the verse-chorus-verse cycle and allow some relief from the sound of the voice. A good instrumental can ratchet up the excitement before the last verse and chorus cycle leading to the outro. Where there is an outro and an instrumental often the instrument that played the instrumental solo will ad-lib throughout the outro, building in intensity to the fade or the end.

I have been talking in the terms of traditional songs here but in a lot of ways the rules still apply in other formats. A hip-hop track may not have a melody in the conventional sense but there are still melodic and rhythmic elements to the vocal that change from section to section. The dynamic elements also still have to change in a satisfying way to make the listener want to add the song to their personal playlist. The producer is really the last stand for a song. If you let poor structure, lacklustre orchestration, weak melodies or meandering harmonic structures slip through to the mix you are dooming the song to obscurity.

e) The Performance

"Production should always come secondary to capturing a moment," says Bruce Fairbairn. "None of the songs on *Pump* would have flown if the guys in Aerosmith hadn't played them great initially. Once you have something great on tape then you have a really good solid base to play around with ... adding the production aspects, mixing in texture and colour to the tracks."

Alan Parsons put it beautifully when he said, "Great records come from great moments – not from great equipment. No amount of knob twiddling can equal someone putting their all into a performance, whether it's a guitar solo, a drum part, even a tambourine part. You can EQ the voice or snare for four hours, but if they finally go out there and hit it properly you have to turn all the EQ off. To me that live thing is to do with the vibe and the confidence from the band all the way through from the beginning. It's got nothing to do with the technology."

When it comes down to it audio production is not so much about getting everything in tune, in time and recorded well. Most hits these days are in tune, in time and recorded well but they were hits for other reasons. Making a great track or album is about capturing a special energy or emotion that actually happens in the studio and then communicating that energy or emotion to the listener. To some extent you can fake energy and emotion using studio trickery but there is an old studio adage ... if you want a great guitar sound – get a great guitar player. You could take this as meaning that great guitar players know, technically speaking, how to get good sounds out of their equipment, but it really boils down to a living, breathing, thinking, feeling, human being's fingers on strings communicating what she is feeling.

The producer's job is to allow the performer the space to feel, and to reach for greatness or as Lauren Christy succinctly puts it – "to dare to suck." When the performance happens the producer has to capture it, discern the great from the good and then protect it all the way through to the mix. Even if everything is computer generated, unless you are actually trying to make a track that sounds like a 1950s robot, it's possible to capture a performance element. It might just be the vocal, but any time picks hit strings, fingers hit keys, sticks hit pads, faders fade or mice click there is an opportunity to capture a performance element. We're on the unceasing quest for the unquantifiable quality where one take can be perceived as being better than another. The differences may be subtle, but when you hit playback, even days, weeks or months later, you still know that take three has something that take four doesn't. Capturing and identifying this hard-to-define quality is in large part what producers get paid for.

f) The Engineering

Bruce Swedien said, "One thing I learned from Bill Putnam (one of the great engineering innovators of the Fifties and Swedien's early mentor) that carries over in my work now is thinking in purely musical terms – as far as recording the instruments – more than in technical terms."

"It's just one of my things, good quality is terribly important to a hit record," says Les Paul. "I don't know how many people have stopped me to ask if it is really all that important, when it's what's in the grooves that sells."

You don't have to look very far to find examples of hit records that don't sound so great. But, the really big records, and particularly the timeless, enduring ones, usually do sound excellent. It would be true to say that if a song is not good, the vocal is less than compelling and the arrangement or performance is under par, then the record will not be successful no matter how well engineered it is.

Having said that, good performances can be obscured by poor engineering. I have seen songs come to life just by being made to sound better. The best example is when an album is remixed because the company isn't getting excited about it. I'm not talking about radical club remixes just the ones where the overall sound quality is improved. Suddenly the whole company can get fired up. It's a wonderful listening experience when nothing hurts your ears, the highs are sweet, the middle smooth, the lows tight and deep. If the frequencies sound balanced, you can hear what's going on in the track, the individual sounds are powerful, you can feel the groove and the vocal grabs you, then the record will undoubtedly be a lot more effective than it would have been if the engineering was under par.

On a great track it can be hard to differentiate between production, engineering and arrangement, they are so symbiotic in terms of the way the track works its magic on you. "Even though in some ways they are discreet entities and may be done by different people they are incredibly interactive," says Andy Jackson. "If you look at [something like a] Frankie Goes To Hollywood record those things all worked together as a package. Not a great song but great records and justifiably big hits."

g) How Important Is The Mix Really?

I decided to remix a track that was about to be dropped from an album. We had serious doubts about the basic song. The remix took a pretty radical approach but didn't change the basic arrangement or instrumentation, just the overall balance and sounds. It worked out so well that the track became the first single from that album. Andy Jackson thinks that the mix is only important as a potential negative. He says, "You can screw up a great one but very rarely can you take a bad song and mix it into a hit." A mix should optimise the song, the vocal, the performances, the arrangement and the engineering. It should sound good on a wide range of high and low-end systems, loud and quiet, be appropriate for the applicable radio format and hold its own in terms of apparent loudness or excitement with comparable material.

h) Timeliness

No matter how perfect the song, the vocal, the playing, the sounds and the mix, if the album sounds like the last big trend (and especially if the band looks like it) you might just see it showing up in the cut-out bins next month. If they're one of the bands that spearheaded the original trend you've got a couple more months before it hits the budget racks. Then again if it sounds like the trend before last or the one before that . . . who knows?

i) The Heart

I have always held that there has to be some belief or heart in a recording for it to do well. Behind even the crassest pop ditty you will find a believer. The creators may know it's not high art, but they believe in what they are doing. Talking Heads' Jerry Harrison says, "I think it's some sort of heart that's the most important thing – really believing in what they're doing. This kind of goes back to what The Modern Lovers (his first band) always stood for, which was this idea that no matter what you were saying, you should really, truly, believe it – nothing should be fatuous in rock'n'roll. I still go along with that. I like people who are a little bit on a mission – things are important to them. It's not just about musicianship, it's about getting an idea across."

T-Bone Burnett says, "I couldn't tell you exactly what it is that makes most hit records successful. And I don't think I'm facile enough to sell out. You have to be able to do something you don't mean, and I'm not good enough to do something I don't mean and have it sound like anything. The only reason what I do sounds like anything at all is because I mean it."

"As producer, I felt that my function was to do the best job I could for an artist," says Mitchell Froom. "And if that occasionally meant going along with things and allowing myself to think in slightly conservative ways – thinking that we had to deliver some-thing that somebody commercially had a chance with – then I accepted that. But over the years I found that for me, personally, wherever I'd been more conservative I had failed." By 1991, he says, "The whole thing had come to a point where I felt that I wanted to go down in flames. I didn't want to be someone who would become more and more conservative. I wasn't happy with that at all. So I said, 'I'll go out with a bang and find people who also want to do that'.

"I don't feel any more as if I'm just there to serve the artists as best I can. That's of course still the ultimate aim of my job, but my focus has changed to trying to get to the bottom of what an artist is about and challenging them to be as innovative and adventurous as they dare to be."

"I learned from Quincy Jones to listen to your instincts," says Bruce Swedien. "That's hard for a lot of people in our business. We have a tendency to cerebralise what we are doing and it's wrong. Music is organic in the human being. What we are doing must provoke an emotional response, not a cerebral response. There is a big difference between a 'beat' and a 'groove.' I'll go for a groove any day. The beat is repetition, but a groove can have dynamics and be very emotional."

Quincy Jones himself says, "I've done three or four things in my life with artists where I really knew that it wouldn't work, where I got talked into it or pressured. I won't bring up any names, but what that confirmed to me was that you have to love and adore the sound the artist makes and adore the person too. Because that's the same sound really, the pain or eccentricity or neurosis or whatever it is, that's where it comes from. Once that happens, you can treat the artist almost like you're an X-ray machine – to go into them emotionally and musically, which is all tied together anyway – I know this sounds abstract – and to feel what is their range and where is their heart, their emotional centre. Then you know what gives them goose bumps; the kind of chord sequences and sonorities and colours or whatever it is that does it. I love to give singers I work for goose bumps all the time."

It sounds like what I'm saying is that you have to have some deep artistic vision that you are pursuing relentlessly and I don't believe that is true. I do think it's hard to make a great production from a cynical point of view. At the same time producers can be chameleons, it's one of the best things about the job, and one person's art is another person's garbage. Ideally you find that point of confluence where love of the music, respect for the artist and sense of satisfaction from doing a great job meet.

j) Are These Rules To Which There Are Exceptions?

There are no hard and fast rules in the music business. There will always be hits that defy explanation. Songs that aren't particularly good, records that don't sound great with singers that can't sing become hits every now and then. If you are trying to figure out what works it serves no purpose to emulate the exceptions. The simple fact is the same basic principles apply today as they did 10, 20, 30, even 50 and more years ago, right back to the earliest popular music recordings. The sound of recorded music has changed almost beyond recognition. But, on most very big hits, there is still a song with a memorable melody or hook, an interesting lyric, a singer with a distinctive character and well arranged and orchestrated instrumental parts. This is just as true if you look at commercially successful rap or alternative records as on 'White Christmas' by Bing Crosby.

If anything, perhaps the biggest change over the last 60 or 70 years has been the increasing dominance of vocal recordings. Through the first half of the history of recorded music instrumental records by artists such as Louis Armstrong, Duke Ellington, Count Basie and Glenn Miller occupied a chunk of the charts. These days, instrumental records are marginally more common than the dinosaur.

Chapter Eleven

Frequently Asked Questions

a) How Much Can You Learn, How Much Is Natural Ability?

Actually a great deal of the job is to do with instinct. Flood said, "So much of what one does has to be based on instinct. From there you use your experience to refine, hone, change and question your original instinct." I wouldn't even venture a guess as to how much of the ability to produce is nature versus nurture but I believe what Flood is talking about is the instinct that develops from being around music, musicians and studios way too much. This is why DJ's with little or no musical or technical ability often become excellent producers. They listen to tons of music, they see first hand how people respond to certain things more than others and effectively program themselves to reproduce the same kind of excitement in their own tracks.

I played in a lot of Top 40 bands when I was young. I resented it at the time because I wanted to play original material but later when I started to write and produce, I realised that having to learn and play all those hits had instilled in me an instinct for what works and what doesn't. I didn't have to think about how to construct a hit. I just knew. Lauren Christy of The Matrix was saying that her partner in life and in producing, Graham, "comes from playing in his Dad's band when he grew up in Scotland and he knows every genre of music inside out. He can write a song in two minutes. He's just amazing." This is a great help when you are producing diverse styles of artists as they do. Production values vary somewhat from one type of music to another and from one era to another. But the basic rules of song structure don't change much and since the music you produce will most likely be similar to the music you like, the more you listen the sharper your instinct gets.

b) How Do You Pick The Right Project?

Jerry Harrison: "I read a thing where [engineer] Dave Jerden said he really only wants to produce bands that he'd play in. And I kind of feel like that, too. Like Poi Dog Pondering – I love them, and it was great to work with them."

Doing projects for the wrong reasons is never a good idea. It's easy if you're a producer with broad musical taste and a good solid musical grounding to look at a project and see right away what needs to be done. You can even do a very good job without really liking the music. I've done it both successfully and unsuccessfully. But, there's not much satisfaction to be gained from working on an album if you don't really love the music.

Sandy Roberton: "It's the right projects. It's so easy to get tempted to take a project just because you need the money. But it might be the wrong project. It's important to be very selective. It's hard because producers panic if they're not working. I think they should really consider doing something else, like actors. The ones who are selective about what they do their career goes on." There's no doubt that it's better to take time off than do a project that is not a good fit.

c) Do Producers Have Their Own Sound?

Some producers definitely do. It's pretty easy to recognise a Jam and Lewis track or Babyface or Quincy Jones. Rick Rubin thinks he has a sound based more on what he doesn't like than what he does. He doesn't like reverb and he likes to capture a performance. He says, "I hate technically slick records that have no sense of emotion or of the artist's performance, and all my records sound like the artist – whether it be The Beastie Boys or LL Cool J or The Cult or Slayer or The Masters Of Reality. I'm not one of those producers who has a stock sound and then adds different personalities on the top as icing."

Flood doesn't think he has a sound but his manager Ros Earls says she can recognise the sound of his records right away. I never wanted to have a sound. One of the things that drove me to produce in the first place was that I was fed up with producers trying to make their album for my band. I thought that the producer's job was to realise the artist's vision. And of course that depends on the type of artist and how experienced they are. The only way a producer can really escape having a sound is to let the artist and the material dictate the engineering and production techniques. To avoid stamping your personality on a record you need to have very broad taste in sounds and musical styles. You either need to be versatile technically and musically or have a diverse range of people to work with.

Nonetheless, if you bother to show up at the studio at all, it's going to be impossible for your productions to be 100 per cent transparent. As Rick Rubin said, your dislikes will define your sound as clearly as your likes. Even the kinds of acts that you choose to work with and the kind of material that you pick can be sonic clues as to your involvement.

d) Should You Get Involved In The Song Writing?

It may be that the very reason why you are producing the act is because you wrote the song. This is very common on R&B and pop projects. The issue of whether to get involved in the writing becomes sticky when you are dealing with a singer-songwriter or a self-contained band. Given that it is the producer's job to make the best possible album for the artist and that the material is the most fundamental element of any record, it would be irresponsible for a producer not to try to improve material that he knew could be better.

It does make a difference how you go about it. In the first instance you can try to stimulate the band into fixing the problem. You might say "You know, that chord change into the bridge just isn't comfortable," or point out that a particular part of a song is weak and could be improved. Sometimes this will work. The band will rise to the occasion and come up with a better idea. Oftentimes the artist either does not agree, doesn't understand, doesn't know what to do about it or comes up with an alternative that is no better. At this point someone (read the producer) has to make a musical suggestion that can be used 'as is' or as a starting point to get to an artist-generated solution. Now you are involved in the writing. The issue is when do you take credit for it.

"Songwriting is not my job," says Bruce Fairbairn. "My job is to help a band create the album they want to make. If I do happen to contribute something writing-wise, unless it's a big, big deal, I'll let it go. If I have an idea and it's going to make for a better song, then it's worth incorporating it. I'm not rewriting choruses for these guys, and

I don't take songwriting credit. I'm more involved in structuring and arranging the song. You've got to work that way, though. If you bring up an idea and the guys in the band aren't threatened that they're going to lose 10 per cent of a song over it, they'll be much more inclined to listen to what you have to say. If you start arguing over every chord change, bridge or word, then that's just counter productive to the project."

What he says here is exactly right. If you are writing choruses you should definitely take the credit. If you're restructuring or arranging material the artist wrote, that's part of a producer's job. If you get into altering chord sequences, melodies or lyrics, you have to make an assessment on a case-by-case basis. You don't want to be stupid about it and write songs for artists that you don't get paid for but as Bruce Fairbairn says you're much more likely to be able to improve the song if your motivation is not in question.

Speaking about their producer Mitchell Froom, Neil Finn of Crowded House said, "Mitchell is a very musical guy, far more so than many who claim to be producers. He gets involved in arrangements and song structure, makes suggestions for the odd chord change here and there."

Even a producer like Steve Lipson (who made his début as the techno-wiz on Trevor Horn productions for groups such as Frankie Goes To Hollywood and Propaganda) says of his production input, "I can write songs, that's how I got started. I'm still 100 per cent involved in arrangements and instrumentation. It varies from song-to-song, and from artist-to-artist. With certain artists I'll reconstruct the song completely from head to foot, play it, not play it, change the chords, change the key, whatever it takes."

Songwriting proved to be the engine that propelled Shep Pettibone from the top of the remix mountain to the top of the production mountain. He had been working with Madonna on remixes of her records and got the opportunity to produce a B-side which turned out to be the massive hit 'Vogue'. Pettibone decided to start putting some more tracks together for her and dropped a cassette of the tracks off to her while she was filming *In A League Of Their Own* in Chicago. She liked all three. This was to be the beginning of Shep's co-production gig on the *Erotica* album; Pettibone wrote the music and Madonna the lyrics. Sometimes he would give her some ideas for lyrics and she would say, "Oh, that's good," or "That sucks." When he did this for the song "Vogue" she very curtly said, "That's what I do." Pettibone adds, "Essentially, her songs are her stories. They're the things she wants to say."

e) New Versus Established Artists?

There is no confusion in Walter Becker's mind when he says, "As a producer, I'd like to work with new artists, and with bands who write their own material. Many established artists have it covered in the studio and know how to do it. I'd like to work with people on their first albums, with artists who need someone to help them capture it."

As a producer you will have a different relationship with a début artist than you will with one who is well established. Even for an experienced producer, working with a musical legend can be intimidating. Barry Beckett produced Bob Dylan's *Slow Train Coming* album. "It took Bob three or four days, while we were cutting, to even trust me. When he finally did, he let me know with a very slight smile, or something like that, to say I was OK. I was pretty nervous when we started."

Most producers will get started by producing new artists. Once you have some success under your belt you have to decide whether you want to increase your odds of having a hit by working with established artists or stay at the sharp end working on début albums. A very rough rule of thumb is that the major label success rate is around four to five per cent. This means that approximately one out of 20 artists signed to a major label will recoup and go on to make more albums. Obviously an established artist is already one of the elite band of moneymakers. Their next album has a greater chance of making money than a new artist's does. They already have a fan base, radio and TV are going to be more receptive and the company wants to capitalise on what it's already developed. The downside of producing an established artist, especially if you didn't produce the initial hit, is that a failure would be highly visible. Creatively you have more control and it can be more satisfying to work with a new artist who really needs your expertise.

Established artists can be more difficult to deal with, they have an identity that they usually want to maintain. You may have to work within fairly tight constraints. They're often surrounded by yes-people and you'll be working on their schedule, in their choice of location rather than yours. On the other hand, it can be very exciting to work with someone whose ideas you respect, you can learn a great deal and it's nice to know that someone other than the artist's mother is waiting for the record to come out.

f) What About The All-Important Credits?

Credits are not to be taken lightly. A credit can in some cases be more important than the money in keeping the producer working and building his resume. Maybe the average person doesn't look at the producer credits but the industry certainly does. Pete Ganbarg talked about how he goes about choosing a producer. "It's a very fun process for an A&R person because all A&R people should be music junkies. This is an opportunity to go through their music collection and say, 'OK, this act that I've just signed really owes a lot to these types of songs or these types of artists.' Usually there are two or three names that keep popping that you feel are kindred spirits to the artist you signed. You start making a wish list [which] is five names, 10 names, 15 names. You have the band do one as well and you cross-reference the lists. You come up with a final wish list of maybe half a dozen names." Obviously in order to get chosen via a process like this you need to have the correct credit on the albums you work on.

i) Executive Producer

The executive producer is often someone in a position of power who has some overall responsibility for the success of the artist or project. It may be the artist's manager (Peter Grant was credited as executive producer on every Led Zeppelin album), the A&R person (Jeff Fenster on the *Fast And Furious* soundtrack) or the president of the record company (Clive Davis on Whitney Houston albums).

Executive producers can be multiple people, each of whom earned their credit in different ways. These may include the person who created the concept for the project, put the deal in place, championed the project throughout the label processes, financed the whole thing, put the team together or was a spiritual guru to the artist. The executive producer is analogous to the film producer as opposed to the record producer who is more like a film director.

The music journalist and Omnibus Press editor (of this book), Chris Charlesworth, is now credited as executive producer on virtually all of The Who's back catalogue. "That was because it was my idea to revitalise their back catalogue by adding bonus tracks and a handsome 24-page booklet to every album," he says. "Of course, I've

196

never produced a record in my life by working with an artist in a studio, but if it hadn't been for me, these new deluxe, remastered re-issues of The Who's old albums probably wouldn't exist. I helped choose the bonus tracks, edited the booklet texts and generally looked after the packaging and quality control."

Charlesworth's relationship with The Who goes back to the early Seventies when he wrote about the band extensively for the *Melody Maker* newspaper. In 1993, it was he who approached Pete Townshend, suggesting The Who release a retrospective box set. Charlesworth wound up compiling the tracks and generally over-seeing the project on The Who's behalf. When *30 Years Of Maximum R&B*, a four-CD Who box set, was released, Charlesworth was actually credited as producer, along with Jon Astley (a 'real' producer, and Townshend's brother-in-law, incidentally) who did the studio re-mastering work, and Bill Curbishley, the band's long-time manager.

The executive producer's role in music is not well understood. Day-to-day involvement can range from active and highly involved to saying "hi" once on the phone. Perhaps because of this there is a sense among some producers and artists that the title is just a credit snatch by someone in a position to do so. In fact the executive producer title really exists to credit those who perform a critical role in bringing an album or track into existence. You may not see this person in the studio on a day-to-day basis but he or she can be highly instrumental in making the project happen in the first place, the overall shape of the album and sometimes the selection of material, producer(s) and mixes.

ii) Album Producer
This is a relatively new descriptor that has begun appearing in the past couple of years. It appears mainly on multi-producer albums in place of or as well as the executive producer credit. Coordinating and guiding the overall direction of a multi-producer album is a task in itself and has traditionally fallen to the A&R person, the artist's manager and/or with high profile artists, the head of the label. Executive producer is not a GRAMMY qualifying category and neither is A&R direction. Producers receive an album of the year GRAMMY, executive producers don't. This seems to be driving those performing the executive producer function towards using an album producer credit or even just a producer credit. The film industry governs the use of such credits via the guild's rules. The Recording

Academy accepts producer credits as listed on an album unless there is clear evidence of deception.

iii) Producer

Short and sweet, the producer credit is usually reserved for the individual who is responsible for the creative and practical day-to-day aspects of making the record. Most of what I talk about in this book applies to the 'producer' or 'co-producer' role. This is the role that qualifies for GRAMMY nomination and the Brit awards.

iv) Co-producer

Usually a co-production credit will indicate an ad hoc team, say, producer with the artist or producer with the songwriter. There may be a hierarchy such as: 'Produced by, 'Co-produced by.' Generally formal production teams even though, technically, they are each co-producers will be credited: Produced by The Matrix, Produced by The Neptunes, Produced by L.A. and Babyface, Produced by Jam and Lewis, etc. Frequently production teams comprise a musician and an engineer, or a songwriting team. Co-production can also mean that the producer collaborated with the artist. Sometimes artists want a co-production credit. This type of joint production credit can be a token gesture to the artist or it can be a full-blown collaborative co-production. It's very rare that an artist makes absolutely no contribution to the production but more experienced artists very often recognise that their contribution is really a normal part of being the artist and are happy to let the producer have the 'Produced by' credit.

v) Associate Producer

This credit was more common in the Eighties than it is today and in the US more than in Europe. Generally it is given to a less-established producer who is working under a veteran. The veteran may not be in the studio all the time and may be leaning towards the executive producer or album producer type of role. The associate producer is very often a musician or songwriter with studio skills who is trying to catch a break into the full production career.

vi) Additional Production By

This is a very poorly defined and often misleading credit. It's frequently given to remixers and it can mean that only minor changes were made to the track such as a little extra percussion in the chorus, muting some tracks, adding a harmony here and there. Additional production can sometimes be added to the credits list without the prior knowledge of the producer. It's less than gratifying to pick up an album that you spent months producing and see an additional production credit given to someone who spent a few days mixing and who is getting their legitimate 'mixed by' credit. If you have some clout as a producer it is possible to contractually bar the use of other producer credits such as this. On the other hand, in the case of dance remixes where considerable chunks of the original production have been replaced, 'additional production' is not only warranted, in some cases it is a major understatement of what actually took place. In a situation where everything but the lead vocal was replaced 'additional production' is, hardly accurate or adequate. Recently 'Remix Produced by' has been used to better reflect reality on mixes where everything but the lead vocal was replaced. Credits such as these should be negotiated up front and may be restricted by the original producer's contract.

vii) Multiple Producer Credits

It used to be that, in most genres, one producer or production team would produce the whole album. In contrast R&B labels have long used different producers for different tracks on an album. In many cases this has been because the producer was also the songwriter. Nowadays all genres are open to the use of different producers for different tracks on an album. The multi-producer album became a fixture in the early Eighties. R&B, pop and hip-hop records are more likely than other genres to have multiple producers because of the predominance of writer-producers. With the advent of radio consolidation in the US and generally pop dominated charts around the world most albums don't sell without a slam dunk hit single. So writer-producers such as The Matrix are more likely to be called upon to generate hit singles for artists such as Avril Lavigne. There are other reasons for using multiple producers on an album. The producer of choice might not be available for the whole project or may be too expensive to do all the tracks. Sometimes the album is delivered but the label thinks it is short of a hit single and another producer is brought in to generate it. Alternative, indie or rock bands that write all their own material still tend to go with a single producer, production team or co-producer for the complete record.

viii) Recorded By

This is really like a chief engineer credit. It usually indicates respon-sibility for the sonic side of the production and, maybe but not necessarily, hands-on involvement. There may be a studio 'house' engineer or assistant engineer who actually does the knob twiddling but the supervising chief engineer or producer still gets the 'recorded by' credit.

ix) Engineered By

This is a pretty self-explanatory credit for the person who twiddles the knobs and generally takes hands on control of all the technical aspects of recording the album or track.

x) Mixed By

Traditionally this was an American credit given to the engineer who mixed the record irrespective of whether the producer was present or not. Lately the boundaries of what constitutes a 'mix' have become blurred. Most commonly 'mixed by' is the credit given to the person or persons who controlled the first released set of mixes. Generally speaking if the bulk of the material used in the mix is the original material recorded by the producer, the person who mixed it will get a 'Mixed by' credit. Some producers feel that they should either get the 'Mixed by' credit or be a part of it especially when they are pres-ent for the mixes and they are mixed by the same engineer who recorded the album. The 'Mixed by' credit will go to someone like Tom Lord-Alge or Bob Clearmountain who specialise in mixing and where usually either the producer is not present at all or is there but makes a minimal contribution.

xi) Remixed By or Remix Produced By

Indicates that this is not the first released mix and/or the mix contains a high proportion of new material. Dance remixes will almost always be credited in this way, as will hip-hop 12" mixes. Generally the person who does club remixes will have replaced a great deal if not all of the original production work. A very common process is for the dance remixer to take just the vocal and build up a completely new track underneath it. They may sample the vocal and just use fragments of it. The track may be at a completely different tempo. The dance remixer's version is often so far removed from the original (for better or for worse) that it is more like a re-production than a remix.

Recently some remixers have been going for the 'Remix Produced by' credit. This is common on hip-hop remixes. A good example is Nelly's track 'Airforce Ones – the Remix' (Nelly, David Banner, 8-Ball), David Banner is credited as remix producer. This mix is a radical departure from the original 'Airforce Ones', which was produced by The Trackboyz. Many hip-hop remixers will utilise most of the original track elements, sometimes stretching the track out a bit, adding a couple of ideas, and then having different rappers performing on top of it all. The track 'Rubberband Man,' by the artist TI, is an example of this. Twista, Mack 10 and Trick Daddy all contributed vocals to the club remix. The track remained pretty much the same (the producer in both cases was David Banner), although just to confuse things, he's credited as 'Lavell DB Crump' on the album version. The album version has a 'mixed by' credit and the club mix has a 'Remix mixed by' credit.

xii) Programmed By
In formats such as dance, hip-hop and pop much or all of the tracks are programmed. Sometimes on multiple levels via machines such as the Akai MPC drum-machine-sampler-sequencers, on software virtual synth and virtual drum machine plug-ins, as well as many kinds of looping and digital recording software. In some cases the producer is also the programmer but the different areas of sampling, looping, beat making and programming are getting so specialised that usually at least one separate programmer will be involved and often there is a long list of programmers credited. Producers very often use the same programmer(s) over a long period of time so this credit is popping up more and more on 12″ labels and in CD booklets.

xiii) Edits By
Sometimes you will see 'remix and edits by' or 'additional production and edits by'. Editing used to be done by the producer or engineer cutting up a copy (sometimes the original) quarter or half-inch tape. In the 12″ remix world editing is a very important part of a successful mix and this function like everything else is now done digitally using software such as Pro Tools or Nuendo. Sometimes the original producer or mix engineer will do the edits but the job is increasingly being farmed out to specialist editors who also get a credit.

201

g) What Are The Best Moments?

Coaxing a great performance out of a singer, or instrumentalist can be a huge buzz. It's especially gratifying when the performer recognises that something special has happened, that he or she has gone beyond anything they've ever achieved before. You can practically measure the electricity in the air when a musician plays an off-the-wall but perfect part that transforms a track from the ordinary to the extraordinary. It's a great moment when you realise that the first take of a rhythm track, vocal or solo you just did, is utterly breathtaking, or when the artist first hears a mix and can't believe how incredible it sounds.

"Great playing, great musicians," says Andy Jackson. "When something fabulous happens, something that moves you. That thing that made us all do this in the first place, that got so fouled and embittered with the years. We stopped listening to music for fun many years ago. Occasionally, you get that spark that you remember, 'This was like when I was 14.' It just occasionally happens."

h) Why Are There So Few Female Record Producers?

There is no clear answer to this question. My best guess is that it's because there have been fewer female artists and musicians in the studio world in general. From the engineering side it is still relatively rare to find a woman who rises beyond the assistant engineer role. I can't account for this, except that maybe women find the hours too socially debilitating, especially in the early years when you have little control over your schedule. As Lauren Christy of The Matrix said "sitting around the studio until 2 in the morning, for women, is probably not the best career to have."

I have worked with several female assistants and a couple of excellent engineers and having a woman in the studio seemed to keep things somewhat more civilised. It can get pretty wild with a bunch of guys locked up together in a studio for months on end. The female presence can be a moderating factor. The flip side of that coin as Peter Collins points out is that "for a lot of guys to have a woman in the studio around is inhibiting." He thinks that might be in part because men tend to curse a lot. I'm sure we've all met plenty of women in and out of the business who can hold their own in the cursing department but oftentimes having a woman in the studio as

Peter says "makes it uncomfortable for at least one person in the band." Odd as it may be there is some truth in that statement. I've had male band members completely nix the idea of a female anywhere on the team.

Surveys by Technet and *EQ* magazine verified the fact that very few women work at the sharp end of record production or engineering. The results showed that women held mainly administrative and support positions. The survey showed less than 20 per cent of all technical positions held by women and less than two per cent of those in 'First' or 'Lead' positions. Evaluating a list of factors that have led to the scarcity of women in audio production, women themselves cited a lack of prominent role models and a lack of encouragement by primary and secondary educators.

Gender discrimination was regarded as being a lesser or secondary force determining the number of successful women in audio. Perhaps the higher incidence of female artists and all-girl bands since the Eighties will result in some of them going into production.

Certainly this is how Lauren Christy of The Matrix got started: "When I was 18, I worked at a publishing company and I thought, 'well, I want my songs heard so I guess I'm going to have to be an artist.' I got a four-track and did these demos at home. In those days you thought you were going to get a male producer who would make you sound amazing and that's it. You thought you would go work with a man and there was nothing wrong with that. Someone said there was a magic on my four-track and I didn't realise that it was my production. I just thought it was my songs. I got a deal and started to work with lots of male producers who were all wonderful in their own way and I'm sure I drove most of them crazy being so involved. I made two albums and the second album I got a production credit on because I was so involved. So I just thought I deserved it.

Then I had a rude awakening that it's really hard to be successful in this business. The stars don't always align for you and I was 27 years old. It was time for me to start thinking about not being an artist. I wasn't an ingénue any more. I met Sandy Roberton, he was trying to get me a new record deal and I realised I was too old for this. That was really a turning point for me where I faced reality and realised I wanted to be behind the scenes. My husband Graham was in a similar situation, Scott Storch had been doing remixes and saw that he couldn't go any further with that, so the three of us decided to do this project and see what it would be like to form a production company.

We had no money. It was all about desperation. We got two gorgeous actresses who could sing a little bit and we realised we could make a superb sound. We'd be up until four in the morning making this big production to make up for their weak vocals and we thought 'wow, this is amazing.' Then someone was looking for something for Christina Aguilera's record and asked if we could write something. We stayed up all one weekend, knocked out a song and that was our big break. We co-produced 'The Fear.'"

I asked Lauren what advice she would give to young women who are interested in becoming producers and she said, "Listen to music. Analyse what you like about it. Try to study writing. Try to get into that. Find a good manager. Find a mentor. Obviously, I don't come from an angle of being a studio engineer. I know that is one way to go, but it's not the route that I took. For me, sharing the success and finding partnerships is the key to being a good producer. I wouldn't have become a producer without my partners. I think at this point I've done so much of it, I know what to do. Give me a great song and an engineer and I could probably do it, but it wouldn't be as much fun. You can't do everything."

On the subject of women producers Wendy Page who produces as part of a team with Jim Marr said, "There ought to be more! I think before the advance of computers and home studios, production in music was a man's world. Many great female artists have co-produced but it is unusual to find a woman who is solely a producer. I think the powerful side of the business, i.e. record labels, are male-dominated and more than a little mistrustful of giving a woman the reins of an immense, creative project like making a record. Remember you are talking about thousands of dollars of budget, intense pressure on the artists/bands to come up with the goods and extra besides. Then there are the sheer politics of fame – Is the producer known? Do they have a good track record? Have they produced hits? So it is hard for women to break into this field. However, if you are determined, patient, obscenely hard-working and have a talent in music, you can break through.

"The ridiculous hours don't attract women, I'm sure. The fact that you go into a recording studio and often don't come out until dawn, does not appeal to many of my female friends! They see behind the glamour of working in the music business and have long come to accept my obsession with music. There is never enough time, of course. I swear, when you are making music time speeds up and suddenly hours disappear down a black hole somewhere! The sacrifices you have to make. I do not have a normal home life. Usually, recording whole albums takes a little shorter than three months. From conception to mastering though can be a longer span. If the experience has been total, i.e. if you have been involved in all the writing, it is mentally and emotionally exhausting. You live and breathe the record. It does not leave much time for having babies. Songs are and always will be my babies, although I hope someday to add a few real ones! Relationships can suffer too with the anti-social hours and shop talk. It is easier if you are involved with someone who understands the creative process and is patient."

Having said all that, Wendy still says, "I love music, I love my job. I consider myself blessed to be able to do this and I cannot imagine living my life without singing and songs." Speaking about particular difficulties that a female producer may encounter in the business, she said, "The difficulties are usually very short-lived. Once people realise that you can do your job, sexism tends to lower its ugly head. I tend to create a happy studio 'family' where everyone is glad to be there, especially the artist. Good communication and diplomacy usually sorts any little problems out."

As to whether there are advantages in having a female producer she points out that, "the studio experience is less intimidating for female artists, particularly if they are very young." She quickly adds the caveat that "if I accept that this is an advantage then I am conceding to a stereotype of female producers being more sympathetic and sensitive." She thinks that it's important to be "the best producer you can be for the artist in question. You want them to be able to trust you with their music. Gender should become irrelevant." For girls trying to break into producing Wendy recommends that they "learn as much as they can about music and develop a thick skin!" She suggests learning an instrument at least well enough to write with. "See as many gigs as you can. Get yourself a home computer set-up. Garageband is fantastic. Remember you cannot fail you can only quit."

Linda Perry is equally perplexed as to why there are fewer female producers, "If this question was asked in the late 1800's I might have had a good reply. But being in 2004, well, I'm a little stumped. I would assume it's the same reason there a few females running major record labels, networks, and most executive positions." Linda has produced a number of female artists such as Pink, Christina Aguilera,

Courtney Love, Gwen Stefani. I wondered if this was something she consciously preferred to do, "Pink and Courtney found me, Christina and Gwen, I went after. All four of these women are incredibly talented in so many ways, how they turned up in my life doesn't even come into question, I just know I'm lucky that they did."

I also asked her if she thinks that a female producer brings a different quality to a project than a male producer or if she thinks that the differences are producer-to-producer and largely gender neutral? "As an artist I have worked with many male producers, three of them completely free of ego, open to my suggestion, very creative and we collaborated well, which made for a wonderful experience because it was equal. Four of them completely full of themselves, made me feel less than, never heard a word I said, not open to suggestion, and very disrespectful. Basically intimidated and threatened by my presence – obviously not a healthy creative environment. I have come to realise that the reason why I had a good experience with the three is that our characters made a connection. The four others . . . we had no connection . . . which caused friction. As a female producer, I feel I bring in all qualities mentioned, but ultimately it comes down to the connection with the artist."

Children's and traditional music producer, Cathy Fink, points out that in the children's music and folk world "there are certainly women artists that get involved in producing their stuff." But there is a big disparity. She thinks that being engineers has helped her and team mate Marcy Marxer. "We're not full-time engineers, we're not the best engineers out there but it's put us in the position where we can know what it is that we want to tell an engineer what it is that we want. There certainly are some really fine women producers but I think it is in line with many other places in the work world where it is a harder place for women. There are not that many people out there succeeding and doing it on a major level."

Gail 'Sky' King got into producing through running errands for Arthur Baker. She became an assistant engineer but preferred production and moved towards that via editing and remixing. The production work evolved out of radical remixes where only the original vocal is kept and the track is completely recreated. She got married and had a child. To try to accommodate this change in her lifestyle she built a home studio. She has had some negative experiences, which she attributes solely to the fact that she is a woman in a man's world. She also thinks that some men are just not comfortable with women in the studio. She says, "Opportunities are so few and far between that you just can't afford to chuck 'em. So if you get a chance to do this, there can't be any half-stepping. Don't go out there and be all fluff and no substance."

Female engineers who have amassed considerable credits for themselves are Leslie Ann Jones who is a staff engineer at Capitol Records and Susan Rogers who started in the business as a field service technician for MCI and became famous for her work with Prince. Sylvia Massy who has also worked with Prince has gone on to engineer and produce alternative groups such as Tool and Skunk Anansie.

There are, of course, many female artists who either co-produce or produce themselves: Beyoncé, Madonna and Kate Bush being obvious examples. Patrice Rushen is an amazing musician who has fired off some blistering jazz-fusion solos behind John McLaughlin and Jean Luc Ponty, wrote and sang the funky pop hit 'Forget Me Nots,' arranged strings for Prince and garnered several firsts as a woman MD for TV award shows. She finally occupied the producer's chair on Sheena Easton's 'The Nearness Of You' for the movie *Indecent Proposal*. This led to an album of jazz standards, *No Strings*, which Rushen also produced.

i) Can You Successfully Genre Hop?

i) Advantages And Disadvantages
Only market research people think that an individual listens exclusively to one type of music. Very few people have singular taste in music. Producers are no exception to this rule. In fact most have much wider taste than the public at large. This is partly because of a general love of music and partly because they have been exposed to a wide range of music. Some producers find it frustrating to be restricted to producing one type of music. I've genre hopped a great deal in my career and there can be a cost to doing that. A&R people have more difficulty placing you with acts.

Veteran A&R person Muff Winwood said, "Artists are very often looking for someone whose last four albums sound exactly the way they want their next album to sound." OK, fair enough. It's reassuring to be able to listen to someone else's record and say that's how I want my record to sound. If the artist doesn't mind a cookie cutter approach to the production of their record then they probably won't be disappointed. The biggest, greatest and/or most influential records were not made this way, they were made by single-minded individuals or groups pursuing a singular vision with creativity and originality, influenced but not dictated to by current trends. The most obvious reference is the man himself – George Martin. His history prior to producing The Beatles was more to do with comedy and classical recordings and it's no stretch to say that his experience in those formats – with both the humour and the orchestration – had a unique influence on The Beatles' recordings that any other pop producer would not have had.

Having a cross-genre track record effectively diminishes the impact of your bio/resume/CV as far as any particular artist is concerned. Artists and A&R people can sometimes be quite limited in their appreciation of other musical types. If you are discussing work with an alternative artist, your R&B or country hits will probably mean very little to them or may even be a negative. They might not have heard of the records you did outside of their genre. Artists and A&R people often have difficulty mentally translating production techniques from another genre into what you might be able to do for them. If anything, the most effective way of using a cross-genre track record is to have successfully produced enough different styles of music so the only logical conclusion is that you can produce any-thing. If the artist is somewhat of a hybrid they are more likely to have broad musical taste and be able to hear that your influences match with the various flavours in their own music. It also helps if your hits were huge, multi-platinum albums allay a certain amount of fear.

I believe if you are capable of putting together a great record at all, then you can probably make a great record in any musical style that you have a genuine passion for. The fundamental rules of production remain pretty constant across the genre lines. The details will change but a good producer sees beyond stylistic details. Nonetheless producers do get genre-bound. The All-Singing-All-Dancing producer may be more likely to become typecast than another type of producer. They are, by definition, responsible for so much of the character of the record, they tend to pin their stylistic colours to the mast.

Of all producers to fall foul of typecasting, the last person you would expect it to happen to would be Phil Ramone. His career has been so long and diverse that you would think his versatility was a given, but when he tried to branch out into country he was thwarted.

"You're typecast from day one as a rock producer," he says. "I was a big fan of Lyle [Lovett], we were about to make a record and then the country people got scared that I would take him somewhere else."

ii) Who Has Done It?
I couldn't bear to be stuck in one format. Although my background was jazz and rock, my first break came producing computer generated pop music. I then went through the pop/alternative of Spandau Ballet and King. Success with urban/R&B projects came in the form of Colonel Abrams, New Edition, Melba Moore and Five Star followed by a hit with the blue-eyed soul group, Living In A Box. I then moved back to alternative/modern rock with Shriekback and XCNN. Along the way were all kinds of pop, dance and ambient projects as well as TV and film music.

Peter Collins has successfully produced artists as diverse as Rush, Philip Bailey and Phil Collins, Bon Jovi, Musical Youth, Tracy Ullman, The Indigo Girls, Elton John and Leann Rimes, Alice Cooper, and Blancmange. When genre hopping works well as in the case of Rick Rubin who jumps from hip-hop (Beastie Boys, Run DMC, Public Enemy) alternative (Red Hot Chili Peppers), rock (Tom Petty), nu-metal (Slipknot) to Johnny Cash, the result is both formidable and mind bending.

Robert John "Mutt" Lange is probably the most stupendously successful example of a genre-hopping producer. He started out producing Graham Parker in the Seventies, moved to Australian hard rock with AC-DC, arena rock with Foreigner, R&B pop with Billy Ocean, American new wave with The Cars, pop-metal with Def Leppard, and eventually pop-country with Shania Twain. Along the way he also worked with Michael Bolton, Celine Dion, Britney Spears, The Backstreet Boys and The Corrs. The common factors in Mutt's productions are the hit songs and radio friendly production.

Genre hopping can be done and it can be done extremely successfully.

j) How Do You Deal With . . .

i) Post-Purchase Dissonance More Commonly Known As 'Buyer's Remorse'?
This very common syndrome most commonly afflicts artists at the end of a long album project. You've hit the home straight, the last

week of recording in the residential studio or maybe you even made it to the mix. As soon as you finish this project you fly to Hawaii for two weeks rest and recreation before starting Jim Morrison's long awaited solo album *Voices From The Grave*. Suddenly the current artist comes down with a severe case of Buyer's Remorse.

The symptoms include an inability to finish the record, characterised by an obsessive need to keep re-recording or remixing tracks. In acute cases the artist will actually start writing new songs for inclusion on the current album in the last few days of mixing, knowing that the record company is expecting delivery by the weekend. Other symptoms are a complete loss of voice the day before commencement of vocals, severe toothache/headache/flu, staying up all night getting completely trashed, disappearing off the face of the earth, having an all-out bust up with their partner and totaling the Harley. A chronic case turns into the endless album.

Tony Visconti says: "It's usually that artists get wacky about 80 per cent into the album, or even earlier, and then they go absolutely nuts. They think it's going all the wrong way, and then it hits the fan when they try to take control. They usually don't know how to do certain things, so they'll come up with wild guesses and all that. The two Boomtown Rats albums I did sort of went in that direction. Sonically, I'm not very proud of them, because they sort of slipped out of my control."

ii) Post-Partum Depression?
The album is actually done, delivered, finito. The label loves it. The artwork is exquisite. The artist is totally depressed. Can't listen to the album/can't stop listening to the album. One minute they love it, the next they want to scrap it and start all over again

The only cure I've ever come up with for post-album blues is to plunge into something else like a holiday, bed, another project, but on no account keep listening to the album. If possible put the CDR away and don't listen to the tracks for as long as possible, two to six weeks should do it. When you come back to it you will be pleasantly surprised. You will be able to hear it without visualising every move you made on the mix. You won't spend entire songs wondering if the reverb on the vocal should have been 0.3 seconds shorter, or whether it really should have been the 'Hall Of The Mountain King' setting as opposed to 'Taj Mahal'. The FX you used and abused won't reach out of the speakers and beat you anymore. You'll be able to hear it more like a normal person does!

k) What Happens When The Fat Lady Sings?

i) How Do You Know When It's Over?
Five warning signs:

1) They don't call you or return your calls.
2) When they do it doesn't lead to work.
3) The royalties become more of a trickle than a torrent.
4) The outgoings exceed the incomings.
5) There are a lot of strangers at the labels these days.

If three or more apply, it would be worth checking your investments and considering your options. Hopefully you don't wait until the phone stops ringing to make plans. Being proactive in finding artists and building relationships within the industry is an effective hedge against enforced retirement. It never hurts to be looking ahead at where things are going, how the business is developing and thinking about where you fit and where you could fit.

Don Gehman said, "Everybody's career has its ups and downs. I had four or five records with John Cougar Mellencamp that were all pretty successful. Then we got to a place where we had basically worked together for 10 years and enough was enough. I moved on to other things. I had *Life's Rich Pageant* (R.E.M.) and enough other things that people were looking at me as a record producer. It was no problem getting work, but getting hit records is difficult. You don't have multi-platinum artists every day." Shortly after making this comment Gehman produced the record breaking, multi-platinum, award winning, major label, début album for Hootie and The Blowfish.

Because the industry is so success oriented, as opposed to quality oriented (hits = quality of work in many music business circles), if you hit a flat spot in your career it can be pretty scary. Both the quality and the quantity of the projects you are offered drops dramatically. You have less to choose from and less of the projects on offer are any good. Do you take projects that don't excite you just to keep working or do you save yourself for the creative marriage made in heaven? It's hard to do a great job on something you don't really believe in. Every producer and producer manager worth their salt feels the same way.

Sandy Roberton thinks it's important to be selective even, if necessary doing something else the way actors do between jobs. It's tough to hold out when money is tight but it's better for your career to stick to artists you like and make albums or tracks you can be proud of whether they are hugely successful or not.

If you really love the job, you've proven yourself to be good at it and you've been sensible with your money through the successful years, things have a habit of turning round eventually. Just when it looks like your career is dead and buried some kid comes along in a hot new band. It turns out that his favourite record was something you produced eight years ago when he was just starting high school and the cycle starts over.

ii) Where Do Old Producers Go?
Some go into record companies as A&R/staff producers. Generally companies that have staff producers seem to have success and produce a higher than average number of great albums. Warner Bros had an incredible run of success in the Seventies and Eighties with their team of all-time great producers such as Ted Templeman, Lenny Waronker and Russ Titelman on staff. Every label should have at least one successful producer on staff. Even if a staff producer doesn't actually produce anything for the company, the inside knowledge of recording, mixing, budgeting and ability to troubleshoot when things go wrong can save a lot of money, heartaches and headaches.

Unfortunately with the massive wave of consolidation and subsequent downsizing that has plagued the major labels in the beginning of the new millennium, there are simply a lot less jobs at labels for anyone. As president of A&M and long-time staff producer, Ron Fair, pointed out in an interview with Doug Minnick for *Taxi* there are distinct advantages of being in-house. "I oversee all of the areas of delivering the record and how they're handled in the various departments: promotion, advertising, publicity, marketing, distribution. I maintain very close relationships with everybody in the chain, so that I can watch over my records. Independent producers have very little input or even ability to get knowledge of what is going on."

Some start their own producer management companies – who is in a better position to understand the intricacies of the business than an ex-producer? Sandy Roberton launched his international operation, as his own production career was winding down, by getting a gig for the engineer he was working with at the time. Studio ownership has traditionally been popular, especially among those who built their own rooms during their 'hot years.' This may not be such a viable option, going forward with the proliferation of inexpensive computer based recording equipment. I know producers who have gone into real estate investment and others who have retired altogether. Many continue to dabble. Some continue their fascination with new technology by inventing, designing and building new gadgets. Producing generates a lot of transferable skills should it ever come to moving back into the real world. You may not need formal qualifications to produce music but producing careers can end too early in life to sit around doing nothing and a college degree can be a good backup for post-producing plan B.

But perhaps, most notably, producers like managers tend to go on to the more senior positions in the music industry. The skills producers develop are right at the core of what makes the industry work – finding great talent and great material then working with teams of people to optimise both. Doug Morris, chairman/CEO of Universal Music Group – the largest record company in the world – wrote and produced The Chiffons' hit 'Sweet Talkin' Guy' in 1966. Andy Slater, who produced Macy Gray, Fiona Apple, and The Wallflowers, is president/CEO of Capitol Records. Matt Serletic, producer of Matchbox Twenty, Carlos Santana's Smooth, Aerosmith, and Celine Dion is chairman/CEO of Virgin Records, L.A. Reid – previously president and CEO of Arista, and now CEO of Island Def Jam, wrote and produced 33 number one singles as half of the L.A. and Babyface production team. The list goes on.

iii) Should You Start Making Plans And When?
If you haven't already started making plans for the future, start today or tomorrow, definitely no later than the following day. Major labels have been merging and downsizing at an alarming rate, putting thousands of lifetime music business employees out of work and dropping hundreds of acts which results in less production work for everyone. There is always going to be room for the next big talent but this is an insecure business at the best of times. Even if you don't get pushed into early retirement it's highly likely you will hit a flat patch when the phone doesn't ring or the demos you hear aren't exciting enough to drag your butt back into the studio. The most relevant question then is "How well did you invest your winnings?"

l) Why Do People Want To Produce Records?

When I was working as a studio musician I always thought the producer's job was pretty boring. I would come in to lay the basic tracks and then several weeks later they would call me back to overdub percussion. I couldn't help but think about all those hours the producer had spent in the same room listening to the same tracks over and over.

Gradually I noticed that certain producers were getting better results than others out of the same group of musicians. This intrigued me. I saw that the great producers were very good at motivating musicians and could squeeze that extra special performance out of them. They also seemed to be better at identifying the good takes. If something was not right they knew what it was and how to fix it. Conversely the lesser producers would miss great performances, not be able to identify problems or be able to sort them out. It is incredibly frustrating for a musician to lay a great rhythm track, only to hear it a few weeks later completely ruined by out of time or weak, inappropriate overdubs that have been piled on top.

In the end it was the bad producers that made me want to produce more than the good ones. It was always harder to see how the good producers achieved their results. There was an effortless, instinctive quality to their work. The lesser guys made it all seem like hard work for everyone involved. Eventually I realised that this was a gross simplification based on a musicians' eye view of the production process. In fact some incredibly successful record producers rank high among the undecided. Results definitely justify the means.

What eventually made me decide to commit myself to long days in padded rooms (sans the straight jacket) was the frustration I experienced as an artist working with producers that seemed to be more interested in making their own record than mine. As a result my production philosophy from Day One would be to make the record that the artist wanted.

m) Why Do People Want To Make Records At All?

Jim Dickinson, producer of Ry Cooder, The Rolling Stones, Big Star, The Replacements and G Love & Special Sauce puts it perfectly, "It is the attempt to capture and retain the unretainable moment that I think makes a man seek to record." Before multi-tracking it was all about 'the decisive moment,' that special take that contained the magic. Now it's a whole series of decisive moments, stacked, manipulated and rearranged to the producer's liking.

The first time I set foot in a recording studio, I fell in love with everything about the recording process. Performing live is a transient experience no matter how great the gig, unless you record a show it lives only in the memories of the performers and the audience. The studio enables us to create, capture and perfect special moments. As a composer and arranger it is appealing to be able to preserve the nuances of a composition and arrangement that can't be captured in written music on record. It would be fascinating to hear recordings of Bach, Beethoven or Mozart produced by them. Their music the way they wanted to hear it. As an audiophile, it is amazing to be able to paint a sonic picture using state of the art equipment to scrutinise and optimise each instrument or sound.

n) Do You Know When You've Produced A Smash?

Mostly I've had a sense, early on, about the records that turned out to be big sellers for me. It can be when the artist plays you the song on guitar or piano or the rough demo. Other times the potential doesn't show until you are in pre-production. Tracks can also blossom during the recording and it becomes apparent that you might have a big one on your hands. But with so many factors in the making of a hit that are non-musical and out of your control there are inevitably records that you believe will be successful that don't make it. Even with the ones that do it's impossible to predict just how big something might become. The difference between a record that will top out at a couple of hundred thousand and the one that will sell millions is not always obvious beforehand.

Arif Mardin told me that when he was working with The Bee Gees on the *Main Course* album, "We didn't realise that we had hits. We were just working and having a great time, very energetic, electrifying sessions, and when The Bee Gees managers and Ahmet Ertegun came to listen to it they said 'Oh wow, you've got massive hits.' We said, 'Really?' We didn't know (laughs). This is a good surprise."

Don Gehman talked about how you hope every record is great, but that great is not good enough to guarantee success. "There is a huge quotient of luck sitting on top of that, in terms of whether something is successful. Nevertheless, you won't get a shot unless you set out to make great records." Speaking specifically about the phenomenal success of the Hootie and The Blowfish record, he said, "There were probably four of us who thought the record had a shot, but nothing like this. We were hoping for a couple of hundred thousand units to start a career. That is all you can really hope for, really. We thought we had songs that could be hits, but the timing was certainly a big part of it. You just never know."

Tom Lord-Alge, co-producer on *Back In The High Life* by Steve Winwood, said, "I had no idea that it would take off like it did. When we were finished and all the mixes were done, I realised the calibre of the record but had no idea that it would go through the roof." When asked if he ever thinks 'this is a hit' early in the recording, Ron Fair said, "The funny thing is the ones when I said that weren't hits, and the ones where I said, 'I don't know what the hell this is,' were."[*]

L.A. & Babyface have produced and written many R&B hits but *End Of The Road* by Boyz II Men was particularly significant in that it became the longest running number one pop single in rock history. L.A. Reid says, "While we were recording Boyz II Men's *End Of The Road* at Studio 4 in Philly, Babyface turned to me and said, 'What we have here is a very good song.' But when it was originally being written, I don't think we even tried to ask if it was going to be a big hit or not. Our responsibility as producers and writers is to create quality music, not to worry about how big a song's going to be or what star is going to sing it."

o) What Is Demo-itis?

I imagine every producer has come across this problem. There are many permutations of demo-itis. The most obvious is when the artist, record company or management gets so used to listening to the original demo that anything you change in the final production will sound wrong to them. Sometimes they're right. One of the reasons I went into production in the first place was because I had a run of producers who made the album without seeing my band live and without any serious reference to the demos. At the end of the production we had records that sounded better than the demos but were completely lifeless, wrong tempos, the wrong atmosphere or

---

[*] Doug Minnick, interview for Taxi, http://www.taxi.com/faq/av/fair.html

missing important parts. The best way to deal with demo-itis is not to ignore the original demos but to examine them with a fine tooth comb. Rip them apart, pull out everything of value to use on the final master and lose everything that's unnecessary or simply no good.

Knowing how all the interested parties feel about the demo helps to arrive at the right combination of what to keep and what to reject. Maybe the demo has nothing going for it and what's needed is to take the song and do a complete re-think of the arrangement, orchestration and production. Other times the demo is perfect except for poor recording quality. These are the hardest records to make. When the demo has a beautiful feel and atmosphere and for whatever reason you can't use any of it, making the master can be a fraught experience. One time I started a track from scratch three times. The first two versions didn't stand up to the demo after the first day's work. I couldn't use parts from the demo because the recording quality was poor. At the third attempt we got it right, bettered the demo by a significant margin and the track went on to be a substantial hit. Part of producing is about having the wisdom to know when to change things and when to leave them alone. These days with most demos being recorded digitally it would be crazy not to use chunks of the demo if it was in the best interest of the record and the artist. "If it ain't broke don't fix it."

When the artist gets attached to the demos a project can become an uphill struggle. Andy Jackson was involved in an album that came to an early demise. The producer and the artist had not been seeing eye-to-eye. It got to the point where it was no longer sustainable and the producer stomped off home. In this particular case the producer was trying to make his record rather than the artist's but there was also a great deal of demo-itis going on. Andy says, "The artist had made his demos and as often happens they fall in love with all these little funny wrong notes. They're so buried in it, they can't see the big picture. In the end [the artist and producer] couldn't communicate in such a way that they could find solutions to the problem. I was asked if we could take a break, and then I saw the producer going home. That was it. That was the last I heard of it. I don't know if the record ever saw the light of day."

Another variation of demo-itis is the attachment to the rough mixes. You finish recording the album at midnight in a residential studio and you or your engineer spend the next three hours running off 'rough', 'board' or 'monitor' mixes to give to the band and the

A&R person. Shortly after, at great expense, you spend a couple of weeks mixing the album in one of the renowned mix rooms in a major metropolis. You deliver the mixes only to have the band or the A&R person tell you that they prefer the roughs. Again, they can be right. The spontaneity and simplicity of the 'monitor mixes' can be a positive attribute. You can definitely overwork a mix. Monitor mixes are so called because, traditionally, recording consoles were divided into two parts, a recording side and a monitoring side. The monitoring side was much smaller and had fewer facilities for effecting the sound. Nowadays most recording and mixing consoles are not built in this split format but in an in-line format where the recording side and the monitoring side are identical. Nonetheless, when a tape label says 'rough', 'monitor or 'board' mix, it means that it was done quickly and has not been highly worked or processed. On the other hand a negative response to the master mixes can be because someone has been living with the roughs, played them night and day and just became attached to the roughs' idiosyncracies.

Of course from the A&R point of view rough mixes are essential and they don't like to wait until the end of the project to get them. Pete Ganbarg explains, "If you wait till the end you could have problems creatively and financially. I like to get roughs as soon as I can and be able to give educated, intelligent feedback as soon as I can. That way they're finishing up the record in a way that there are no surprises."

Don Gehman says, "I don't have a problem with certain people coming and listening. In fact I like that. It's a great way to get reactions, so you can see if you are on the mark or not. On the other hand, I don't give anybody copies of anything. I've been very strict. I've always been that way. I don't let people have cassettes of anything, until it is finished. We are basically signing people's lives away, even in the band, to let copies out. I think you're taking your life in your hands. It's a chance for someone to make a judgment in a fixed point in time on something that is still a work in progress. For that reason alone, it's a great way to shoot yourself in the foot. I can't tell you how many managers and A&R guys have come to me over the years and said, 'Man, I do this for a living. I know what I am listening for.' I tell them, 'No you don't. You have no idea what you're doing. The only way that this makes sense is if you are here every day. Otherwise, it's going to be something that you lock in time. Further on down the road, when I decide that this is the record, and you still have that older mix, you're going to think that your mix is better. That's because you've got used to it, and you didn't take the time to listen to the new mix and understand where it is going.' If I give that mix out, I risk having a back seat driver or producer that I am going to have to deal with for a long time. Many times, it taints the whole project, if that person is in any position of power or has played it for people in positions of power."

Peter Collins tries not to give out roughs, "unless it's really, really required. I'd rather have them come down to the studio and check it out and if there's anything wrong we can solo instruments and deal with it on the spot. But I hate rough mixes going out, as I'm sure you do. When you do roughs and people have them they get used to them. If they love them, you are sunk when you come to mix the thing."

The flip side of this situation can be just as damaging. This is where you let out rough mixes to an influential player or to someone who then plays it to a powerful person at the record company. Out of context and, by the time it reaches the third party, unaccompanied by explanation, an unfinished mix or early rough can cause major panic in high places. The next thing you know, you have delegations flying in from Los Angeles to protect their investment and to make sure you haven't completely lost your marbles.

p) What Kind Of Person Becomes A Producer?

Going to work for a large company is like getting on a train. Are you going sixty miles an hour or is the train going sixty miles an hour and you're just sitting still. (Paul Getty)

I realised some time back that I have two basic needs in life, autonomy and creativity (maybe they are wants but they feel like needs). I can survive extremely adverse conditions if those two qualities are actively present. Stress cannot easily grow in a field of autonomy. Boredom melts in the fire of creativity. Fortunately I have been lucky enough to have occupations that supply both the freedom of autonomy and the thrill of creative pursuit. Anyone who can sustain any kind of producing career is going to have to be independent, self-sufficient, confident in his or her abilities and sure of their opinions. A helping of patience, some amateur psychology and a dash of streetwise, survival techniques will not go amiss. Diplomacy

219

can be a lifesaver. Babysitting, hand holding and nose wiping can be called for. I try to stay clear of those projects. Politics can definitely affect what you do but the beauty of being freelance is that you don't depend on one employer for your livelihood. Then again, neither do you have a regular pay cheque. Those who produce independently by choice are not, by nature, company people.

Quincy Jones went on staff at Mercury Records in 1961 as an A&R person and had risen to become the first black VP of a major label by 1964 but, despite his success, he had a tough time with the constraints of the nine to five. He said, "I was behind a desk every day. Awful! I had to be in there at nine o'clock, and you had to wear these Italian suits. You had to fill out expense reports and all that kind of stuff. That really made my skin crawl." Staff producers at major labels enjoy the regular pay cheque, have the inside track on who is being signed and which acts are being prioritised in the system. They are often able to carve out their own space within the company and, somehow, ride the range a little more freely than other employees.

Arif Mardin really liked being on staff at Atlantic for most of his career. "I think it was maybe security. I had a financial arrangement. Also, it's a legendary company and Ahmet Ertegun is still there and I love to be with him, you just feel attached. I'm not too much of a freelance person, where I would have to hustle. They come to me." Arif also enjoyed the various duties he had to do as one of Atlantic Records officers.

George Martin started working in the industry in 1950, before the term record producer was even used and well before the evolution of the freelance producer. He produced The Beatles while on staff at EMI and if that were all he ever did he would still be a legend. He left EMI, started the world famous AIR Studios in London and built a substantial track record of productions with other artists including the Mahavishnu Orchestra, America, Jimmy Webb, Neil Sedaka, Cheap Trick, and Paul McCartney. He says, "The role was something that evolved. Producers come in all shapes and sizes. A good producer has got to really have an understanding of music, and a catholic love for it. Unless you're very specialised, I think that you have to have a very universal approach to music, to have the temperament to like a lot of music. Which, fortunately or unfortunately, I do! If you're very narrow in your outlook, you're not going to make a good record producer, because you have to be pretty tolerant, too. But in terms of music, it is very important to have an understanding of how music works, although I don't think it's absolutely a pre-requisite that you have a musical education."

q) How Do Producers Feel About Remixers?

The peak of tolerance is most readily achieved by those who are not burdened by conviction. (Alexander Chase)

Some producers really resent having their work remixed without any discussion or consultation. In order to be an effective and creatively active producer you really need a passion for what you do. To hand your work over to someone else to remix is for some the equivalent of being forced to give away their baby at birth.

Some producers don't want to do the mixing themselves, or don't regard it as one of their strengths. In that case as long as they are able to have some input, such as helping to choose the remixer, discussing the mixes with the remixer or even participating in the mix sessions they are likely to be happy with the outcome.

Peter Collins says he doesn't mind having his work mixed by someone else but he does prefer to be there. Linda Perry goes even further by saying, "I am a horrible mixer. Mixing is another art form, a very important one. I oversee the mixes. Dave Pensado is my mixer. He is incredible, he understands what I'm trying to accomplish in the production then drives it home on the mix. Dave experiments a lot with the mixes. He knows I don't want the same old tricks. We work really well together."

The Matrix cover both options. "We mix most of [our stuff]. We always present our mix. We also kind of like to get someone else's point of view on it. Bob Clearmountain has been doing a lot of our stuff, just because he is so amazing." Sometimes the label will choose the remixers' mix over the producers and the producer doesn't think they are as good. Lauren Christy puts that in perspective, "Yeah, that happens, but then sometimes our mix gets used like on 'Complicated.' Our mix got used on the radio and they put on our mix as well as a hidden track on the record. To be honest, you can't get too attached to it. A mix is important and sometimes you hear it and you're, like, 'That's fucked up, that blows,' but it's still a hit."

Wendy Page is generally positive about her mixes. "They tend to be mixed by other people and this can be a really good thing, a fresh set of ears, etc. However, often the original vision of how a song should sound is right and it gets blurred or lost in the mix. The trick is to make the monitor mix as close to perfect as possible." She also points out that sometimes the choice of who mixes the record can become politically important. "Often when it comes to mixing and putting out a record, the politics of putting out that record can take as much of a priority to the record company as the sound of the record itself. Part of the producer's job is being able to take this on board and make sure that everyone is happy. The goal is to not compromise the artistic vision and deflect sabotage if possible."

Sandy Roberton sees that mixes are one area that an A&R person likes to think he can have some involvement in. "Generally the band tells him who's going to produce the record. He's worried that he's not going to have much to do with the project. He says we should get this guy to mix it and generally gets his way."

When a track gets remixed without your input, you breathe a huge sigh of relief if it turns out even reasonably well. You have to break the outside mixer issue into two categories – the straight mix and the radical remix. Most rock or alternative mixes run pretty close to the original production concept, using the basic material recorded by the producer. Sometimes club remixes use hardly any of the original production ideas. Most producers seem bemused by, but less concerned about, dance or club mixes. They accept them as a specialist thing designed for a specific purpose. Most producers really want the album and single versions to be somewhat close to their original concept. The 12″ versions can be off the wall. What's really upsetting to many producers is to spend months obsessing over the details of a production only to have someone else come along and mix the track with complete disregard for the intentions of the producer or artist. And even though it's less of a concern, in the case of the radical club type of remix, it's nice when the remixer bothers to get the chords right or attempts to be sympathetic to the vocal attitude, timing or melody. Sometimes they don't when they are trying to unnaturally jam a track into a current trend. The producer is left wondering why the record company didn't have the remix person produce it in the first place.

Mixing cannot be divorced from the overall production process. It's especially difficult to accept if you came up through the business at a time when mixing was part of what the producer did. The best you can hope for if someone else mixes your productions is that they are good at what they do and enhance the production rather than detracting from it. Unfortunately many producers have had bad experiences.

Tony Visconti, talking about who makes the decision to have the project remixed, says, "Sometimes it's the artist. They want the benefit of all possible worlds. They keep remixing with people, they might even edit your mix into someone else's mix. Or some A&R person might think it's cool to have someone else mix the album. A lot of times, it's not the best decision to get someone on the outside to remix the album. They don't know why you put a certain track in a certain place, they don't know what level it should be at, and the whole original concept is being placed in the hands of a third party who doesn't know what went into that concept."

It's very frustrating to put in all the little tweaks and idiosyncracies for the artist, only to watch them get completely lost at the remix stage. Often the artist is not there and the remixer doesn't have to consider what either the producer or the artist wanted. "They're bypassing the months of blood, sweat and tears that went into making those sounds, and that's what music is about – not technical tricks," says Visconti. "The technical tricks might make the music sound good sometimes, but they don't make the music. We, the musicians and the producer, make the music. In the Seventies, the vision of the producers and artists was always respected – you would never tamper with a Led Zeppelin album or an Elton John album or a Queen album. You'd get your balls cut off. The manager would have your guts for garters if you went near it. Now there's no protection from it. If someone told me they got their six-year-old son to remix some-one's album, I'd believe them. It's lawless."

George Martin says, "This modern tendency for mega mixes, the 12″ mix, four inch mix, 1972 rehash mix and the 1994/95 rap mix is boring. It really is. Leave it as it is. If you want to create new work, create new work."

Part of the problem is that, very occasionally, a remix really works. The right marriage of timing, track and remixer gets pushed into the machine and something inspired plops out the other end. Unfortunately, perfectly good records are subjected to remixes by infinite numbers of optimistic monkeys, in project studios in obscure places, in order to achieve an occasional success.

r) What's The Remixer's Point Of View?

The Lord-Alge brothers have built awesome and well-deserved repu-tations as remixers. Chris talked about what they find when the multitracks arrive for them to mix. "Sometimes you have to be 'Audio Maid'." Tom adds, "You gotta get in there and clean it up. I get tapes that are recorded well, and I get tapes that aren't. The ones that I find challenging are the ones that are butchered. There are great engineers out there, but unfortunately there are too many bad ones. There are a lot of guys who cannot record live drums." Tom adds, "What I've found in the tapes that I mix is that often the drums sound dull. On vocals, you find a lot of guys who aren't careful enough with the vocal comping and the vocal punching, breaths, words, bad punches all the time." Chris interjects, "The worst thing about mixing, aside from bad-sounding recordings, is getting track sheets that make no sense. They're not notated properly, there are no tempos written down. You'll have four or five vocals, and it's not written what happened or how they did it, no notes. You feel like the engineer didn't care who got the tape next. You have to get their mix to figure out what the hell was done with the vocal."

Arthur Baker says, "I was one of the first to get the 'additional production' credit. On certain records it becomes a category all to itself when you're keeping only the vocal and re-cutting everything else. It's really a step beyond production, because producers often use the act's arrangement. But when you're working off nothing but the vocal, you have to do a lot of arranging. A remixer sometimes does a lot more than the original producer did."

s) What's The A&R Person's Point Of View?

I asked Pete Ganbarg if he prefers the producer to mix his or her own tracks or if he prefers to bring in somebody. "It depends on the producer and their track record. How good they are as an engineer. With some guys it's not up for debate if they produce they mix, if you say 'no, you can't mix' then they don't do the record. If you let them know up front that you don't want them to mix then there are no surprises."

Usually if you are one of the producers that insists on mixing it will be in your contract. As Pete says, "It can say that you are hiring so-and-so to produce and mix the record or it is understood that producer has first right of refusal to mix the record. A lot of it is about how badly you want that producer. The label doesn't want to give up control. Nevertheless you are trying to hire somebody who wants you to give that type of concession. As an A&R person representing the label, you want to reserve whatever right you can to finish the record with the best people."

There are probably only about a dozen producers at any point in time who are in that league and can command that level of contractual control. I asked Pete how much of a difference an outside mixer can make to a project. "It depends on the outside mixer. If all they do is mix and you listen to their records you know why it's worth giving up a point and the fees and taking it out of a producer engineers' hands. They are the best there is. If you know that this is the guy for the job because of his track record then it brings a lot to the project. There are only six to 10 mixers in that league. There's so few A&R people out there that the majority of veteran, seasoned professionals have worked with these people. So there are no surprises. So if you are working with a band, it's like, 'Is it Tom Lord Alge, Chris Lord Alge, Jack Joseph Puig, Alan Moulder or Andy Wallace?' The names are not mysterious names, they have great track records and reputations based on their work, not with smoke and mirrors but because they are great at what they do."

That's absolutely true. I've worked with all of these guys with the exception of Andy Wallace and not only are they good but they are fast. Tom will mix two tracks a day without blinking. I asked Pete if he thought the speed was a factor. "Most of these guys are quick. Most of them we hire regardless of whether they spend five minutes on mix (which one of these guys who shall remain nameless is known to do) or a day on a mix, it's going to sound good. I don't care how much time they spend on a mix as long as it sounds good. The majority of these guys are getting a flat fee and they've done so many records that singles budget is X, album budget is Y, the fee is the same, the studio time is the same, there are no surprises."

And that really is the key. Labels don't like surprises. They don't like budget overages or albums that are delivered and don't sound good. That's why it's so hard to break in and why a small core of producers and mixers remain on the A list because they are consistent and reliable.

t) What Is The 'Sophomore Slump'?

This is the American term for the difficult second album. There are a number of reasons why the second album has been the downfall of many a promising career. The first album is usually written over a long period of time, starting when the band is formed and continuing right up to the time the first album is recorded. If the band is lucky enough to make it to the second album they often have to write all the songs in hotel rooms, on the road, while they are promoting their first record. Some artists can't write on the road so they have to come up with a whole album's worth of material between the end of the first album's promotional campaign and when they have to go into the studio. That can sometimes be a matter of two or three weeks.

There is a tendency to try to reproduce the first album. First time out the only objective was to make a great record. Assuming the first release was successful, the pressure will be to repeat the formula, sometimes from the label or management but often from the band themselves. Songs written under those conditions can tend to be inbred reproductions rather than inspired originals.

The opposite and probably even more dangerous option is when artists go out of their way to demonstrate their versatility, credibility or a completely different side of their talent. In very few instances, a completely different second album can be the mark of genius and establish a substantial career, more often it alienates the fans that bought the first. Artists are often under the label's thumb on the first release and with success they want to step out and assert their creativity. What the producer has to do is assess whether the new direction will be perceived as artistic growth by the same fans and media or whether it's a complete reinvention that will leave everyone puzzled. I always thought that Motown had the right attitude – "The Same Old Song." I know that wasn't exactly what they were talking about in that lyric but the second Motown single was usually very similar to the first and any significant change would happen after the artist was established. It worked well for them. Unless your gut, the band's management and the label is telling you that the new direction for the second album is flat-out genius you might want to start thinking about a group intervention or an exorcism.

Back in the Eighties there was an artist's whose sales had slumped from more than seven million units on the début to below 200,000 by the third album. The label continued to support the act in spite of the looming inevitability and because, let's face it, artists pay for most promotion costs out of their pipeline royalties. Nevertheless they believed the talent was there. In the end the idiosyncratic offerings became too much and they dropped the act. Nowadays with falling sales and digital piracy, major labels are even more conscious of the bottom line. It is not uncommon for a previously multi-platinum act to get dropped when the follow up album sells less than gold, particularly if the demos for the proposed third album don't get anyone other than the artist excited.

Muff Winwood, ex-producer and long-time CBS/Sony A&R person says, "The worst problem with second albums is that you just can't tell the artist what to do. They know best and they don't want to listen." He said that sometimes the best commercial decision you can make as a company is to drop the artist if they are in decline after the second album. "They get more and more expensive to maintain at that point, they want to fly to all the gigs instead of riding on the bus, they demand first class hotels and hospitality at the shows even if the sales do not justify it." Most companies do continue to feed out the rope to an artist who has had début success; at least for as long as the artist's own royalties from the prior blockbuster are paying for it.

Chapter Twelve

Working Outside The Mainstream

a) Classical

Andrew Cornall is one of the most influential and widely-respected classical producers in the world. He is a multiple GRAMMY nominee and winner in the category for 'Best Classical Producer.' He started at the Decca Record Company as a producer in 1977 working his way up to Senior Executive Producer and General Manager of the revamped classical label Argo. He has won many awards and worked with a glittering array of artists including the conductors Vladimir Ashkenazy, Bernard Haitink, and Michael Tilson Thomas; the singers Joan Sutherland, Cecilia Bartoli, Luciano Pavarotti, Angela Georghiu, Andrea Bocelli, and the instrumentalists Joshua Bell, Viktoria Mullova, Jean Yves Thibaudet, and Mitsuko Uchida. His very thorough education was in composition and oboe at the University of Manchester and the Royal Northern College of Music, and then electronic music and recording techniques at the University of East Anglia.

Speaking about how he got started, he explained, "Like most people in the record business I fell into it by accident. I don't think anyone ever decides to do classical music production as a career move. I know I didn't." Most music producers I know did not start out in life with a burning ambition to produce. They usually evolve into the role via the unique set of skills they pick up along the way.

The differences between pop (for lack of a better term) producers and their classical counterparts are probably best explained in Cornall's own words. "All producers are there to get the best out of the artist so that you create the best recording possible. But the fundamental difference between classical and pop is that classical producers are primarily there to get someone else's musical interpretation down on tape and are not part of the creative team to

228

the extent where they are responsible for the orchestra's sound. Classical orchestras and musicians already have their own sound and all the producer should do is capture it. Producers are the bridge between artists, engineers and the technical crew."

For sure the All-Singing, the Collaborator and Merlin are not going to be content without creative input. But, interestingly, Andrew Cornall's description of the classical producer as somewhat of a transparent mediator comes quite close to Steve Albini's opinion about the relationship that he thinks the rock producer should have with the band.

Cornall goes on to say, "The producer runs the session and represents the artist's view to the engineer and vice versa. Our role is to help everyone do the best job they can. I'm not hands on with the equipment – I leave all that to the engineer – so I'm not rushing about moving faders up and down. Of course I discuss what I want with my engineer and will ask for specific things such as more woodwind or advise caution if there is a big 'tutti' coming up. The engineer reacts to me as though I'm the map-reader – the navigator who steers everyone through the session. Another fundamental difference between classical and pop producers is where they record. Classical producers are rarely, if ever, studio bound. Usually, they are out on location, going to wherever the orchestra is based."

Composer and orchestrator Michael Torke was referred to as the "Ravel of his generation" by the *New York Times*. He said of his long working relationship with Cornall in an interview with Michelle Ryang on classical.net, "It's a great fortune to have someone anticipate my needs before I am aware of them. His ears bring about the best aural advantage for my music. It's nice to know someone can read my mind."

It would not be easy to be a classical music producer without a substantial music education. The classical producer is always dealing with highly trained instrumentalists, composers, and singers. The job involves interpreting complex scores and discussing details and nuances of the performance at a highly sophisticated level with musicians and composers who are the very finest in their field.

b) Jazz

In some cases producing jazz can be quite similar to producing rock records and in other cases it can be more like a classical role. Mostly there is an element of improvisation involved in which case the recording session will be about capturing the interaction between the musicians and everyone will be playing together. In recent years jazz has diversified greatly and now albums that fall under the many sub-genres of jazz are put together in all the various ways available to a producer ranging from entirely live, through layered overdubs, to entirely programmed on the computer.

Teo Macero is probably most famous for his work with Miles Davis. He studied at Julliard, was friends with Edgar Varese one of the pioneers of electronic music, plays saxophone himself and recorded with Charlie Mingus. He has worked with Count Basie, Tony Bennett, Duke Ellington, Ella Fitzgerald, Lionel Hampton, Johnny Mathis, Glenn Miller and Thelonious Monk, and many more. He pioneered new techniques in the production of jazz, editing and reworking Miles Davis' groundbreaking music. He treated the studio very much as his laboratory and modified equipment and editing techniques became an integral part of the music. Unlike the stereotype of the purist jazz recorder, Macero was willing to try new ideas, techniques and equipment. The tape was kept rolling during the recording sessions for the breakthrough album *In A Silent Way*, capturing all the bits and pieces that the musicians would play and improvise. Macero was never averse to adding effects and electronic treatments later. The album was edited down to its final LP length using razor blade edits and as many as 20 reels of tape. His view was that he was like the editor of a book; Miles would supply the material and Teo would edit it into its final shape.

Legendary jazz producer Orrin Keepnews has had more than 500 releases to his name. He prefers live recording for jazz. He says, "I think there are instances in which I will believe in the validity of overdubbing and layering, but I also believe that it can be drastically overused to undercut and do away with the spontaneity that's a very important part of jazz." Keepnews has started three labels of his own. He thinks that the problem with jazz and music in general, as it functions in a capitalist system, is that it has to be an art and a business at the same time. He went on to say, "That's one of the most anti-creative things imaginable. I believe it is the function of the producer to gain control of the environment so I spent as much of my time and ingenuity as I could, working against all those ticking clock situations. Then all I have to worry about is getting product – good, creative finished music – which of course is what it's all about anyway. The single most important ingredient in creating jazz records is to remove all the unnecessary tensions, while being careful not to remove any of the necessary tensions, and there is a distinction."

In his book *The View From Within*, Keepnews said that he tries to maintain the attitude, the perspective, that it's the artist's album and not the producer's. "What you need to accomplish, more than anything else, is there has to be a very real working partnership between the artist and the producer, which means a recognition on both sides, sometimes implicit and sometimes explicit, that each has his areas of being the decision maker. I am never going to say to an artist, 'That was the take, I'm not going to let you lift your horn on that tune again,' but I'm not going to let somebody say to me, 'Yeah, that was good enough, let's go on,' if I don't believe it was. If you are able to establish a workable, creative relationship with the artist, you're going to come out pretty good or better. If you're not able to establish this, then neither of you belongs in the studio.'

"My philosophy of sound with jazz is that the sound is only a means to deliver the performance. I don't want extremes of sound. The sound should be as unobtrusive as possible. I don't want a kick drum that calls attention to itself."

Jazz producers range from the purists who simply capture what is being played to the studio alchemists who bend and shape the sound and music during and after the session. You're either going to need to be a top notch audio engineer and/or a well trained jazz musician to hold your own in this field. Recording any form of improvised music is a lot about creating a studio environment conducive to musical chemistry. As always the relationship with the artist is vital. In some cases the producer is the one who pulls together the musical elements such as material, musicians and arrangers. You need at least sufficient knowledge of the technical considerations to be able to hire the right people and communicate with them, enough tact and diplomacy to make the artist feel comfortable, and enough musical knowledge and strength of character to be able to keep the session on track.

c) Country

Country music producers are a unique breed. They are very often on staff at the record label. The top producers often run the labels yet they remain active in the studio and since they often come up through the ranks of the musicians, they even play on their records from time to time. Most country recordings are made in Nashville and that's where the producers live.

Tony Brown is one of the all time great Nashville producers. His unparalleled run of success from the early Nineties included Vince Gill, Reba McEntire, George Strait, Steve Earle, Kelly Willis, Lyle Lovett and Nanci Griffith among others. He played piano for Elvis Presley in the 1970s, moved to Nashville in 1980 and eventually became president of MCA Nashville at a time when it dominated country radio. In 2001, he launched Universal South with Tim DuBois, founder of Arista Nashville.

Country music superstar, Tim McGraw says that he loves producing and that he tries to bring an artist and fan perspective to the studio. He went on to say, "But I really rely on [co-producer] Byron Gallimore. He and James Stroud have been my teachers in the studio. Any success I have had as a producer, I owe to them."*

James Stroud, has been vice-president of A&R for Giant Records, Nashville, and label head of DreamWorks Records. He worked as a studio drummer alongside Tony Brown, producers-to-be Paul Worley, Keith Stegall and others making gospel records. He remembers, "In the beginning, people like Paul and Tony and me had a hard time getting productions. There was a standard here. The town had gotten to a certain place and was happy selling 150,000 records. Nashville then was a branch town in the music industry. After Eddie Rabbitt went platinum and other records were starting to sell 750,000, it sort of blew the top off. We learned to make Country records with a pop edge."

Stroud cut his production chops on R&B records in Los Angeles and Muscle Shoals and was well positioned for the new style of production. His productions included The Bellamy Brothers, Eddie Rabbitt and Dorothy Moore's *Misty Blue* that sold three million units and was nominated for five GRAMMY awards making him a force to be reckoned with in Nashville.

Jimmy Bowen was largely responsible for bringing Country music production techniques up to date. When he first arrived in Nashville, budgets were so low that artists had to cut three or four tracks in every three-hour session. Bowen wanted to spend a day or two on each song, as he was used to doing in New York and Los Angeles. By bringing in recording techniques and sounds from New York and LA, he was able to reach a wider audience than had previously been thought possible

---

* Tim McGraw biography, curb.com, http://www.curb.com/artists/tm/tmbio2.html

with Country. For his innovation and success he was rewarded with the presidency of most of the major labels in Nashville.

Bowen spoke about getting started in Nashville, "Of course, getting in on the ground floor of engineering and producing is difficult any time, any place, but if I were a young man looking to break into the industry now, Nashville would be the place. I'd go around and knock on every door until I got a chance to start my way up the ladder. Engineering and producing is still essentially an apprenticeship process, so if you have to start by custodial engineering and producing a shine on the floors of the studio, then do it. Then, finally, you'll get that first chance to sit down and work at the board and everybody will see if you've got what it takes, or not. It's very much a trial by fire, but that's how it works. There are, however, a couple of colleges in Nashville which offer courses in music engineering. From what I've seen of them, they're giving out useful information. We've had a few students in as trainees and have just taken on a couple of graduates in our hirings. That's an opportunity that didn't exist when I was starting. It's not easy to break in, but it's not impossible. As a major record company president, I also think the new project studios are great. I only wish that when I was young we'd had them. When I started, at college, we recorded straight to disk. We had a band, and at night we would go in and use the college studio for a few hours. Anything you learn about working with music, about getting it down properly on tape, can only help you later on. There's still a vast difference, of course, between producing music on a home set-up, regardless of how elaborate, and working in a major studio. I think, though, that it's the difference between flying a Lear jet and a 747. Many of the basic principles are the same, but there's a lot more hardware to know and to handle in the jumbo jet."

d) Traditional, Folk, Roots and World Music

"We now have cultural machines so powerful that one singer can reach everybody in the world, and make all the other singers feel inferior because they're not like him. Once that gets started, he gets backed by so much cash and so much power that he becomes a monstrous invader from outer space, crushing the life out of all the other human possibilities. My life has been devoted to opposing that tendency." (Alan Lomax)

Daniel Sheehy is the Director and Curator of Smithsonian Folkways Recordings – the record label of the National Museum of the United

States. Smithsonian Folkways Recordings specialises in releasing ethnographic albums of traditional music styles representing cultural diversity from all over the world. Their releases feature extensive notes with in-depth background information on the music and the artists. Dan has produced many traditional world music albums and has had albums nominated for GRAMMY awards in the traditional world music category. He has a Ph.D. in ethnomusicology from UCLA and in addition to running Folkways and producing albums, is a talented and actively performing singer and multi-instrumentalist. He leads somewhat of a real-life Indiana Jones type of existence bridging the gap between academia and the practical realities of producing music and running a record label.

He frequently jets off to exotic, sometimes dangerous places and returns clutching digital masters of the most incredible music you have never heard before. Producing in practical terms for Dan is "a lot of cultural brokering. There is usually some sort of mission that helps you make your decisions – this artist or that artist, this piece or that piece, this style or that style. Fortunately for me I have managed to land in institutions in which my own personal mission fits very well. There's a social hierarchy that is keeping [certain musics] down. I left my hometown went to UCLA and learned about all these musics. I realised, 'Hey, where's James Brown in my music education, where's Kwasi Badu (he's my master drum teacher from Ghana), where's the Jarocho music from Veracruz.' And I got mad, there's something unjust in the world and that is the channeling of people by major social institutions, educational institutions toward a very limited view of what's valuable in music. So I said, 'Dammit, I want to do something about this.' Fortunately that's where I ran into what some people might call the Alan Lomax school of folklore and ethnomusicology and production of music of grassroots people in the United States.

"I started to work with his sister Bess Lomax Hawes working on the Smithsonian Folklife Festival. Probably the most challenging part for me is coming up with the sense of what needs to be done to satisfy two sets of needs – getting things out to the public and somehow benefiting the artists and the communities they come from – the traditions they represent. There's no substitute for knowledge and experience there. The main tool of my trade is fieldwork by [which] I mean really getting to know the people, the dynamics of the community networks, the repertoire of the music within the tradition, the larger context of the dynamics, social cultural and musical. If you don't hear it firsthand from individuals who live the life and are right in the middle of it today you really can't move ahead with much confidence.

"There are two ways to get that kind of expertise. One is to do it yourself the other is to have somebody else involved who knows it. There are different kinds of views that you can bring to bear on that. There is the artist, the insider, the person who has a particular story to tell – their view of the musical terrain at the time. And there is the specialist with a broader view. Sometimes those are scholars and sometimes those are other people who just have a broad view of what needs to be done. If you can get to the point of having that [expertise] as a tool to use with whatever production you are doing then you are going to be positioned much better to have the effect that you desire – getting something out there, that maybe isn't known, to the public. Or somehow calling attention to something in a very public way that [may] have a positive effect on society in general and the community that is being represented.

"So, for example, why do a recording of Mariachi Los Camperos de Nati Cano? If you go into record stores especially Latin stores in Mexico or the southwest there will be lots of recordings of mariachi music. Some of them are by a single group Mariachi Vargas de Tecalitlan that's the preeminent group, they are really the model, most other groups cover whatever they do. There are a lot of cheaply done grassroots groups that you don't find much anymore because it is not economical. Why Mariachi los Camperos? They are a pioneering group and they have a story that's tied in with cultural identity. A story that's tied in with the efforts of Nati Cano who created a new context for Mariachi music and broke through to social classes that hadn't felt comfortable with cantinas and bar music. He didn't have anything circulating at all in the marketplace. They are an extremely accomplished group, they're successful concertisers. They're positioned where with a recording sponsored by the National Museum they can make a big difference in society through [playing] greater venues.

"There could be a lot of impact by having that particular group recorded and out there, doing their style of music along with their story. None of these [other Mariachi] recordings have lots of notes that tell the story behind the music. That's an important part of the production for me too.

"OK, let's jump to another kind of music. Why do a recording of Musica Llanera from Colombia? Musica Llanera is in Venezuela and in Colombia, it has been identified as the national music of Venezuela, but has not been recognized as being important except for in the plains region. It is very difficult to get anything but watered down versions of this extremely exciting music – the 'prophet in your own land' thing. This is great music by great musicians but not valued at home on the Colombian side of the border because that nation did not select this as their main national music (the Bambuco for a lot of people is the national music). So by taking this music out of this rural area and putting it on the Smithsonian Folkways Recordings label and then distributing it in the United States we've had enormous feedback from the musicians themselves. From the Colombian end of things this is a great breakthrough for them, people are looking at them with new eyes now. In the United States our hope is that their appearance at the Smithsonian Folklife Festival, and being featured on the Global Hits section of the BBC World Service, is going to get them more opportunities to perform outside their country."

This doesn't sound easy – finding and authenticating traditional talent buried deep in other countries and cultures. I asked Dan what the practical steps are. "In the case of the Mariachi recording I went to Nati Cano and said, 'We want to tell your story, what you do is important and we want to have a record that is an introduction to Mariachi music. There's nothing like this out there.' We went with the mission of the institution and the mission I saw as someone who has been close to this music for sometime. [He] said, 'Great that's exactly what I want to do right now' so it was a very easy collaboration from that point on."

"In the case of the Colombians I relied on others to take me to a person that I had heard of years ago as a leader of this music. So I did a little fieldwork and located this person. He worked for the Ministry of Culture so he had the big view. He was an activist in teaching people to teach in cultural centres throughout Eastern Colombia. He was totally frustrated, like I was, by some of the general, commercial pressures on traditional music that deracinates it, that takes the real zest, the excitement, the energy out of it and relegates it to the whims of a star singer who is basically motivated by profit and personal success in one way or another. Carlos Rojas saw this as 'Hallelujah, (*laughs*) where did this guy come from?' and I was on the other side of the fence saying 'Hallelujah, where did this guy come from?' It was another one of those magic moments.

"I came with a knowledge that he did not have about the audiences in the United States. About what would accomplish this mutual sense of mission that we both had; getting the music out and around, getting it more respect in the form the musicians play it for themselves at parties on the plains, in the cattle country out there. So we went into the recording studio with a basic understanding of what our mission was and what we needed to do to reach our mutual goals and it just clicked – bang, bang, bang – another one of those magic moments. We got a recording that they can't stop saying enough good things about it and I'm pretty fond of it myself."

When something so complex sounds so easy it piques my curiosity so I asked Dan if it always comes together this well. "Let me give a bad example. There was another group representing another tradition that was very convenient to record. I didn't really know the tradition that well but I had a lead through an ethnomusicologist to the group leader. I realised that it was kind of a risky venture going in. We had talked about all of our deal points before we got together to start the recording. We had talked a bit about the style of music at the traditional end of the spectrum without lots and lots of the fashionable bells and whistles that would appeal to the new age sound. We got in the studio and many things started to fall apart, most importantly the interpersonal understanding – the collaboration between me and the co-producer.

"He pulled that particular group of musicians together and worked up a repertoire. I did not know him well enough, I did not know the tradition well enough and the contact that got me there in the first place was not part of the equation. It was a pretty good example of some pretty serious things that can go wrong in the production process. At some point during the recording session he wanted more money for himself, not for the musicians and he wanted to add rainsticks which is not part of the tradition. Basically he had a very good product. At the business end of things it was really, really disastrous. He runs in more popular circles than the musicians that he brought to the session. He had some sense of what would appeal to more popular audiences. That was outside of the mission for me, outside of our understanding that we had reached. I didn't know him well enough and he didn't know me well enough.

Producing traditional music with traditional artists who might not have had a lot of experience in the profitability of traditional music in the global marketplace was at the root of the failed part of the production. The collaboration has to be there, knowledge has to be there, the sense of shared mission has to be there."

It strikes me that the problems Dan outlined are extremely similar to the kinds of problems a commercial producer can experience. You start out trying to achieve an apparently common end, people have different viewpoints, sometimes there is a hidden agenda and that's where it goes horribly wrong. Dan: "I dealt with grassroots musicians many times before and this was the only disaster I had encountered and it came about by moving too quickly. The fact is that human relationships were made and business arrangements were half made and it's taken a lot to salvage that relationship and come out at least neutral, not ahead of neutral (*laughs*). In societies where people don't really depend on the written word very much at all they depend on human relationships, on knowing somebody, or somebody else knowing somebody, or knowing that a community knows somebody where there are all these ties that are in built controls of trust." This is a particularly insightful comment because even in a major label environment where you are protected by a contract, when relationships break down things become difficult. You might get paid because of the contract but when the relationships are damaged it's hard to salvage the project."

Dan also brings two vitally important ingredients into the production relationship – the finance for the project and academic rigour. Classical music and this area of authentic traditional music are two of the only styles of production that really require academic qualifications. Dan's Ph.D. in ethnomusicology is focused culturally on Latin America and more specifically on regional Mestizo, Mexican music. "The resources that are brought to bear on folk music are meagre compared to a lot of commercial situations but that doesn't mean they are not significant. A lot of times [Grassroots artists] don't have much money, access to the studio, to the label, to distribution. This is a great opportunity for a lot of the artists."

"A lot of academics are scholarship driven. They are looking for the article, the new thought, the new theory, the new paradigm. That's not how I use my tools. I didn't go into the academy partly because I didn't see that I could get this much done in the context of the colleges and also because I was a musician and what I was excited about was the other musicians and the music they made. It took me a while to build my own idea of what I was doing getting back to the idea of the mission. The idea was to get this music out and around to make people excited about something they may not know anything about. We had one artist who was really keen to record 'The Flight Of The Bumblebee' on his instrument. He thought that it would put his instrument on the map by showing off his technical ability. The fact was there wasn't even a map yet for most people. The core repertoire was what was important to the label and my own mission. So I wasn't sure that our relationship was going to work out. Then when I explained the context that this artist would be playing into he understood or he said he understood (*laughs*). He started to see that, 'Well, maybe I should get the grassroots repertoire out there so that people can understand the basics of where I come from before I do 'The Flight Of The Bumblebee."

"I'm looking for something beyond just the sound. There is a certain sound with certain grassroots music that is so heartfelt, it has a sense of strength that a people have given it over time. I think some of that conveys to people who don't know anything about it. But, really, people are what give meaning to music. Music doesn't have any meaning at all. People create music and in creating music they give meaning to it. You can take the same music and it can have different meanings for different people or different meanings for the same person at different times. That's what makes it important to tell the story, to make sure people have an understanding of the cornerstone and the building blocks of that musical tradition so that they can have some place to start. Otherwise they are just grasping, they are saying, 'The Flight Of The Bumblebee'? I've heard that before and is there a slightly different sounding instrument here? That in my view undercuts the basic aims of that musician because it references back to Western European music."

"And like everything else things have gotten more complicated. The way it used to work but not so much anymore because the market doesn't allow this, was that ethnomusicologists like me would go off to a place like Chile and record all this great music. Up on the high plains two miles high in the Andean Mountains, down the central plains with all these different kinds of flute musics, little regional styles of music. I had a friend who was starting a world music series for ABC records and she said, 'Hey, I want to hear your stuff.

We are looking for material to publish.' That was easy, the hard part was figuring out how to get money back to Chile."

Dan commented that rights issues have evolved since the early Seventies. "Rights issues have become increasingly important. You can't just release something that you recorded somewhere no matter how far away from western civilisation it may seem to be without permissions from the performers and composers or, sometimes in the case of traditional music, the community.

"The reason folklorists are working with the people that they are recording is because they have a passion for this music and the people and they want to do right by them. That assumption was enough back then. Things evolved over time so that the written-word, signed contracts became injected into the situation. I did a CD to accompany a textbook 10 or 15 years later and I wrote to the folklorist [in Chile], sent him a form to take to this pea farmer on a farm about an hour away from the nearest town. He was happy to help out, he got their signature and we got them an honorarium. We had it all locked down in terms of permissions. Fifteen years earlier it was regarded as an ethical issue and scholars were on their own in following it through. As a result you had some good ones and some not so good ones in terms of doing right by the people. In any case there were never significant sums of money being made that I know of. It was like what Moses Asch [founder of Folkways Records] did, as I understand it. He was focusing on letting these people's voices and music be heard because he felt that they weren't and so it was really social and cultural equity. He just did what he could to keep the label alive so that he could follow through on [his] social and cultural mission. That was pretty much typical in the Sixties of how people were thinking."

It's very hard for someone to make a living producing traditional music unless they are doing it in the context of an institution. As Dan confirms, "I can't think of any person who has made a living producing traditional music who is not either employed by an institution like the French government, the Smithsonian, a non-profit organisation such as the World Music Institute or they started their own business." An excellent example of someone who started and has run for many years a successful traditional music label is Chris Strachowitz, founder of Arhoolie Records.

Dan: "You could say that they were successful at doing it and making a living but that is being much more than a producer. You can either get a job with an institution like the Smithsonian or you can start your own business but you still have to pay the price of doing all this non-production stuff. (*laughs*)"

e) Children's Music

When my kids were little I wanted to introduce them to quality music as early as possible and I had great difficulty finding really good children's music that they would stay interested in and that wouldn't make me want to jump out the window. Cathy Fink and Marcy Marxer achieve this balance. They don't talk down to kids, in fact they make sophisticated and varied productions featuring very high standards of musicianship. Cathy and Marcy have been nominated nine times for a GRAMMY and won the children's music category in 2004. The same year I was fortunate enough to work with them on *cELLAbration* – a Smithsonian Folkways Recordings tribute album to perhaps the most influential children's artist of all time, GRAMMY Lifetime Achievement Award recipient, Ella Jenkins also known as the First Lady of Children's Music. Suffice it to say that the quality of their output is a direct result of the quality of their input. The level of professionalism and musicianship, which they apply to the entire recording process, is as high as I have seen from any producer in any genre.

Marcy described how they developed their skills. "I volunteered to work on people's albums in exchange for them working on my albums. With two of us in the studio one of us might be playing but the other was paying attention to what was happening at the board." They now encourage other artists to learn the same way. Marcy explains, "I've said to them, by the second or third album, that I really want them to speak up, give me your opinion, don't leave it all to me. Within a couple of albums you should be producing your own stuff."

Cathy and Marcy adjust their roles within their team as the project demands. Marcy: "We have the advantage that both of us have separately produced so many projects that when we get together we know exactly what the jobs are and we divide them up. Cathy is much better at taking care of the paperwork and contracts. She is generally the contact person. For years I would do the tape formatting, the advance work, if I'm playing a bunch of instruments I will do those arrangements. We'll confer on the arrangements but I'll write the

241

charts. It's great working as a team." In children's music budgeting is a critically important part of the process. "We plan it very carefully because nobody has huge budgets. So far we have never come in over budget." They try to keep a couple of days recording time as a contingency for fixes at the end of the project. In order to stay within budget they have to be very detail oriented. "For all the songs that are going to be recorded I'll make a huge spread chart that hangs on the wall of the studio. As each thing is finished it is checked off and coloured in so, always at a glance, we can tell exactly what there is left to do, nothing is going to be missed. I love to do a track over until it is right. I'm somewhat of a hole-filler. We bring in other musicians and if something isn't working I'll usually be able to play some kind of instrument or do something that makes it work. Cathy adds, "We are incredibly flexible and each project has it's own direction, so that sort of dictates how we are going to operate."

Cathy and Marcy are good examples of musician-producers who were empowered by the recording technology revolution. Marcy: "As soon as we started making records I wanted to get into producing but the equipment end of it was so cost prohibitive at that time. As soon as home recording became available I really wanted to do it. Luckily at that time I didn't have the money to go into MIDI or I might have gone into computer work early. I ended up learning to play more instruments, which has served me well in the long run. Then we met up with Greg Lukens from Washington Professional systems and he became a mentor. We've been lucky with people who will help us out and show us the ropes."

Marcy started out in an old time string band in Michigan. "My grandma was a barrelhouse blues honky-tonk piano player and also dabbled in hammer dulcimer. My mother and her two sisters used to sing jazz songs. But I had some family members who played traditional music. I grew up playing music with everybody." From the beginning she played for children. "I did my first school assembly when I was 12. I played for summer camp groups, whatever gig came in. That's the wonderful thing about traditional music you find it in every corner, every pub every old folks home. So alongside the old time string band we would play some school assemblies, concerts and festivals but I never stopped doing the kids stuff. Cathy was the only musician I had met that played a wide variety of music. She could sing so well I couldn't believe it, she could sing any style, country, jazz, swing, she could've sung pop if she'd gone that way but luckily she did exactly what she should be doing. She had done kids things since the Seventies."

Cathy and Marcy approach producing children's music much the same way they would any other music but with more musical and stylistic freedom. Most albums have to fit a genre or style so that the retail sales clerk knows where to put it in the store. But as Marcy says, "With kids stuff we're bringing the world to kids, we want to bring as many experiences as we can and we want it to be a complete picture, not only educationally but also with fun. It's almost like looking at a plate of food, we want a sampling of this and a sampling of that and it's all going to be good for you and then we want dessert. So we can bring any style we want in the studio and it all works because the glue that holds it together is that it's for kids." As Cathy says diversity is one of the trademarks of their kids albums. "We both have different strengths there but we share a love of lots of different kinds of music." The biggest difference with children's production that Marcy identifies "is that kids judge how much fun they are having by what they are doing and not by what I'm doing. We use real kids that are very good and work hard and they sound great. That is so inspiring to other kids."

Like producers in every other genre Cathy and Marcy regard the choice of material as the most important factor in a successful kids album. Activity songs are crucial as well as having kids voices on the recording, Marcy adds, "We try to make the music as good as it can be. We really figure that if the music is not inspiring to us it's not going to inspire kids to take up music or even to think about it enough to realise what the differences in the instruments are. If an instrument takes a solo on a kids' record of ours, it's up front, it's kind of in your face. We tend to like to hear the instruments in a space and to hear it clearly. My opinion as a producer is generally that if you can't hear it clearly then take it out."

As I mentioned Cathy and Marcy's productions are sophisticated and have a degree of complexity. Marcy explains, "We've always done our best and we feel like kids deserve the best. There are lots of ways to cut corners and we really try not to. Some of that also comes from remembering what we liked as kids. I remember thinking that [some kids albums] were pretty bland. Whereas playing a honky-tonk tune with my grandmother was great music. The traditional stuff is really where my heart lies, and I think it's great for kids. Part of my heart really wants kids to have a personal connection. Computers are really great but it's hard to have connection with a computer."

Cathy describes their process, "Step One in our teamwork is immerse ourselves in the material and whatever the project goals are. We have to match those goals with some kind of budget. Then see how we can achieve them. We outline what we think the possibilities are. Obviously they've hired us because they want our influence but it is definitely our job to help them achieve their dream and there's an assumption that there is a partnership between Marcy and myself and the artist for the purpose of trying to make that dream come true." Cathy says that they don't have the same need to steer the artist as they would in the commercial world. "Let's face it – in children's music there isn't any real pressure to see if you can have a hit. There's hardly any place to get any airplay. However, I do think that our 30 years of experience in this field, both as performers and producers, puts us in a good position to give sound advice to an artist. That advice can come in the form of critiquing the songs. They may have an idea about a direction for a project that we feel just isn't viable or that we feel that audiences aren't going to connect with. It is certainly our job to have that discussion with them and we have that discussion in great detail before we even come to an agreement that we want to do a project together. So we don't enter into a project unless we feel like everybody's on the same page."

Because the budgets are small, careful planning is imperative. Cathy is emphatic about having, "an agreement with these budgets that says 'this is what this budget covers.' If, in the course of doing the project, we go in a different direction or we add musicians or you decide to change four songs and record four more songs these are things that change the budget."

Nobody is going to go into producing traditional children's music for the money. Neither Marcy nor Cathy thinks that it would be easy to make a living exclusively as a children's music producer. Cathy's advice to young producers is, "make sure you have a couple of other things that you like to do. Part of what makes this work for Marcy and I is that we are musicians. We play a lot of different styles of music and our producing feeds off of what we can do live and that feeds off of what we can do as producers." They are hardcore about using real musicians. Cathy: "We probably hear 20 things a year that are one guy with a synthesiser doing all the parts. They are doing that because they can afford it. But I don't think it gives kids the best. When we have a Dixieland band we want kids to hear a real horn section and a real drummer. When we play old time music we want them to hear a real fiddler and a real banjo player. Whatever style of music it is that we are doing we want them to hear the real thing."

When the budget is very small they limit the number of musicians rather than resort to MIDI. Cathy also likes to see the artist live and see how the songs work with kids. "After 30 years, [we] have a pretty good idea of whether a song is going to fly." Cathy acknowledges that some material works in concert that won't work on a CD and vice versa. "Even when a great artist like Tom Paxton comes to us and says 'I've got a whole bunch of kids songs and I'm just about ready to make a kids album.' We'll say, 'Let's go to a local elementary school classroom and try some of these songs out.' You want to know if kids are going to connect with this stuff. I can't tell you how many times people will say to us 'Well my kids love them.' That's not actually a good barometer. Your kids are going to love anything that you do. It's a good sign that you haven't turned them off of your music but it doesn't tell you that other people's kids are going to love them. When you see some of the great kid's artists, they are out there working, sharpening their material honing it, tweaking it before they go into the studio with it."

So producing is part of a whole, 'life of music' package for Cathy and Marcy. They enjoy doing many other things such as children's and traditional music performances and they have deep motives for doing what they do. Marcy: "We do what we love and it's important, the kids stuff is good for the world. I'm really proud of our work, we have albums on many different subjects. We don't make an album unless we think it is really important and unless we know that there is nothing like it out there in the market place. It helps [kids] grow into emotionally healthy people. We all know the arts helps kids learn how to think. By feeling complicated rhythms it automatically helps them to understand math and fractions better. Beyond that it's culture and culture is the only thing we have left of some civilisations and groups of people. It's the one thing that we judge them by, we judge their intelligence by it, and we judge their technology by it. It's so important. There are types of traditional music that are so strong that cultures develop within and around the music and old time music is that way. There are people that we've known since we started playing. We all get together and it's a big party. You have this automatic group of friends across the country and you stop in, you play more music, it's a lifestyle."

Cathy echoes Marcy's sentiments. "We are very lucky people in that we only work with music we love. There are definitely producers out there that get stuck with stuff because it pays the bills. We only work with music that we love. You can't ask for more in life than to do something you love, something you feel is worthwhile and be able to make a living at it. Even if it doesn't make you wealthy it makes you rich in every other way."

f) Regional Producers

The proliferation of inexpensive and high quality equipment has allowed many musicians and engineers to set up their own studios in cities, towns and out in the country all over the world. For whatever reasons they were set up in the first place many of these studios become the local mecca for bands and artists of all shapes and sizes. Very often the owner is the operator/producer/engineer and the time is billed 'all in' with them producing and engineering or there may be a small team of people with a menu of options and charges. Either way the rates are reasonable often as low as twenty-five to fifty-dollars an hour, which may even include amps, drums and guitars from the owners personal collection along with all the usual mics, outboard and recording gear. Often all that stands between these producers and the big time is the lack of the right artist. John Kurzweg produced the first Creed album in his home studio in Florida for six thousand dollars and it sold ten million copies. John Alagia had been producing regional bands in his Maryland studio for years and eventually hit the bigtime with John Mayer and Dave Matthews.

There are many reasons why this is a good way to get started on the road to success as a producer. You get to experiment with producing many styles of music and that could open the door to working in genres that you may not have initially considered. Usually the budgets are small so you become very fast at getting the initial sounds, recording and mixing. You get tons of practice dealing with all kinds of personality types. Your work is very often being shopped around to major labels and the larger independents as the artist is looking for a deal. Sometimes producers get picked up when an artist doesn't if an A&R person is more impressed with the production than they are with the artist. You are in a great position to assess the local and regional talent early on since most artists have to pass through a studio like yours to make demos in order to get signed. You may be able to help them get a deal but at the very least you have the opportunity to build a relationship with up and coming artists who may carry you with them as they rise or even come back and get you when they are successful. Artists often have to work with 'name' producers for their first couple of albums on a major but as their success matures they gain more control and are able to choose to work with people they are comfortable with.

Chapter Thirteen

Technology Rules:
Will the Internet Kill the Video Star?

a) Has Technology Made Studio Life Easier?

> *"The first rule of any technology used in a business is that automation applied to an efficient operation will magnify the efficiency. The second is that automation applied to an inefficient operation will magnify the inefficiency."* – Bill Gates, *The Road Ahead*

Computers are totally invaluable in the studio by relieving many of the pressures that characterised studio life. Before the advent of computer-controlled mixing, the process was done manually. This entailed many pairs of (often willful) hands on the console, moving faders, pan pots, effect sends and equalisation knobs from one little grease pencil mark to another, hopefully on cue. These multiple pairs of hands, in addition to the engineers' would often belong to the band. Band members are invariably deaf to their own instrument. The bass player never thinks his bass is loud enough, likewise the guitarist and so on. The exception to this is the singer who, strangely, for the rampant egomaniac that he needs to be, hates the sound of his own voice. Throughout the mix each musician, secretly nudges his or her own fader up a little. Except the singer who pulls his down. The drummer 'gooses' the tom fills a little more on each pass until they leap out of the speakers and strangle someone. What you end up with is a mix that you'd have more luck selling to a karaoke club than commercial radio.

The best way around this is to have the drummer ride the guitars, the guitarist – the bass, the bass player – the drums. I'd better take the vocals and the singer can go hang out with the girl he just met at the video shoot.

In the days of 'steam' mixing, the whole process had to be figured out and memorised in one day. If you didn't get it finished that day, by the time you came in the following morning, everyone would have forgotten their moves or would want to change them. It could take several hours to get everyone up to speed again. Only when you had committed the mix to tape could you really sit back and listen to what you had done. So, at four in the morning, you'd turn it up to a notch above painful, lean back in your chair, desperately will the mix to be right and try not to doze off. If you did fall asleep the trick was to wake up right as the track ended (the booming silence snaps you out of it), stop the tape and quickly turn to the band saying, "What did you think?" If they were studio savvy, they'd come right back at you with, "I dunno, what did you think?" The only dignified response was, "I need to listen one more time." When you finally made it right through the track in a conscious state there would invariably be at least a couple of things that were still not right. At this point there were only two practical options. You could muster up your last vestiges of self-discipline, send your *girl du jour* (who'd been sitting in the lounge dressed and ready to go out to dinner since 10 p.m.) home in a cab and go for one more take. Or you could live with the mix you had and pray that those little problems you heard don't assume mammoth proportions tomorrow when you play it for the A&R person.

If it turned out that someone couldn't live with something about the mix, the whole process would have to be repeated from scratch. Unfortunately you could easily solve one problem and create another. Before the coming of the computerised console, it was very difficult to recreate a mix. Say, for instance, the problem with the earlier mix was that the guitars in the choruses were not loud enough. You'd set the mix back up and fixed the guitars but when you compared the new mix to the old one you might find that the vocal sound was not quite as good as before. Once SSL introduced the total recall console it became relatively easy to set up a mix exactly as it had been even months before (providing no bright spark has modified the console in the meantime). The computer remembers all the settings, levels and moves you made during the original mix. Now, with digitally con-trolled, fully digital or virtual consoles that reset themselves, it can be a '10 minute walk in the park' to push those guitars up or fix an EQ.

That's the theory and the theory holds true if you and all involved parties are decisive, in an unmodified state of consciousness and know precisely what you are looking for. The actuality can be frighteningly different. Creative endeavours are not filled with certainties. Creative people are not renowned for being precise and decisive. In the manual days of old many decisions were made by default. Maybe the budget was running out or everyone was simply too tired to do another take. The sheer difficulty of setting the mix back up might be sufficient to deter them from going on and on and on. This was not necessarily a bad thing.

Recently I listened to a multi-track tape of 'Einstein A Go-Go', a track that I had produced with my band Landscape in the late Seventies. I clearly remember the mixing session for this song. It was long and arduous. We went right through the night and there were hundreds of intricate little moves and changes and much technical jiggery-pokery going on. When I put the multi-track on again I simply pushed up the faders in a straight line just to see how it all sounded. To my astonishment what I heard was pretty close to the finished record. It had been a hit in the early Eighties, so I'd listened to that track thousands of times as I went around lip-synching to it on dodgy TV shows all over Europe. I know how the track sounds; it's engraved into my grey matter. But here was the original multi-track tape unequalised, with no effects and no moving faders, sounding eerily similar to the mix that we had laboured and sweated over using the state of the art analogue, digital and computer technology of the time.

This experience reminded me that for all the obvious attractions of new technology we spend large chunks of our studio lives functioning in that twilight zone where the inverse-square law of diminishing returns applies. We labour long and hard to improve things in extremely small increments. I'm not saying that it's not worth it. I'm not saying that it doesn't make a difference to the quality of the record or to its chances of success. Some recordings stand out because of the sheer quality of the production and engineering. But computers and digital technology have been both a blessing and a curse. If someone's unable to make a decision then the technology allows them to procrastinate and fuss over details of ever decreasing importance.

I once spent three days perfecting a computer-generated string part for an R&B track. When we wrote the part in pre-production the artist was happy with it. We got to the studio and as we were about to print to tape the artist innocently asked if we could shorten one of the notes a little. Of course having shortened one, some others had be shortened also. After about the first six hours I mentioned that it would be quicker and cheaper for me to write out the parts and hire a real string section. The amount of studio time that we were burning up trying to satisfy his attack of obsessive compulsive disorder would more than outweigh the cost of the string section, the part would be recorded within an hour or so and sound a million per cent better anyway. 'No!' he said, 'it's sounding good and there's only a couple more notes to change.' Three days later we had an over-worked, underwhelming, sampled string part. I'd still be working on the part if exhaustion hadn't finally set in. He decided it sounded fine and when it came to the mix, the part was, mercifully, buried somewhere behind the reverb.

Anyone who says that computers make things easier, faster or more efficient is trying to sell you one. Or they own the studio and love that you just spent a month programming parts you could have nailed in three days with real musicians.

Still, when they work, they're great. There are projects that have to be done on computer because that's the sound the artist needs. Some bands use machines because they can't play. Increasingly computers are the only way to go. What computers have allowed us to do is to keep adjusting, refining and polishing. But no matter how much you polish a turd, it won't get any more attractive. Assuming the project you are working on is not a turd and you have enough objectivity and restraint to know when your work of art has been polished, refined and adjusted sufficiently, then the computer will have been a wonderful, tireless assistant. It's very easy, however, to adjust, refine and polish down to the micro-molecular. You get mesmerised by the process, lose sight of the objective and become a slave to the machine. Album projects that should take three months drag on for a year because of a deadly combination of indecisiveness and maximum flexibility. When there are no fixed parameters adjusting, refining and polishing every facet can actually make a gem disappear.

"It's like moving a snare beat in the computer," says John Leckie. "If it's a sample triggered by the snare hit, the dynamic is the same no matter how hard you hit it. So you have to move it because the first hit is a little late and suddenly everything's shifted. Six hours later, you're still fiddling with it. Six hours! This is what goes on . . . Techniques – potentially they hold all the secrets of turning a live performance into a record – but techniques are frequently at the mercy of equipment developments and the promise of progress can readily translate into poor performances and missed opportunities. And sometimes it becomes difficult to distinguish between innovation and indolence, direction and distraction, model and muddle. It's generally accepted that *Sgt. Pepper* made a great contribution to recording techniques, but you could also argue that it was the worst thing that happened. It made the recording process abstract. It made the band's performance secondary."

Leckie also thinks that automation has affected the band's involvement in the studio processes. He says, "I'm often surprised nowadays. In the old days bands would be much more involved than they are now, particularly in the mix. It would be four people, hands on the desk – everyone would have their fader to move, or the panpot, or the echo sends. It may be just to do with automation but the band's involvement in the studio process would be a lot more than it is now. I often do records now where the band doesn't even touch the mixer."

b) The Revolution Will Be Digitised: Where Is It All Going?

"Technology is a queer thing. It brings you great gifts with one hand and stabs you in the back with the other." – C.P. Snow

Technology has had a huge influence on the job of music production. As in all other areas of life, the new technology will not entirely replace the existing ways of doing things but will take its place alongside them. Newspapers and books were not replaced by movies, which in turn were not killed by TV. Radio was modified by TV but not replaced. The Internet has not yet superceded TV and most likely will not. History shows us that new technologies eat away at the market share of old technologies but rarely completely replaces them in the short-to-medium term. Nonetheless, the demand for traditional production methods is diminishing. As new technology bites deeper into society and the music business there will be less and less opportunities for the traditional producers of the type who originated the job description in the Fifties, Sixties and Seventies. More and more artists will produce themselves.

For the creatively ambitious who are musically challenged, there are sample CDs and pre-recorded MIDI sound files to help them make music by numbers. There are various kinds of music software with wizards and templates to aid the creative process. Programs such as Acid and Adobe Audition make it possible to point, click, cut and paste your way through a substantial part of the creative process. Pro Tools, Nuendo, Digital Performer, Cubase, Logic, Cakewalk and the many other makes of recording software make it possible to see on the screen what you used to have to hear. You can adjust timings and tunings by dragging or clicking with the mouse. Various software companies have ventured into compositional software with limited success. Melodies are subject to mathematical rules and are logically related to the underlying harmonic structure and rhythm of a piece of music. Compositions and arrangements have an underlying mathematical logic to them. Since music and math are inextricably linked there are no reasons why it should not be possible for software to generate compositions or parts of compositions based on general parameters entered by the user. Hybrid Arts dabbled with this kind of idea with their "Ludwig" program in the Eighties. If as Eno said, "Artists are people who specialise in judgment rather than skill," then the artistry would be in defining the parameters and then selecting the ideas to be used in the final composition from the range of possibilities offered up by the software.

Lyrics could be more of a problem. Even though it seems unlikely in the near future that a computer is going to generate lyrics that can touch a human being's soul it does seem possible that ideas that could form the basis of a lyric could be generated by software. Artists such as David Bowie have been using literal cut and paste techniques for many years. Choosing from and rearranging lyrical ideas generated by software isn't any different from rearranging paper cutups of words and phrases on a tabletop. Sampling and waveform emulation techniques were in use at IRCAM in Paris and Stanford University in California for many years before the first commercial sampler, the Australian Fairlight CMI, became available. There were several years of limited commercial availability (due to the hefty price tag). Eventually mass proliferation via the cheaper 'knock off's' such as the Emulator, the Ensoniq and the Akai S900 led to the sampling and looping techniques which have now become the cornerstones of certain styles of music production.

Mass proliferation is an important factor in the success of any new technology. TV was not conceived in order to deliver a daily diet of never-ending chat, game and reality shows. Mass proliferation, corporate economics and, supposedly, public taste has reduced TV to just that. Once music is digitised or reduced to bits and bytes, we immediately have the potential to manipulate it in a way that was previously not possible. The early days of digital recording (on tape) were more about the market perception of what the DDD markings on the packaging meant. Less tape hiss and the ability to copy without degradation were the main advantages. The technology was expensive in the beginning. Consequently it was available only to the most successful artists and producers who were most likely to use it in a traditional way. Initially the only storage medium for digital information was linear reel-to-reel tape. The recorders were expensive and the possibilities for extensive manipulation of the music were limited and complicated. ADATs brought digital recording within everybody's reach. Manipulation was via two machines but at least they were affordable and the synchronisation between two machines was relatively painless. The inexpensive samplers and their big brothers, the hard disk recorders, were really the beginning of the revolution. Once the ability to manipulate large chunks and little bites of music came within the economic grasp of anyone who could afford a computer we began to see some extremely creative uses of the new technology.

During an interview in the Seventies I said that the exciting thing about making music on a computer is that you can separate an idea from the technique required to execute it. It democratises the process. Unfortunately computers also allow a lot of music to be made that is divorced from both the technique and an idea. But, if someone has an idea in their head they no longer have to spend 10 years learning to play an instrument, studying arranging techniques, trying to get Arts Council grants or major label backing just to be able to hear their idea. Perhaps more importantly, anyone can create a demo to play for other people so it's become easier to get feedback on what you create in your mind. After the initial capital outlay the ability to express and preserve your ideas is available, close to free, 24 hours a day.

Some successful artists would not have been able to get a foot in the door before the computer became a platform for audio production. New technology has affected audio production in a significant way because artists can create works of art or commerce in their bedrooms and deliver them in digital form to the labels. All sonic snobbery aside, the results you can get from a good pair of ears and a $1000 to $30,000 digital recording system can be functionally identical to recordings made on $500,000+ professional studio equipment (I can hear the e-mail coming!).

On top of that labels are increasingly turning ears to the Internet to find new artists. Most bands that are serious have websites with MP3s of their music and there are many unsigned band outlets on the web where it is possible to audition new bands from the comfort of your own computer. The band Steriogram, from a small town in New Zealand, were signed to a five-album deal with Capitol in the US. Frank Ahrens reported in *The Washington Post* that they were discovered online by Los Angeles talent scout Joe Berman. It beats spending days on planes, in airports and late nights in smelly clubs and means that bands from far off places have the same shot as a band based in New York, Los Angeles or London. It also opens the door wider for artists who don't or can't play live but simply create compelling music.

If the artist is technically and musically savvy, there's no point in going into a major recording studio and re-creating everything with a producer who's going to take a big chunk of your advance and subsequent royalties. In this situation the only reasons for hiring an outside producer would be either because the artist did not have the technical skills to fully utilise the equipment or is missing certain key creative ingredients. Project studios reduced certain kinds of recording budgets dramatically. You can set up an amazing digital project studio for a tiny fraction of some commercial recording budgets. The studio is usually situated in a no-rent place like the artist's house or garage. The engineering is often done by the artist and frequently all the instruments are played/programmed by the artist or the members of the band. Labels are waking up to this fact and buying home studios for the artists with the requisite skills.

So digital technology is taking an ever-increasing bite out of the amount of production work available. In keeping with the general societal trend, computers are allowing people to do things for themselves that they would have previously paid someone else to do or perhaps would not have been able to do at all because of prohibitive costs. As Thomas Whisler, professor of business at the University of Chicago, said in 1964: "Men are going to have to learn to be managers in a world where the organisation will come close to consisting of all chiefs and one Indian. The Indian, of course, is the computer." Music is going the same way.

c) What Does This Mean To The Professional Record Producer?

It means that our own profession is experiencing the same pattern we are seeing in society generally – shifting responsibilities and job requirements. Certain jobs disappear altogether. There is already a reduced demand for producers who are totally dependent on the professional studio environment.

Sandy Roberton: "If there is a producer who doesn't really use Pro Tools or understand it, if he's one of those guys who just hits the talk-back button and says 'Let's try that again.' I think those guys are over. You really need to bring something to the table. Every producer should really be able to use Pro Tools, Logic or whatever. You have to have some technical knowledge now."

The trend is swinging towards the more versatile and creative producers. Engineers like Alan Moulder, who collaborates with bands who have a strong idea of what they want. Writer-musicians like The Matrix and The Neptunes, who will work with the artist at the writing stage and have an implicit understanding of how sampling and technology interweave with the writing and production process. There will always be a demand for the All-Singing-All-Dancing, Jam and Lewis/Babyface/Max Martin type of producer as long as there are singers who can't write their own hits and don't get involved in the production process. The guru will still have a place because Merlin can function in a project studio environment just as well as a five-star studio. At the very high end there will always be artists who want and can afford to use the very best studios with the very best equipment and the very best technical and creative expertise. Retro analogue studios and productions will continue to have a fervent but dwindling band of devotees.

Paul Saffo, Director and Roy Amara, Fellow of the Institute for the Future, identified a tendency toward 'forecasting double vision' in which mass excitement over a coming technology – or for that matter, mass fear – leads people to overestimate its short-term impact. They tend to forget that technology diffuses slowly, and when cold reality fails to conform to overheated expectations, that disappointment can lead us to underestimate impact over the long term. Personal computers are a good case study. Saffo says, "In 1980 everybody said that, by 1983, everybody would have one. It didn't happen. So by 1985–86, people said homes would never have them."

The same thing happened with digital technology and the project studio again with the Internet and digital downloads. When digital recorders first became available in the early Eighties, there were all kinds of predictions that analogue would be gone within five to 10 years. Here we are twenty-something years later and analogue tape is still the medium of choice for a small but determined group of artists and producers. Right through the Nineties, rock and alternative/ indie artists still tended to prefer analogue. At the same time digital was sneaking in through the back door. Project studios, most budget studios, and mid-priced rooms embraced some form of digital recording devices in large part because of the cost to quality ratio. In the mid-Nineties Alan Parsons' said that, "Eight-track modular digital recorders are probably the most significant thing to happen in the last 10 years. I think you will see a lot of major studios shutting down as a result of that technology."

The proliferation of the project studio in the Eighties caused panic among major studios. In Los Angeles they lobbied to have home-based project studios eliminated using idiosyncrasies of residential zoning laws. Ironically, at the same time, governments and corporations all over the world were espousing the potential benefits of telecommuting from home offices. Subsequently many corporations, including major labels, eliminated unnecessary office space such as regional sales offices. This saves them the cost of the office space and has the positive side effects of reducing fossil fuel consumption, road congestion and pollution from commuter vehicles, alleviating the stress on city centres. Now some individuals are enjoying the 15 second commute from the bedroom to the home office and the improved quality of life that working from home can bring.

Telecommuting is upon us and will affect an even greater proportion of the population in the near future. Technology that enables this is in full swing. Broadband costs are dropping and speeds are increasing, making uploading and downloading of large amounts of data more time efficient for small businesses and residential users. E-mail transformed the way we communicate. Now we can communicate voice, complex images, and video in real time. The 'videophone' is finally somewhat of a reality via the Internet. You can patch into large central networks from anywhere that has a high-speed connection. As predicted in the previous editions of this book, these technologies are having a sociological impact by reducing the amount of physical traveling we need to do. Broadband costs still need to come down so that the technology becomes ubiquitous. Speeds need to increase to accommodate real time audio and visual needs. Countries that have short sighted or greedy telecommunications suppliers will continue to fall behind in the world market place. Wireless and Satellite systems are leapfrogging wired systems in Third World countries and may eventually challenge the hardwired model.

As I write, about 50 per cent of Internet users in the US are estimated to access the web by broadband connection as opposed to just over 40 per cent in the UK. According to Nielson//Net Ratings about 38 per cent of US households are wired. In the UK several sources reported significantly less than 15 per cent of UK homes as having broadband access. In late 2003 the BBC reported the UK as being ranked ninth globally in terms of broadband connections. In contrast some cities in South Korea have over 80 per cent broadband penetration and according to CNET News.com it is not uncommon for a user there to have a connection speed of eight megabits per second – several times the typical broadband speed in US households in 2004.

Personally I hate commuting. It's a waste of life. Fax machines and e-mail sped up communications significantly in the Eighties and Nineties respectively. ISDN lines showed us the way artists, producers and the business could collaborate remotely on audio projects. Broadband is moving communications to the next stage, transforming the way we work and play in a dramatic way. Many of us operate from constantly changing locations all over the world using by landline – phones, faxes, broadband, wireless, dial-up, couriers and even old fashioned mail. Sending mixes in real time or instantaneously as a file to the label or overdubbing musicians from another city by wire, wireless, laser, fibre or whatever, would save a lot of time and inconvenience. If we had visual contact at the same time so that we could interact with the musicians in a virtual studio with video as well as audio fold-back, it would be even better.

In 2003 Avid bought the assets of Rocket Network. Dave Lebolt, vice president and general manager of Digidesign said at the time, "Rocket Network developed technology that has greatly excited and creatively charged the Digidesign Pro Tools audio community. By integrating this technology into our current offerings, we plan to provide Pro Tools customers, who are the world's leading producers of audio media, the means to take advantage of smooth, collaborative workflow between Pro Tools systems over local area networks or the Internet. With powerful tools for easy and secure digital delivery of large media files of any type, including audio or video, this new technology will help our customers move vast amounts of media over the Web at high speed."

I have wasted a lot of hours in studios waiting for an A&R person who is stuck in traffic or a marketing meeting. High speed remote communications technologies can enable label executives and management to listen from their own location, on speakers they understand, in an environment they are used to listening in so that they can make meaningful suggestions at a time when they are needed by the producer. Broadband transfer of audio files definitely beats the old 'listening to the mix over the phone' routine. It also eliminates a lot of Fedexing of mixes and roughs around the globe and should speed up the creative decision making and approval process hugely. Hopefully at some point it will be possible to send a file to someone's mobile phone for him or her to listen at full fidelity – either in real time or at their convenience.

Film and commercials composers in New Zealand are already over-coming distance and using time differences to their advantage by digitally sending their work at the end of their day, halfway around the world, to where the director is editing the movie. The difference in time zones allows the director to receive the music early in the morning, in time to try it against the movie. Then the director sends the updated edit of the movie back to the composer in time for the beginning of his or her next day's work. James Hall has been co-scoring a movie with another New Zealand based composer, Bruce Lynch, but they hardly ever meet. They do alternate cues using a large sampled orchestra, running "gigastudio" on a PC as a sound source. They each use a consistent set up of midi channels, for strings, winds, brass and percussion. Jim sends his cues as mp3s to Bruce who assembles the score mixes. When they've done a reel, Jim prints his parts, records any live performances and sends out final mixes as Left/Centre/Right AIFF files via the Internet. Pictures are often delivered to Jim and Bruce the same way. As convenient and fast as it is Jim says, "It is still beset with problems, technical ignorance being the most common." Clearly as compatibility between systems improves this will be the way music is moved around.

Mixing albums on a laptop is now a reality. More mobility and flexibility as well as more seamless communication about the project with the decision makers, has to be good for producers. Of course there's always a time lag between the availability of technology and the widespread use of it. Saffo notes, "You've got to look beyond the common wisdom. The expected future always arrives late and in utterly unexpected ways."

Nonetheless, in time, many people will spend at least part of their working lives operating out of home-based offices. The amount of time spent commuting will be reduced. Studio use has been going this way for a while now. Just as some people still prefer to record on analogue tape, some still want to go to a professional recording studio. Sometimes a pro-recording room is necessary where, for instance, a large amount of space is required for an orchestra or live band; a great deal of noise is being generated or very expensive, high end equipment is needed. Apart from that a lot of recording will be done at home or in project studios on computer-based recording systems. At least some portion of society will return to the pre-Industrial Revolution, cottage industry way of working. Except it will be the iCottage or eCottage. There's also the developing mCottage.

Daily commuting is no fun but traveling across continents and oceans for business or pleasure can be. I like having the capability to be operational from wherever I am. I wrote a large part of the first edition of this book on a laptop, sitting in a park, watching my kids play. Laptops, PDAs, mobile phones and the Internet are gradually morphing into one portable unit that helps us to stay in touch with our businesses and families. Being able to be where you want or need to be and have access to everything you require to be fully functional can either be an imposition or liberating. It's nice to know that you can pull up stakes and head to the beach, the lake or the islands without having to organize your life like a military operation. People don't even have to know where you are in the world these days with instant access via cell phone and e-mail. If a situation arises that only you can deal with it's usually preferable to handle it at the time than to have a disaster waiting for you when you return to civilisation. Lack of personal downtime can become an issue but you can always turn off the technology.

Tony Visconti thinks that we may eventually see an end to the record producer role altogether. "It's no longer a great mystery – how to make a record," he says. "There are zillions of books on the subject, whereas when I started 25 years ago, there were none whatso-ever. Now, the information is available to anyone." There's definitely truth in what Tony says about the proliferation of information but Tony's career wasn't built on just information. The basic talent still has to be there. I know from working with him that Tony is a great engineer and a great arranger as well as having all the people skills, the smarts and the musical ability. What the increased availability of information and inexpensive equipment is doing is democratising the opportunities for talented individuals but it is still going to take talent and hard work, along with that good measure of luck to succeed.

It's certainly true that there seems to be an explosion of new names under the production credits on recent albums. Not only that, more and more artists are producing themselves, in part because they do have the knowledge and confidence gained from college courses, books, magazines and practical experience in either their own home studio or in one of the many inexpensive semi-pro studios that have emerged. Andy Warhol's 15 minutes of fame for everyone is starting to look optimistic. It may well be more like 15 seconds.

Not only is the status quo under fire from freely available information, greater tech-savvy and a glut of inexpensive equipment, but the information dirt-road is finally turning into the promised super-highway and is now offering unprecedented delivery and distribution systems for anything that can be digitised. As negative as they may have been for the music industry the illegal, free peer-to-peer networks have given us a real insight into what can happen when you can access any music, anytime, anywhere. The overall consumption of music has shot up. Unfortunately the creators are not getting paid. Although it still only accounts for a small proportion of music downloaded online iTunes' resounding success has shown an industry, which had its collective head in the sand for the previous few years, that there may be such a thing as a legal digital download business model that enables musicians, producers and copyright owners to get paid.

Until we learn to dematerialise and rematerialise anything made of atoms such as clothing, cars and computer hardware, we will still have to move things about by road, rail, sea or air. At the time of writing CD sales have been falling worldwide for the past three years. The CD is now over 20 years old. It will be superceded and most likely by some form of digital download. The demise of vinyl began 30 years after their introduction with the advent of CD. The CD was the first alternative to the album that, arguably, sounded as good or better and was more portable. Cassette tapes were introduced into the market about 20 years after the LP. Pre-recorded tapes including the archaic eight-track represented a more portable alternative to the LP and they opened up the in car market for pre-recorded music.

However it was the Phillips blank cassette tape and home recording boom that really changed things. Although there were other factors involved, it was no accident that the transistor radio had coincided with the Sixties boom in record sales and new music acts. These battery-operated, pocket-sized portables enabled people to have music wherever they went. Recordable cassette tapes personalised the concept. For the first time we could travel with our own personal playlist. Only 20 or so years after music had emerged as the killer-app. radio finally had some serious competition which it responded to with the almost subversive spread of FM stations and increasingly subdivided, youth oriented formats. Towards the end of the Seventies the Sony Walkman was another major victory in the mobile revolution which has arrived at the inevitable but musically liberating iPod experience. Pre-recorded cassettes accounted for a significant portion of music sales at their peak but were never a serious threat to the existence of the vinyl record because of the greatly inferior sound quality.

Sales of cassette tapes started to drop off in the mid-Nineties with the wider introduction of inexpensive car CD players. The blank tape business took a dive as recordable CDs dropped below the price of a blank cassette and CD burners came as part of every computer. It will be a few years before CDs die away completely, as many people still like owning a physical disc with accompanying artwork. But the idea of being able to carry around your entire music collection in a portable digital music player such as the iPod is very attractive. It's standard practice for the 'digital natives'[*] – the kids, born on the cusp of the new Millenium who have grown up with videogames, PCs and cell phones. MP3s and other compressed digital music codecs don't sound as good as CDs but compression algorithms will improve and there are loss-less codecs such as FLAC, which will become more viable for downloading as access speeds increase. South Korea currently has broadband access speeds many times the rate of the US and Europe.

---

[*] Marc Prensky from *On The Horizon* (NCB University Press, Vol 9 No. 5, October 2001)

Since the film and video industry is moving inexorably if un-willingly towards the download model it's inevitable that download speeds will increase at least to the point where a full-length movie can be downloaded quickly. The band width required for movies is such that downloading three or four-minute FLAC or even uncompressed WAV files will be practically instantaneous. Once it becomes standard practice to package digital downloads with substantial metadata – including artwork, images and extensive notes, with a choice of compression codecs and the digital media players that can play audio, video, and text – it is hard to imagine why anyone would want to buy a CD. Combine these capabilities with the cell phone-camera-voice recorder which is already a fashion accessory as much as it is an all purpose communications device and we are only a few steps away from "Beam me up, Scotty."

The obstacles of physical distribution are gone. An artist can now create music (and visuals) in a home studio and collaborate with other e-musicians in a virtual cyber-studio without ever meeting them. Then he or she can take the finished product, eliminate the whole manufacturing and distribution part of the chain and upload from the studio to one of the virtual stores. The concept of a finished album could become irrelevant for certain artists. In the same way that websites are works in progress, it's now possible for artists to make tracks available as they create them and continue to adjust and modify the music, text, graphics or moving images after the point of release. A consumer accessing the work at one point could potentially hear and see something different a few hours, days or weeks later. When real time, high quality, audio and video access becomes available, ownership of a hard copy of music or video may become pointless. The illegal peer-to-peer networks have given the public access to virtually all recorded music for the past few years.

If the rights holders and creators can be remunerated it is clear that this model is massively preferable to the current major label system where the majority of their music holdings are not available to the consumer at any one point in time. Currently there are many business models being experimented with. Apple's iTunes with its $0.99c digital downloads has been far and away the most popular so far with hundreds of millions of downloads. Other models are working also, such as downloads by monthly subscription, streaming by subscription, pay per listen, advertising and sponsorship. Labels currently spend fortunes to get their product on listening stations in music retail locations. Clearly consumers like to hear before they buy. Music websites offer the 30 second promotional clips which make it easier to discover music that has not been bought onto radio by a major label. As hard copy ownership falls by the wayside consumers will be able to try things out either before they buy, at low cost or as part of their overall subscription package. Ratings will be more dynamic and will reflect repeat usage rather than the initial purchase, much the way radio and television works today. The consumer might revisit not only because they liked what they heard and saw but to check on the latest updates. It could cut down on the number of albums that you buy, listen to once, and file away under 'Never To Be Played Again.'

There are still many questions about digital delivery. Royalty shares have to be established and will probably be tested through the courts. Downloads are being treated as a sale by the labels and on-line stores but there is a strong argument that they should be regarded as a license thus entitling the artist to a substantially bigger slice of the pie under the current generation of recording contracts. The performing rights organisations' rates are still not established to everyone's satisfaction. Digital rights management systems that limit use and prevent consumers from downloading music for free get cracked five minutes after they are released.

One system currently in place is TouchTunes®, which delivers music via the internet to thousands of digital jukeboxes at commercial venues. These jukeboxes are refreshed daily with new releases and catalogue updates via network access to TouchTunes® Tune Central music library, which contains hundreds of thousands of songs (at the time of writing). The consumer at the venue can access music by song title, artist, or album. Early reports show that customers are very excited about being able to quickly access virtually any song they want. An added benefit is the ease and accuracy with which music usage statistics can be compiled since every request is automatically logged.

The biggest problem with Internet radio at this point is that the listener is tethered to a computer. Many thousands of channels of listenable-quality streamed audio are keeping office workers, students and computer users everywhere a little happier. Depending on what happens with wireless Internet, previously inconceivable amounts of radio-like streamed audio should be available in your car and on a personal, portable unit such as your cell phone in the not-too-distant future.

Two separate satellite radio stations now deliver coast-to-coast US coverage of one hundred channels each. Unfortunately the two stations have incompatible signals requiring different receivers and separate subscriptions. XM radio has taken the lead in numbers of subscribers but Sirius is picking up steam also. Most of the rest of the world is or will be covered by signal from Worldspace satellites. WorldSpace broadcasts 100% digital audio via their own satellites to receivers throughout a global area that includes more than four billion people. If ten dollars a year could be generated for each one of those potential listeners that would create as much revenue as the entire worldwide recorded music industry currently makes.

Legitimate digital download companies initially struggled and in most cases failed, in part, because they did not offer access to enough of a spread of recorded material. The major label initiatives such as Pressplay and MusicNet were akin to starting a label-specific music store. These days music is branded by artist or genre. The average consumer doesn't know which labels their favourite artists are on and wouldn't go to a store that only stocked music from one label. The solution finally came in early 2003 in the form of Apple's iTunes, which is an ingenious marketing program designed to sell more of their iPod digital music players. Apple was launched with all of the major music copyright holders on board, giving iPod owners unprecedented legal access to a broad selection of relatively inexpensive music. Music lovers responded en masse and tens of millions of downloads per year are now bought from the iTunes servers. Personal digital music players like the iPod will do for legal digital downloads what the Sony Walkman and in-car players did for cassette sales.

Napster was such a huge overnight success because the user could find anything they wanted quickly and easily and this continues to be true for the current epidemic of free peer-to-peer services. Even with iTunes, at the time of writing, you still can't find everything you are looking for. Free is obviously a huge bonus for the user but consumers also value guaranteed quality as well as virus and spam free transactions. Royalties have been flowing for well over a year from iTunes but it remains to be seen whether businesses and careers can be based on the income that labels, artists, producers and all involved with creating and financing a recording can derive from the various streaming and digital download models. It also remains to be seen whether the consumer conscience will decide to pay for music rather than just taking it for free. Early calculations indicate that iPods are not being entirely filled with $0.99c downloads. (It would cost nearly $10,000 to fill a 40GB iPod).

Although some of the world's collective hard drive space may be taken up with tracks ripped from the owners own CDs it's a safe bet that many iPods have substantial amounts of illegally swapped or downloaded tracks on them. Free music for the consumer equals no royalties for the producer and the producer doesn't have touring or merchandising income to fall back on.

More music is consumed now in one way or another than at any other time in history. Adjusting for inflation, music is cheaper now than it was in the Sixties. The previously non-existent ring tone industry exploded to over three billion dollars worldwide in 2003. To put that in perspective US domestic sales of recorded music in 2003 were around 12 billion dollars. At the time of writing ring tones cost around two dollars which for a few seconds of music is not cheap. They are easy to pay for as the charge goes right on your phone bill. Compared to a ring tone the 99 cent download looks like a bargain. Most of us accept the idea of paying for cell phone minutes. The same principle could apply to music. It could even go on your cell phone bill. When we get to the point that music can be streamed or downloaded at good quality to a personal portable wireless device for a reasonable monthly fee or per minute charge the amount of music usage will explode. Cell phones have caused a revolution in the amount of remote communication that goes on in the world. My family didn't even have a phone in the house until I was ten years old. Now families have multiple land lines and cell phones. Per minute costs for local and long distance calling have tumbled to the point where it is cheaper to call than to write a letter. Under a similarly changed digital-music business model we could start to see very different sales patterns.

We've all had the experience of buying the latest offering by a favourite artist whose previous album we loved only to be horribly disappointed. If actual usage was measured and paid for, rather than the one-time, outright purchase where most sales emphasis is on the first few weeks after release, patterns of success and revenue flows could change drastically. We are very close to a time when virtually all recorded musical will be legally available on demand. The free, peer-to-peer systems already offer something close to this. How will we know what to buy? This is why radio is such a powerful marketing medium for music. The program directors pre-select music based on a voodoo mix of research, gut instinct and legalised payola, before hammering it into your brain 40 or 50 times a week. At least you can go online now and listen to 30-second promotional samples of music to find out what you might be interested in buying. Still, with all the music that is generated now, it's a daunting task to drill down to the tracks you are prepared to pay money to own. Maybe virtual agents can do the auditioning for you by crawling the Internet looking for things that might appeal. Whatever happens many marketing dollars are still going to be spent to try to influence your purchasing decisions.

Maybe the album is going to die out. How many times do you buy an album because you like the single only to discover that the single is the only decent track. For promotion purposes labels are allowing consumers complimentary or timed-out free downloads. This opens up the opportunity for new artists to get their music heard by a large number of people. Most people will check something out if they can do it when they want to, for free, from the convenience of their computer. On-line delivery potentially offers artists and producers greater creative freedom, and the ability to get something out to a worldwide audience without being 'filtered' through the gatekeepers at radio and the labels.

The benefits to labels are the elimination of manufacturing costs and greatly reduced distribution costs, no overstocks, no returns, no physical warehousing costs. The battle for consumer attention and, ultimately, dollars will be fought once again on the fields of marketing and promotion. If you doubt this, try going onto any site that offers large quantities of new music and see how many tracks you have to listen before you find one that you like. As frustrating as it is how good music gets filtered out by record labels and radio, life in an unfiltered e-world can become overwhelming.

Recent history has shown that when a new technology or format is introduced the record companies use it as an excuse to reduce the artist and producer's royalties. When CDs first came out, labels wanted to pay only 50 per cent of the normal royalty rate as well as increasing packaging deductions. The excuse was technological development and start-up costs in addition to increased manufacturing costs. In the beginning they may have had a point. Today they still try to reduce the royalty from 100 per cent for no good reason. I fully expect that when the time comes for full-scale distribution by wire (or wireless) we will see additional contractual reductions based on a label's start-up investment and increased costs. The labels are still taking all the reductions and deductions that should only apply to physical goods on downloads.

d) Why Will We Even Need Labels In The Future?

Even with ever increasingly sophisticated search functions and specialist websites, focusing on precisely the music you like, it will still be hard for the consumer to find the music they want to buy without some guidance from the media. Media guidance costs money. Magazines pay for the space they devote to reviews with advertising and although you can't directly pay most reputable magazines to review your music the label that doesn't advertise with a particular magazine may find the number of reviews they get diminishing over time. I think this is called 'you scratch my back and I'll scratch yours.' Radio and TV are the same and one way or the other, money gets spent which results in a certain piece of music getting played more often than others. The methods of doing this, so as to remain on the legal side of the fence, become more and more sophisticated and convoluted but somehow the end result is always the same.

In this the music business is no different than, say, the supermarket business. If you tried to launch a new brand of corn chips you would have to spend a lot of money to make the consumer aware that they exist. You would also have to pay to get them placed in a favourable position on the shelves in the supermarket so that people could find them. Now even if we are not talking about physical distribution and shelf space, there is still prime real estate on a website just as there is in a record store or supermarket. All those endcaps, listening stations, and in-store displays have to be paid for by the label in the first instance and ultimately by the artist. Likewise, if you see music advertised on the home page of a large commercial website, for sure money has changed hands somewhere along the way. The same with the 'If you liked that, you might like this,' type of promotion. You get the idea. You still don't get 'something for nothing.' Marketing muscle, which translates to expertise and money, is the primary reason why major labels will continue to dominate in an on-line distribution world.

Variety is the spice of life and it would be very boring if everyone made albums the same way. There will always be artists who need a bigger canvas and more colours on their palette than they can afford to finance. Not every artist values his or her artistic freedom so highly. Some would prefer to have a bigger budget and a shot at stardom. They are prepared to trade off a good deal of freedom for help, advice, a large advance and more production and marketing dollars. Talent comes in all shapes and sizes, very occasionally some-one comes along with the ability to write, play, sing and produce but mostly the young artist needs help in many areas to complement their particular gift. It takes a lot more than musical ability and the desire to be rich and famous to be able to set up a home recording studio, to produce, engineer and master an album and then traverse the complexities of digital online distribution.

The 30 second promotional sample is a potentially industry changing Internet innovation. Once again you can hear music before you buy it, just as you could in the old record-store listening-booths. A little bit of power comes back to the people. Remember that music store listening booths nowadays are 'paid-for–marketing-oppor-tunities' priced for major label budgets. Almost anything can be auditioned on-line now. In his excellent book *The Tipping Point*, Malcolm Gladwell talks about the 'Law of the Few' – the people he calls connectors, mavens and salesmen. These are the people who always know about new things before anybody else does and widely spread the innovation, sometimes causing trends and societal change. This phenomenon is the basis of viral marketing. Trends grow out of certain locations because of one person or a small group of people. The rhythm and blues movement in the UK in the early Sixties that ultimately spawned so much great music and the so-called 'British Invasion' goes back to a small handful of enthusiasts such as Alexis Korner.

In the past, specialist music stores run by total fans of a certain genre had a field of influence that included the town they were located in or as far as they could afford to spread the word through paid-for-print advertising. Now, with the Internet, a specialist's knowl-edge can extend around the world and although the physical goods can be ordered from anywhere, as we move increasingly to the down-load model, there is not even a time lag. Online DJ stores are a very good example of this. They usually specialise in very narrow slivers of club music, selling very short runs of 12″ vinyl. Club DJs locate stores on-line that cater to their specialty and can audition and order the vinyl from anywhere in the world. The DJs in turn spread the word to their communities via the trendsetters who hang out at the clubs. Trend epidemics infect the world at light speed. Hopefully this will help to counterbalance the unhealthy use of expensive, brute force marketing techniques by corporate conglomerates that bias charts against the quirky outsider, the newcomer and the unpredictable. Most major trends grow out of movements that are initially regarded as weird, unusual or left of centre.

e) Charts

Charts are marketing tools. There are all kinds of charts; some based on sales, others on airplay. Charts serve as a feedback loop to the industry at large. The feedback reinforces or diminishes confidence in a release at every level. Chart success will trigger continued or increased interest from the label. Although charts can be manipulated by a label using promotion and marketing techniques, a decent chart position or the lack of one, affects the label's enthusiasm for the release thereby establishing a positive or negative feedback loop. The resulting increased or decreased expenditure of marketing resources magnifies the release's movement towards success or failure. Positive progress on a particular chart, whether it be club, airplay or sales charts, encourages the label to pump more marketing money into the project. Low, slow or declining figures will cause them to abandon, even allegedly or contractually, pre-committed promotion and marketing campaigns unless there is a commitment from senior management to break that particular release or act.

Chart action not only affects the label but also the amount of radio play and television exposure a record will get. If stations are spinning a track and it doesn't chart in a predetermined time period, they drop it unceremoniously from their playlist. A major chart showing can influence a station to add a song (assuming it fits their format) that they may not have previously liked. Tour promoters and booking agents also watch charts carefully and that can affect the amount and quality of gigs an artist can get. Like every other business the music business is becoming more and more research driven. Sales are the ultimate research and the important charts are the ones that either reflect, or are proven to be the precursors of, increased sales.

Major label marketing money is still the dominant influence on the most important charts. So far no one has had a major hit based entirely on Internet marketing and/or distribution but the Internet can offer some alternative ways to get things started. An enterprising artist with basic computer skills can create, market and distribute entirely from home. The music, of course, will still have to find its audience. The difference between using the Internet and the traditional method of pressing up a thousand CDs, getting them into local stores and going out and playing shows to promote yourself, is that now an artist has the whole planet instead of a small local area as a potential market. There are many on-line competitions – genre specific, area specific and voting sites – that can help to make people aware of new music and the Internet is very much a word of mouth medium. Building a mailing list is much easier and cheaper using e-mail. And if people find something they like it's extremely easy for them to let all of their friends know about it by e-mail or instant messaging. Viral guerrilla campaigns growing out of a local market via a live fan base is still a great way to get started but the web puts a new dimension of possibilities into the equation. It won't completely replace the tried and true 'tour and build an audience' system but it is a very significant augmentation of the road-warrior methodology where you build a fan-base and stay in contact with them via a mailing list. And, after you do all the hard work, if you are still interested, major labels do look for developing stories – A&R departments use on-line research to uncover new talent in addition to all the traditional methods.

How does this all affect the record producer? Well, there are many more albums being made on a regional level now than ever before. For the fledgling producer this is an opportunity to cut their production teeth under much less pressure than in a major label environment. And there is always the chance of selling millions of albums from a project studio recording as John Kurzweg did when he produced Creed's blockbuster debut album before they even had a deal.

From the financial point of view there are many copyright issues still to be resolved in the digital distribution world. The DMCA or Digital Millennium Copyright Act in the USA goes some way towards resolving the issues of payment to labels and artists. Artists, producers and labels have to be paid for their work in order to keep making music. Terrestrial analogue radio (the AM and FM stuff) in the US doesn't pay performers, producers or copyright owners for the use of their tracks. The DMCA was created to ensure this would not be a problem with digital broadcasting. Although the amounts are small right now at least artists and labels are getting paid something when their music gets played on satellite and Internet radio. The media in particular seems to have latched on to the idea that rock musicians make too much money. Many journalists and music fans seem to think this justifies pirating music at every turn. Artists and music face the biggest set of threats ever in the digital age. Perfect digital copies can be made on CD-ROMs in much less than the time it takes to listen to the album. MP3s can be downloaded at no cost for nearly every song ever recorded and disseminated around the world at the click of a mouse.

Obviously if an artist is highly successful with personal wealth in the tens or possibly hundreds of millions, then even losing 50 per cent of their sales to various forms of piracy won't significantly affect their lifestyle. My concern with piracy is not so much the effect it has on the super rich. Those at the top of the Hill will still be at the top but the Hill may be a lot smaller and a lot of musicians, artists and producers at the lower levels get squeezed out. What this personal piracy does is it effectively shifts the wealth from the creators, producers and distributors of the music who are the rightful owners, to the hardware and firmware manufacturers who make the recordable and rewritable CD-ROM drives and the CD-ROM and CDRWs. In the case of the peer-to-peer networks, multi-million dollar companies have been built on the backs of artists, producers and labels. By allowing business models based entirely on the theft of artists' copyrights we are starving the host and feeding the parasite. Like any other profession making music is a career that requires full time commitment. In times past composers were supported by wealthy patrons. Some forms of music are still subsidised by government grants and donations. Patronage and subsidy are not healthy democratic systems for supporting freedom of speech and artistic innovation. We live in a predominantly free market world. Music should exist in that world too but it will not be able to if we allow businesses to monopolise profitability based on the misappropriation of others rights.

In the US, when tested by the courts, the law has mostly upheld the rights of the artist and copyright holder. Peer-to-peer distribution is a simple yet powerful means of distributing music. If the copyright creators' and owners' rights are acknowledged, respected and rewarded, there should be no reason why music should not be as easily available as it has been through Kazaa. Even the 'free to consumer' model could work if the wealth generated is distributed fairly. Broadcast television has always been free to the consumer but the writers, directors, producers, actors and TV executives all get paid handsomely from income generated by advertising. It's worth noting that the film industry has not made its movies available in unprotected digital form. While it's true that DVD copy protection systems can be easily cracked it is also true that your car can easily be broken into. Nonetheless, a lock is still a somewhat effective deterrent, so you don't stop locking your car. Copy protection will always be cracked but a protected music file will deter basically honest people from casually copying music.

There are many ways that music can be paid for. Advertising brings with it the same ratings problems as we currently have on terrestrial radio. Sponsorship has the same drawbacks as patronage when it comes to freedom of speech and innovation. Subscription as with cable TV could be a promising model as long as all or at least most titles are available for one monthly fee. Consumers don't like partial catalogues unless there is some sort of editorial factor by someone they grow to trust. Micro payments systems will come into their own for purchases, as more and more intellectual property is made available for small amounts of money. Despite all the scaremongering about on-line fraud, credit cards have worked just fine for larger payments but as they stand they're not practical for multiple small payments because of the bank fees that the vendor has to pay each time they charge your card. A service that monopolises their particular niche can aggregate your charges on a monthly basis thus reducing the impact of the bank charges. A universal micro payment system that can be used with different vendors for different types of low priced products will be more useful. Payments can very easily be added to your phone or cable TV bill but not too many parents of teenagers will authorise their kids to make unrestricted charges.

The biggest problem with online purchasing is that it's the very kids under the age of 18 who can't get their own credit cards who are the most likely to be interested in downloading single tracks. They also have totally disposable income. A pre-loadable phone card type of system or an online account that can be replenished is much safer for them and their parents than an unlimited monthly billing account like a phone or credit card bill.

f) Will Record Producers Survive The Revolution?

Jazz records are still being made even though they represent a smaller proportion of the market than they did in the Thirties, Forties and Fifties. I'm sure in 20 years' time there will still be record producers making records in exactly the same way they've been made for the past two decades. As with jazz, current and past styles of production will continue to be valid alongside newer methods but in order for a producer to survive with any degree of certainty it would be wise for them to broaden their skill base. To go back to what I said at the beginning, the producer is like the blank piece in Scrabble. He becomes that missing letter, completing the word, whatever the word is that the artist needs to make the winning play. In the future the missing factors may be more than a few engineering, arranging and people skills. In a world where video, graphics and music are communicated in exactly the same way and through the same channels, the clear dividing line between the different creative disciplines may blur or even disappear.

Early recordings were merely captured moments, sonic photographs of events that actually took place. When Les Paul did his first overdubbing or sound-on-sound experiments he took that all important first step, a giant leap away from capturing an event towards artificially synthesising an aural picture. He utilised the recording medium and the studio in a more direct and creative way.

Many artists, engineers and producers subsequently contributed to the fits and starts development of this process, most notably Phil Spector, The Beach Boys and, of course, The Beatles and George Martin developing from *Rubber Soul* to *Sgt Pepper*. An artist such as Prince would have been almost unimaginable in the Fifties. It was inconceivable that an artist could have such a spectrum of abilities from composing, to arranging, to performing all or most of the instruments in addition to understanding and controlling the audio production techniques. The technology is cheaper and more user friendly whilst at the same time many pre-schoolers know their way around computers so the technophobic barriers are being torn down. As with all human endeavour, the next generation stands on the shoulders of the previous and regards what has already been done as the new starting point.

As I predicted in previous editions of this book, while recording has evolved from a technical skill to being an integral part of the art of making music so multi-media is becoming an all-in-one conceptualisation for some artists. The past 25 years has seen a change in the use and the purpose of the movie soundtrack. Movie music is no longer used just for dramatic reinforcement of the visual action. For many Hollywood films, a carefully put together soundtrack has become a powerful marketing tool for the movie and the featured music artists. Video clips very often feature footage from the movie intercut with the artist's performance. The right soundtrack helps target a specific audience demographic for the movie. The right movie can launch music careers and boost already successful ones. MTV and the subsequent explosion of video music channels have welded music and visuals together in the minds of viewers. The lines are getting blurred between sound and vision.

It is no accident that Avid Technology, the creators of the Oscar winning professional, non-linear video editing system, bought Digidesign – the GRAMMY and Oscar winning creators of one of the leading computer-based, digital audio production systems. Avid's slogan is 'Serving the industries that make, manage and move Media.' With random audio and video access it's a cinch to manipulate both together allowing complete interchangeability in the prioritisation of the music or the visuals. With the trickle down effect making cheaper versions of the technology widely available and increased connectivity, interesting hybrid projects are emerging. As I predicted we are now seeing the evolution of young, computer literate audio-visual artists who produce full-blown multimedia works out of their own home-based, audio-visual project studios.

As reported in that May 2004 *Washington Post* article, Steriogram got their US deal via their website, using an Apple Powerbook G4 laptop and Logic Pro to record and edit their album and iMovie software to make a tour video. They refer to themselves as a 'geek' band. Video has become more and more important in the marketing and development of an artist. Professional video production costs are completely out of hand. Hopefully the falling prices of technology will democratise the process and help level the playing field for the more creative and enterprising artists. Perhaps we will see the emergence of producers or production teams who include the visual element in their arsenal of skills.

When you boil it down producing is really about problem solving and technology is just one of the tools we use. Albhy Galuten is a renaissance man who produced 18 hit singles, won two GRAMMY awards and went on to develop the enhanced CD format, which mixes data with music carrying full band-width, uncompressed audio as well as text, graphics, photos and video. He explained this remarkable career move by saying, "As a producer, I learned to listen with my guts and solve problems with my mind. You do a lot of left-right brain shifting. Producers may be well suited for these new media forms. Artists are usually visceral, and computer people tend to be quite analytical. The ability to make viscerally engaging multi-media 'objects' is going to require the ability to shift back and forth, to communicate. To me it's no different from trying to use a tape loop on a Bee Gees record, or two 24 tracks instead of one. Technical innovations can be very stimulating, and I enjoy hanging around at that intersection, working with artists and programmers."

Producers came into being because the intersection of technology and music needed some traffic control. Producers are sonic artists. They paint with sound. Maybe in the future they will be painting with sound and vision. Since the first edition of this book we've seen artists evolve that are creating not just music but their own websites with graphics and visual content. Websites have a voracious appetite for content. They need to be updated constantly. The marriage of visual and aural via the Internet offers a more versatile program for the creative artist than the current album cycle that we are locked into because of physical product. Tracks can be posted as soon as they are completed and updated or changed at any time.

It's inevitable that producers will emerge who are equipped to respond to these trends but not everyone will have to deal with multimedia. In the same way that film, television and video have not replaced books, there will always be a need for pure audio. One of the greatest things about music and radio is that you can enjoy it while you are doing other things like driving, working, even reading (I'm listening to Paco de Lucía while I'm writing this chapter, but I couldn't watch TV and write). Anything with both audio and visual content demands a great deal if not all of your attention (except, perhaps, prime time television). Undoubtedly multi-media with all its ramifications and implications will offer a window of opportunity for the producer who has cross-disciplinary skills or enough savvy to put together and manage a team of people with the technical and creative skills in computing, video, graphics, text and music.

Chapter Fourteen

The Final Cut

After a lifetime of working with the legends of the music business, Phil Ramone is not resting on his laurels. "I've always been worried that somebody is going to do it better. There is a competitive side to making great music and finding ways for it to slot better, to sound better, to be heard in a different way than ever before. I'll be honest with you, when you start a new record there is no cushion under your ass."

This kind of attitude is all the more remarkable when you consider all the technological changes that someone like Ramone has had to deal with over the years. He embraced digital audio very early on, picked up on the advantages of the low priced modular digital multi-track machines, and was one of the first people to utilise ISDN to record artists from remote locations.

John Leckie: "Just be into the music and try not to worry so much about technology. Do whatever it takes, but you have to enjoy the music you're recording. Never stop looking for different kinds of music to work with – there's a tremendous amount of it out there."

Jack Douglas feels that the trick to working with an artist is to let him realise that you're on his side. "I like to work with new artists and new artists have always been suspicious of people that are on the other side of the glass. They feel that in some way or other we're out to get their music and do something to change it. I want to convince an artist that all I want to do is take his music and help him get it on the record so that it is, in fact, what he wanted to begin with. New artists especially get very insecure about their own stuff. If I can keep an artist's confidence up in the early part of building a record, that record is going to work."

There are a handful of producers who get mentioned again and again as influences and sources of inspiration to other producers. A partial list would have to include George Martin, Quincy Jones, Phil Ramone, Jerry Wexler, Arif Mardin and Tom Dowd. Phil Spector had a relatively short career but in that time he established the idea that the independent record producer could be a creative force in his or her own right. He had such a powerful creative identity that people often refer to the hits he produced as 'Phil Spector records' rather than by the names of the artists.

Quincy Jones: "Our whole life is about the blank page: 'What are we going to do, because right now we have nothing!' Ideas are the sustenance of creative life. What's always amazed me is how one person will take the first idea that comes or the second surge of inspiration and say, 'Fine'. Another person will say, 'That's not it yet.' They get to the 27th layer before they say, 'That's it.' How do you know that? "I'm the 27th through the 40th. I don't know how, but somehow you know, you just say, 'That's it.' But that's a very important decision in creativity. "I guess the trick is to dream real big. But if you do that, you have to get off of your ass and execute real big! That's the killer. I think our higher power likes our dreams to be very specific. Don't just say, 'Oh God, I wish I was happy.' Give me a break, man! It doesn't have to be like a machine, but I think when you start dreaming and visualising, you've got to be very specific or it won't happen."

Clearly there is no such thing as the average record producer. Producers come in all shapes and sizes, with disparate talents and abilities. What you can say about a person who produces music successfully for a living is that he or she is 'someone who gets the job done and gets it done well.' There's zero job security for the freelance producer - you are as good as your last couple of projects. Experience and knowledge are vital but not always valued. Previous and recent success is the most sought-after qualification. An excellent network of connections is essential – you'll never see an ad for a record producer. Job satisfaction is extremely high. If you stand still you go backwards. The only constant is change.

Richard Burgess
Washington DC, August 2004

Featured interview with legendary producer
Arif Mardin

July 28, 2004

RJB: You came to the music business relatively late after studying economics in Turkey and London. I assume you had a background in music before that in order to win the Quincy Jones scholarship?

AM: Here's how it happened. I was a jazz fan since I was 10 years old. My sister used to listen to American pop music, which at that time was big bands, The Andrews Sisters and all that. We are talking about the early Forties. I acquired a taste for big band music then on my own, later in my teens, I was a bebop music fan, Charlie Parker and Dizzy Gillespie, I was a modernist. So I did have the musical roots and the taste. At one point I started to take piano lessons. It looked like I wasn't going to be a concert pianist but it gave me enough technique to be able to pick notes and chords, I also took harmony lessons and things like that so I was into music parallel with my education in economics.

RJB: That's very interesting. So when you got the Quincy Jones scholarship your level of musical ability was not so high but you had enough appreciation and understanding and I guess Berklee transformed you?

AM: Not exactly. The level of my musicianship was actually high. At Berklee I learned to formalise it and learned new techniques, it opened up new horizons. The reason I got the Berklee College, Quincy Jones scholarship was that I wrote compositions and arranged and orchestrated it for two trumpets, one trombone, three saxophones and three rhythm. I did that, I copied my own parts and sent it to Quincy. Quincy recorded them for Voice of America. He used an A team of New York musicians – we're talking about Art Farmer, Phil

Woods, Hank Jones. So these guys played my music, in fact when I received the tape I said 'Did *I* write this music?' they were so fantastic. So I was able to actually write. In fact, a few years before that I was a piano player and arranger in a businessman's big band in Istanbul. They would come after work at six o'clock and we would play stock arrangements so I had all the experience but of course Berklee opened up totally new horizons.

RJB: In my experience most producers in the popular music arena don't have formal music qualifications. How much do you think your formal training has helped in your career and in what way?

AM: It's interesting. I think you have three kinds of producers. I'm talking about when I started – today there are many other kinds. You have the songwriter producer who is in control of his or her composition and records the song with an artist. We are talking about Gamble and Huff, Lamont Dozier, Leiber and Stoller, songwriter producers. Or you have music lover producers, like Ahmet Ertegun, Jerry Wexler, the Chess brothers, Berry Gordy they don't have music training but they love music and they have a song sense, they know lyrics and things like that, they can analyse a song. Then the other would be the engineer producer – Hugh Padgham, Tom Dowd, they sit behind the controls and help shape the sessions. Of course, today, and I don't want to put people down, but you have tin-eared producers too.

So how did it help me? First of all when I joined Atlantic Records I had all this knowledge of all these modern chords, great harmonic variations and things like that. When I was writing an arrangement for horns I said I had better forget this knowledge because what they are doing is triads, three part chords, one, four, five, that's blues and rock. So I had to forget my augmenteds, diminisheds, major sevenths and all that and write the orchestrations in a simple, pure way. So it didn't hamper me but it was a big shock, wow, I can't use my major seventh here (*laughs*). But of course I would sneak them in too, like the wonderful, late Dusty Springfield. On some of my arrangements I have all these little things in it but they don't sound jarring.

RJB: And of course Chaka Khan?

AM: Chaka Khan as well.

RJB: And Norah Jones?

AM: Well Norah Jones plays her own piano [parts] – nobody tells her what to do on the piano. So far I only did one string arrangement for her which was a viola and a cello. Norah Jones was an exercise in restraint because she is such a purist and a wonderful artist, anything superfluous will stick out. I'm known as a person of excess – put the background vocals here, strings here but with Norah I was totally the opposite, I just directed it and shaped it in a subtle way.

RJB: I was going to ask you to define the producer's role, which in a way you just did? What I thought was interesting when you defined the three different producer roles was that you left your own role out?

AM: OK, yes. Like David Foster, there are musician-producers, the fourth category. I should have said that.

RJB: Like Quincy?

AM: Yes, Quincy.

RJB: George Martin.

AM: George Martin. David Foster for example was an incredibly sought after keyboardist in Los Angeles in the Seventies before he became a producer. In fact he played a bassline I wrote out for synthesiser for Chaka Khan's 'Nights In Tunisia'. He was the guy who played (*sings bassline*), all that stuff. And then of course he slowly went into production and writing great songs. He became a musician-songwriter-producer. He also has that side.

RJB: He produced 'Through The Fire' on the same album.

AM: Right.

RJB: I loved that track. That was an interesting record the way you merged Melle Mel in with a mainstream R'n'B artist and song.

AM: It was an education for me too. I was working with John Robie, the day's hip-hop master. I was looking at his edits. He was cutting half-inch tape like there was no tomorrow, putting things together. So it was very interesting. Melle Mel was working with Reggie Griffin who arranged and played on Grandmaster Flash's 'The Message' and we were working with him. Before that Chaka's brother was at my house, at my keyboard trying to get a beat on a drum machine. I said to him, 'You know your sisters' names are so percussive, Chaka and Taka Boom'. So [sings], 'Chaka-Khan-Taka-Boom-Chaka-Khan-Taka-Boom.' We tried to get a drum beat and we didn't succeed but that remained in my brain [sings], 'Chaka-Khan-Chaka-Khan.' So I said to Reggie, 'Why don't you go to Melle Mel, and I want a love rap. I don't want anything about women or gold chains, try to get a love rap using her name as a percussive thing [sings] 'Chaka-Khan-Chaka-Khan.'

So he brought the tape in. It was very short, we liked it very much and I inserted it in a rough mix. We had a party and I was playing it. People's ears pricked up and said 'Oh, this is great, this is great.' So I said we should use it many times in the song. In the old days there was a sampler called the AMS and my finger slipped on the key so it became [sings] 'Chaka-chaka-chaka-khan' so we said let's keep it. It was an accident (*laughs*).

RJB: It was a turning point. That was a very important single.

AM: Very important for me too because it was a learning process. I was in hip-hop territory which I wasn't in before. It was, like, 'Let's do this. Aah, it doesn't fit, let's take this, aah, it fits!' that attitude. Even with Stevie Wonder, I said, 'He will never come and play today,' because it was Marvin Gaye's funeral. He showed up and he was fantastic. It was a wish list. I also wanted to have Prince play guitar but he was touring so it didn't happen.

RJB: Your discography, and I'm sure it's abbreviated, is six pages long. Every record on there is something that was successful and that people know about. You must have been inundated with offers to produce projects throughout your career. I'm curious to know how you evaluate a project and what makes you say 'OK this is the one I am going to do'?

AM: The artist must first of all be a genuine artist, I can't work with concoctions – with a beautiful girl or a handsome young man – put the voice in Pro Tools and correct it. I don't do that. First of all I am too old, I am 72 years old, it needs too much energy and I don't do that. Artists have to be genuine. Willie Nelson for example is an American classic. Are we looking for a Pavarotti voice? No. He doesn't have that but he's got a beautiful voice. Then I worked with Patti LaBelle she can sing rings around anyone. These are genuine, genuine people. I think I analyse the artist first and say, 'Yes, I'd like to do this project because I love his or her voice'.

RJB: What do you think are the most important ingredients in a hit record?

AM: I think it has to address a certain section of the record buying public. We have a few kinds of records. You have a novelty record which can be a dance record, 'Who Let The Dogs Out?' or something like that. I'm not saying they're bad. The other kind would be 'Wind Beneath My Wings.' I was extremely gratified when I received letters from the public, they were more important than GRAMMY awards to me. [The letters would say things like] 'I played this song when my mother was dying and it gave us solace.' 'My wife and I were about to divorce and we heard this song and we got together again.' Things like that. I thought, 'Wow, I feel like a priest or something' [*laughs*]. She [Bette Midler] touched a certain part of the record buying public.

I think also with Norah Jones' success, especially at that time in 2002, there were too many manufactured records, they were uncertain times with the 2001 memories. Then this pure voice, unadorned beautiful songs, simple, touched people's hearts. So I guess it's a spark that makes a hit record. There are these idiotic software programs, I think they developed one in Spain, they put in a lot of hit records and they come up with a formula saying you have to have this tempo but they don't analyse language – lyrics.

RJB: So you put lyrics very high up on the list of importance?

AM: Yes, the lyric is very high up, unless it's a novelty song, lyrics are very important.

RJB: So the artist could come without the song and you'll find the song. Do you do a lot of that?

283

AM: Yes we have to find the song. You write to your publisher and songwriter friends and collect the material. As you say some artists come with their own songs, they write the songs or they find them or we have to find them for the artist.

RJB: Have you had that experience where you get to the end of a record and you think, 'I don't have that hit song, that lead single yet', or do you know up front what you have?

AM: Well you know I think I go with the flow. Working with The Bee Gees on the *Main Course* album, we didn't realise that we had hits, we were just working and having a great time, very energetic electrifying sessions and when The Bee Gees managers and Ahmet Ertegun came to listen to it they said 'Oh wow, you have got massive hits.' We said, 'Really?!' We didn't know (*laughs*). This is a good surprise. I don't know if I ever scrapped something and started all over. I don't think so.

RJB: I didn't mean the whole album but where you might say 'I've got ten good tracks but I need that one extra single.'

AM: Well, yes, and if you are lucky you have got this extra beautiful song and you go and record it, of course.

RJB: So generally you don't always know when you've got the hit?

AM: You just feel it. It's a very, very rare feeling. With 'Jive Talkin'' we definitely knew we had something after hearing it so many times. With Bette Midler for example, 'Wind Beneath My Wings,' 'Oh, you recorded another ballad with her,' that was the record company talking. All of a sudden it started, especially with the movie, affecting people. The other one was 'From A Distance,' you have the word God in there. I don't think any station will play this.' And then (*laughs*) it was proven wrong.

RJB: 'Wind Beneath My Wings' was recorded many times previously

AM: Many times, many, many times, and 'From A Distance', too.

RJB: So how do you explain that, was it the magic between . . . ?

AM: The magic of Bette's delivery and also the very sad situation in the film *Beaches*. If you have a good film and your song is featured in the film, it definitely is a plus.

RJB: You have been on staff, pretty much your whole career at Atlantic, since 1961 and now at Blue Note.

AM: I am retiring from Blue Note in September.

RJB: I'm sure you are not retiring though?

AM: No, I have projects.

RJB: There must have been something that you really liked about working within a company setting. When you are in a company there is usually a lot of work other than music or production that has to be done as well. What did you like about working for a company rather than being freelance?

AM: I think it was maybe security. I had a financial arrangement. Also it's a legendary company and Ahmet Ertegun is still there and I love to be with him, you just feel attached. I'm not too much of a freelance person, where I would have to hustle, they come to me. I was also one of Atlantic Records' officers. I had duties to do there too.

RJB: Did you mind that side of it?

AM: No.

RJB: You say that it was a legendary company but you helped to create that legend.

AM: Well I was part of it but they were legendary before I even joined. They had all of these wonderful pioneering R'n'B records and John Coltrane and all that. When I joined in 1963, I became part of that phenomenal motion.

RJB: It was an incredible time. It seemed as if every record I liked was on Atlantic, Stax or one of the subsidiary labels. Do staff

producers generally get the same kind of points on records they produce as freelance producers or do they have a completely different arrangement with the label?

AM: First of all when I helped produce The Rascals, Tom Dowd (my mentor) and myself, we received the smallest percentage. We were salaried, it was like a bonus, 'You did good work so here it is.' It's the individual understanding or contract. I don't know if an A&R person produces an act for a label what he will get. Will he get a percentage from the general A&R pool? There are so many ways he can get paid. Does the A&R person have permission to produce an act belonging to a rival company, which I did. Ahmet Ertegun gave me permission. He said, 'Hey, produce anyone you want.' So I worked with Clive Davis. I also stayed within the WEA family, I was doing Warner Bros. It all depends. Today's way of payment for a producer/A&R man can vary. Will he get a great bonus at the end? Will he get a percentage of all the acts from an A&R fund? How much of a percentage he will get on sales is hard to say. It all depends on salary and the understanding he has with the label. With a freelancer he can say I want this much but [as a freelancer] you are judged by your last success.

RJB: Always (laughs)

AM: There are incredible amounts of advances given these days, I hear. Especially in the hip-hop field, young producers like to get more on the advance and less on the points. That's one way of looking at things.

RJB: I always preferred the points over the advances myself. I heard that there is a book in the works?

AM: Yes, my memoirs. It went on the backburner a little bit when I started at EMI. I am on my sixth chapter, it's going to be very interesting, it's not a tell-all. It's all musical and funny anecdotes with Bette Midler, in the studio, funny things, what was recorded when and with which musicians, my childhood in Turkey, World War Two. My father was a bank manager in Alexandria, Egypt in 1941 and '42 and we used to visit him. In 1942, Rommel was at the gates. Every night we would have air raids. It was almost like that Spielberg film. So these will be the things that will be in the book.

RJB: I will be the first in line to buy it. Thank you for taking the time to talk to me.

AM: You're welcome.

Further Reading

For full transcripts of other interviews in this book, more information and further reading please visit: www.burgessworldco.com

Glossary

A&R	Artist and Repertoire – the department in a record company that signs artists and supervises the making of records
advance	Money paid by a record company or publisher to an artist or writer in anticipation of sales. The advance is recouped from future royalties.
album	A collection of tracks on vinyl, cassette, CD or future format
alternative	Guitar-based rock also known as indie rock and modern rock which grew in response to the mainstream rock of the 1970s. During the Nineties, alternative rock became a mainstream format
ambience	The acoustic characteristics of a real or imaginary space in which a sound occurs.
analogue	In the case of recorded music, audio that is represented by a continuously variable electrical signal
analogue console	An audio mixer with input and output channels which uses analogue technology (as opposed to digital). Also known as a board, recording console or desk (UK)

arrangement	The adaptation of a piece of music for performance by a particular set of voices or instruments
ASCAP	The American Society of Composers, Authors and Publishers is a US performing rights organization www.ascap.com
Big Band	Large dance or jazz band sometimes featuring vocalists and improvised instrumental solos
Billboard	Weekly US music industry trade magazine www.billboard.com
BMI	Broadcast Music, Inc. is a US performing rights organisation www.bmi.com
Board	US term for an audio mixer with input and output channels. Also known as a console, recording console or desk (UK)
Business Manager	Professional who helps the artist with tax matters, monitoring of income from contracts and other financial matters. Preferably a different person than the personal manager who takes care of running the artist's or producer's career
channel	The end-to-end transmission path connecting any two points in which specific equipment is connected
chorus	An effect that tries to make a single voice sound like multiple voices in unison utilising a series of delays whose delay times are slowly being modulated. Although it is no substitute for multiple instruments or voices chorus does add depth and resonance to a sound
Class A circuitry	Considered to be the best sounding circuitry it is an active device such as a vacuum tube or transistor biased to conduct all the time throughout the waveform giving the best possible linearity at the expense of efficiency
Clearchannel	The largest single corporate owner of radio stations in the US. They also own and operate billboards, venues and promote concerts. www.clearchannel.com
codecs	Short for compressor/decompressor, any

technology for compressing and
decompressing data

compression
An electronic method of reducing the dynamic
range of a signal by a variable amount when
the signal exceeds a preset maximum

Console
An audio mixer with input and output
channels. Also known as a board, recording
console or desk (UK)

controlled
composition
Royalty-reducing provision which
contractually reduces the mechanical rate for a
songwriter/producer and publisher on songs
written or otherwise "controlled" by the
producer

copyrights
The rights which permit the various owner(s)
of a musical work to restrict others from
reproducing, displaying, performing, or
distributing that work

cutouts
CDs, Cassettes or LPs marked, notched, drilled
or punched to prevent them from being resold
or returned at full value. The record company
is not contractually obligated to pay artist or
producer royalties.

cutout bins
Dump bins in record stores containing cutouts

cutting
These days a generic term usually used to
mean 'make a recording.' It dates back to the
days of vinyl, 78s and cylinders when the music
was encoded into the media using a cutting
lathe. In the vinyl mastering process the lathe
uses a slightly heated sapphire or diamond
tipped stylus that etches the groove into a soft
oil-based lacquer

deal
Short for record deal – a contract to make a
recording for a record label

delay
Single or multiple discrete echo(s) which can
occur naturally by reflection off of a hard
surface or be created by analogue or digital
signal processing. Delays form the basis of
many other effects such as filters, reverbs,
flangers and can also be used to synchronise
out of phase or out of time signals. Delay can

	also be the unwanted byproduct of other acoustic or electronic signal processes
demos	Low budget recordings created as rough sketches of the final audio production.
Desk	UK term for an audio mixer with input and output channels. Also known as a board, recording console or console
digital	Digital recording technology utilizes information encoded using binary code of zeroes and ones – discrete, non-continuous values – to represent the audio information
digital formats	Recording formats that use digital technology as opposed to analogue
Digital Millenium Copyright Act	Also known as DMCA – provides for revenue for sound recording copyright holders from digital cable, satellite and webcast transmissions. www.copyright.gov/legislation/dmca.pdf
digital workstations	Self-contained computer based recording devices utilising digital technology
discrete	A discrete circuit has the specific parts it needs, carefully selected for that application. Most audio circuitry nowadays is assembled with integrated circuits (ICs) or op amps that are versatile, small and inexpensive but include extra parts that can cloud the sound and add noise
distorted	Used to describe a sound that contains distortion
distortion	Any change, during recording or playback, of an audio wave form from that of the original wave form. Usually used to describe an overdriven sound that occurs when an audio signal is pushed above nominal limits for the device it is driving
drop-in	British terminology for commencing recording part way through a performance on one or multiple tracks see punch-in
drop-out	British terminology for ending recording part way through a performance on one or

	multiple tracks see punch-out. Drop-out can also refer to a momentary loss of audio information on the recording media either due to operator error or faulty media
drum machines	Digital device that has a built-in sequencer to play programmable or preprogrammed patterns using internal synthesised or sampled percussion sounds
dynamic mic	A dynamic mic generates the audio signal by the motion of a conductor within a magnetic field. Generally less expensive than condenser mics, robust construction, can often handle very high sound pressure levels, does not require external power to operate, often used to record electric guitar and drums
dynamic control	The control of the dynamic range of a sound or a music piece usually done by using some form of compression, expansion or gating
dynamic range	The range between the loudest and softest parts of the music or sound
dynamics	The variation of intensity of the sound
Echo	A signal which has been reflected or otherwise returned with sufficient magnitude and time delay to be detected as a signal distinct from that directly transmitted
Effects	Any form of audio signal processing including reverb, delay, chorusing, compression, limiting, aural exciting, etc
EQ	see equalisation
equalisation	Equalisation is the increase or decrease of signal strength for a selected portion of audio frequencies. A simple equaliser such as a bass control increases or decreases the strength of the lower frequencies, affecting the tone by changing the relationship between the fundamental and harmonic frequencies
ergonomics	The science of equipment design intended to maximize productivity by reducing operator fatigue and discomfort
ethnographic	The branch of anthropology dealing with the

	scientific description of specific human cultures
ethnomusicology	The study of music styles of the world focusing on the cultural context of music
expansion	The increase in dynamic range of a signal or the restoration of a compressed signal to its original dynamic range
Fairlight CMI	The first commercially available sampling device. The first recording of which was by the author on Kate Bush's album *Never Forever* released in 1980 and Visage's 'Fade to Grey' in the same year
FLAC	Free Lossless Audio Codec. flac.sourceforge.net
flanging	Mixing a signal with a time-delayed copy while the delay time continually changes in order to produce a swept comb filter effect
foldback	A UK term for the signal sent to the performer's headphones or monitors
folklorist	Person who studies the traditional beliefs, knowledge and culture of a people, transmitted orally
formats	Can refer to the type of music such as alternative, hiphop, country. Can also refer to the recording medium such as two-inch 24 track, ADAT, hard disk
48-channel	Refers to the number of independent channels in a recording console
frequencies	The number of complete oscillations (cycles) that an audio wave makes in a second, usually expressed in hertz; or cycles per second. The frequency of a signal is directly related to the pitch
gating	The process of selecting the portions of a soundwave which exist during one or more selected time intervals or which have magnitudes between selected limits. Generally used to eliminate extraneous noise from between the desired signals or to shape a sound. Gates can be triggered externally and used to drastically change the shape of a sound

Gobos	A mobile barrier used to create some acoustical seperation between individual microphones assigned to specific instruments. Sometimes called a baffle, a screen or a partition
Go-go music	Fusion of Funk and hip-hop from the Washington DC area invented by Chuck Brown in the mid-1970's
Grunge	Label applied to a form of rock music originating in Seattle and popularized bands such as Nirvana, Pearl Jam and Alice in Chains
Harry Fox	National Music Publishers' Association www.nmpa.org
hook(s)	A catchy and memorable melody, phrase, or sound used to capture the listener's attention
in-line	Refers to the type of recording console which uses the same channel strips for recording and monitoring the sound
instrumental	Music performed using musical instruments and without vocals. Could refer to the whole song or just a section of a song
instrumentation	The instruments used in a musical score, arrangement or recording of a band or orchestra
IRCAM	Institut de Recherche et Coordination Acoustique/Musique – a centre for education, research and creativity at the Pompidou Centre in Paris. www.ircam.fr
Level	Loudness or gain
limiting	Where an audio signal is not allowed to exceed a permitted dynamic range
LP	Long Playing vinyl sound recording to be played back at 33⅓ rpm
major	One of the big four global record companies which, combined, command over 75% of the international market share
major label	*See major*
marketing	The process of identifying and reaching specific segments of the population for the purposes of selling the music to them. This

294

	includes setting prices, giving discounts, placing product in appropriate physical and online retail outlets, getting airplay, TV exposure, tour coverage, the creation of point of sale display materials, paid-for media advertising, free media coverage via interviews, reviews and features, product endorsements, direct marketing to consumers via mail and email, online marketing via websites, newsgroups and blogs
MCPS	Mechanical Copyright Protection Society (UK) collects and distributes 'mechanical' royalties generated from the sale of recorded music on all formats. This income is distributed to their members – writers and publishers of music. www.mcps.co.uk
mechanical copyright	The form of protection provided by law to the authors of original musical works when their works are reproduced on any format such as vinyl, cassette, CD, MP3 and other digital codecs
Mechanical copyright royalty	The royalty which is paid to the publisher and the writer of the song upon the sale of a performance of the song on a physical format such as a CD and also in a virtual form such as a digital download
Mechanicals	Abbreviation for mechanical copyright royalty
merchandise	In the music business merchandise generally means associated products such as branded T-shirts, baseball caps etc
Mic pre	Abbreviation for microphone preamplifier which raises the level of the signal from the output of the microphone up to the level required by the mixing console, processing equipment or recording device
mix	Used as a verb: to blend audio signals together into a composite signal. As a noun: the signal made by blending individual signals together
mix engineer	The engineer who does the signal processing and balancing to create the final mix

mixer	Can refer to the recording console which mixes signals together or the person who mixes the music
mixing console	An audio mixer device with input and output channels. Also known as a board, recording console or desk (UK)
monitor speakers (a.k.a. monitors)	Loudspeakers or speakers convert analogue electrical signals into audio. Monitor speakers in recording studios allow the producer and engineer to monitor signals as they have been and are being recorded
MP3	Most widely used compression codec for music downloads and streams on the internet
multi-track tape machines	A digital or analogue, linear tape recording device with more than one track for audio recording. Being superceded by computer based hard disk recording systems
Music Week	Weekly European music industry trade magazine www.musicweek.com
musique concrète	Music composed by manipulating electronically recorded acoustically generated sounds
NMPA	see Harry Fox. www.nmpa.org
orchestration	An arrangement of the instrumentation and/or vocals for performance or recording
outboard equipment	Discrete pieces of signal processing equipment that are not part of the recording console or recording device
out of phase	refers to two identical or similar signals that are 180° out of synch with each other causing cancellation of frequencies
overage	Refers to the amount by which the agreed upon recording budget is exceeded
overdubbing	The process of recording live onto one track whilst listening to the audio from a previously recorded track
override	When used in context of a recording deal means a percentage paid to a third party as part of a contractual agreement

parametric equalisation	An equaliser that allows the continuous adjustment of all equalisation parameters including amplitude, center frequency and bandwidth in order to change a signal's tonal characteristics
pass	One complete run through a song usually in overdub mode either for rehearsal or recording purposes
perfect pitch	The ability to listen to and identify any note without any visual, musical or tonal reference
Performance royalty	A royalty that may be generated for the writers, publishers, copyright owners and in some cases the artists, performers and producers any time music is played anywhere in public
phase	The time relationship between two signals. Identical or similar waveforms that are out of phase cause cancellation of frequencies which may be an undesired effect
phase check	Checking that two similar signals are in sync with each other
phasing	The hollow sound that occurs when two identical tracks are run in near-perfect sync with each other. *See: flanging*
pipeline royalties	The royalties owed but not yet paid to the artist from records already sold
plug-and-play	The ability of a device to detect and configure new hardware components
Points	Refers to the percentage of the retail or wholesale price that the producer or artist gets paid as a royalty. 10 points = 10% of either retail or wholesale price
PPL	Phonographic Performance Limited (UK). An agency that collects performance royalties for artists, musicians, singers and the copyright owners of recordings. www.ppluk.com
pre-production	The planning phase before recording begins. Includes budgeting, production planning, scheduling, studio booking and equipment rental but mostly refers to the selection,

	rehearsal and refinement of the music and musical arrangements prior to recording
PRO	Performing Rights Organisation (generic term). An organisation that collects royalties for public use or recordings and compositions
production company	A company with which artists sign an agreement to produce tracks or an album. Depending on the agreement the production company may cover recording and production expenses. The production-company then endeavours to sign an agreement with a label or distributor to release records by the artist.
promotion	The marketing a track or album to radio and TV with the intention of getting airplay
PRS	Performing Rights Society (UK). Agency that collects royalties for airplay and other public uses for songwriters and composers. www.prs.co.uk
punch-in	American terminology for commencing recording part way through a performance on one or multiple tracks *see drop-in*
punch-out	American terminology for ending recording part way through a performance on one or multiple tracks *see drop-out*
Quad	Quadraphonic sound was an early attempt at surround sound using a system of four channel sound where the channels are designated as left front, left back, right front, and right back. It fell into disfavour in the early seventies
quarter or half inch master	The final mix that is recorded onto quarter or half inch analogue two track tape
radical dance mix	A remix of a track aimed at a specific type of club DJ that involves using little or no material from the original recording
random access	The ability of a storage device to go directly to the required place without having to read from the beginning every time. This is one of the characteristics of disk type of recording

	media. LPs and CDs can be thought of as random-access, cassette tapes are sequential or linear access
recording console	An audio mixer with input and output channels. Also known as a board, mixing console or desk (UK)
recording media	The physical objects on which the audio data is stored, such as hard disks, CD-ROMs, floppy disks, and tape
residential studio	A recording studio which has accommodation for the artist, musicians, engineer and producer
reverb	Multiple reflections of delayed and attenuated sound waves against room boundaries and objects within the room persisting after the original sound has ceased creating the sense of spaciousness of a room
RIAA	Recording Industry Association of America www.riaa.com
riding the levels	Changing levels relative to time and the other instruments. Can include panning of instruments and vocals. These techniques are both used to improve the dynamic flow of the track, to draw attention to different facets of the orchestration at different points in the song
rights clearances	The process of obtaining permission from the various copyright owners
scratch vocals	A quickly done rough vocal-take often recorded at the same time as the basic track. Scratch vocals are usually discarded later but because of the lack of pressure when they are recorded sometimes they have a special quality which can not be emulated or improved upon
screen	*See Gobo* – also called a baffle, screen or partition. Screen/pop-screen/pop-shield can also refer to the sonically transparent mesh that is placed in front of or covering a microphone to minimise vocal pops and moisture accumulation on the diaphragm of the mic

SESAC	US performing rights organization. Agency that collects royalties for airplay and other public uses for songwriters and composers. www.sesac.com
single	Any format which primarily features one song. MP3 files and other digital codecs are the descendent of the 45 or single which was introduced by RCA in 1948 as a 45 RPM seven inch vinyl disc. They featured the primary song being promoted to radio and for sale on the A side and a secondary song on the B side. This evolved into the cassingle on cassette tape and the CD single, both of which could contain between one and four songs or remixes but primarily featuring one
SM58	Widely used multipurpose Shure dynamic microphone. www.shure.com
SMPTE	Society of Motion Picture and Television Engineers – sets standards for audio visual synchronisation timecode among other things www.smpte.org
solid state	Devices which control current using transistors and integrated circuits instead of moving parts or vacuum tubes
sound field	The recording area detected by the microphone(s) including the presence or lack of discontinuities or boundaries
Sound-on-sound	A method in which new material is combined with previously recorded material on one track. Done by re-recording to another track while simultaneously adding new material or by disabling the erase head and entering record on a track containing previously recorded material. Differs from multi-track recording in that the balance between the newly recorded and original material cannot be changed post recording
Sounds	Used to describe the individual recorded sounds before or after the addition of effects. *see also Tones*

spec.	Abbreviation for specification. Describes the properties, characteristics, ranges or requirements of a part or device
staff producer	A music producer who is employed on staff at a record label
state-of-the-art	The most advanced level of knowledge and technology currently achieved
Synclavier	early digital synthesiser developed at Dartmouth College, New Hampshire, USA in the seventies www.synclavier.com
talkback	The system, usually located on the recording console, that enables the engineer and producer to speak to the musicians in the studio through their headphones or the studio speaker system
Technics SP1200	The most commonly used professional DJ turntable
Terrestrial right	Public performance right which would require terrestrial broadcast stations to pay royalties to performers and sound recording copyright owners for the broadcast of sound recordings
tone	Can be used to refer to lineup tones which are single-frequency signals used to ensure that the frequency response of the various recording machines are aligned consistently from day to day and studio to studio. Also used interchangeably with the term sounds meaning the particular sound of an instrument or voice
tones	Used to describe the individual recorded sounds before or after the addition of effects. *see also sounds*
tracking	The process of recording sounds to tracks on an audio recorder. Also known as laying down tracks and just recording. Tracking is the first stage of the multitrack recording process
TV advertising clause	A provision in the producer and/or artist contract that modifies their royalties when TV advertising is used to promote the sale of the recording

two-inch tape machines	Multi-track analogue recording machine which uses two inch wide magnetic tape. The recording and erase heads (headstack) are usually configured to record 24 tracks across the width of the tape but they can be configured in other ways, the most common alternative being 16 track. Some other configurations such as 32 track machines were manufactured. They were the most widely used professional recording format from the early 70s to the late 90s. Becoming obsolete with digital technology
valve	UK term. The US term is vacuum tube or tube. A valve or tube will amplify a small AC signal voltage into a larger AC voltage. The key element in early electronic recording technology. Largely replaced by transistor technology but still beloved by audiophiles

Printed in the United States
104178LV00002B/11-54/A

9 781844 494316